THE EARTH'S GALACTIC HISTORY AND ITS EXTRATERRESTRIAL CONNECTION

Constance Victoria Briggs

Adventures Unlimited Press

"I believe that we should expand the mind and consider all things extraterrestrial, so that as a species we are not stagnated in our efforts to move forward into a better world, a more fulfilled life, a safer planet and the desire to become a spacefaring race that will one day become a part of a galactic community. We are on the cusp of something big."

--*Constance Victoria Briggs*

THE EARTH'S GALACTIC HISTORY AND ITS EXTRATERRESTRIAL CONNECTION

Constance Victoria Briggs

Earth's Galactic History and Its Extraterrestrial Connection

by Constance Victoria Briggs

Copyright © 2023

ISBN 978-1-948803-62-5

Published by:
Adventures Unlimited Press
One Adventure Place
Kempton, Illinois 60946 USA
auphq@frontiernet.net

www.AdventuresUnlimitedPress.com

THE EARTH'S GALACTIC HISTORY AND ITS EXTRATERRESTRIAL CONNECTION

Adventures Unlimited Press

Dedication

To Ghobad
Thank you for encouraging me to write this book!

Other Books by
Constance Victoria Briggs:

The Moon's Galactic History
The Encyclopedia of Moon Mysteries
Encyclopedia of the Unseen World
The Encyclopedia of Angels
The Encyclopedia of God

TABLE OF CONTENTS

Earth seen from outer space.

Introduction

We have entered a time when information about Earth's galactic history and its connection to extraterrestrials is coming out very fast. The evidence suggests that we are not alone, and we never have been. In fact, whether there is other intelligent life in the universe is no longer a question. There is proof that shows that we have been visited by extraterrestrials from the beginning of human history and that Earth is being visited today. The question is whether humanity will accept this reality. I believe that we are on the verge of the next step in Earth's extraterrestrial connection. If we are to enter a time when we will evolve to be greater than we are now, then we need to examine Earth's galactic history and its extraterrestrial connection. Only then will we be able to move forward into a time when we can join what I believe is a galactic community.

Therefore, it behooves us to examine as much information from our past on the subject as possible, as well as explore the theories and possibilities of how we are connected to the stars. *Earth's Galactic History and Its Extraterrestrial Connection* explores the many aspects of humankind's interactions with extraterrestrials starting from our ancient past to the present. The timing of this book is apropos because the topic of Earth's connection to extraterrestrials is being closely scrutinized today.

In fact, more information than ever before on the topic is becoming available. Even some governments are declassifying documents on strange encounters they have had with what appear to be otherworldly phenomena. Perhaps needed to reach a level of development before this information could be widely disseminated. The information presented in this book will allow people to draw their own conclusions as to what they think about Earth's galactic history and our extraterrestrial connection. We may just have reached a point in human history where we are ready to accept the reality that we are not alone in the universe. Perhaps we are now ready for that spacefaring, *Star Trek* future that so many have been anticipating.

We just may find that learning where we are headed in relation to the cosmos, and the fact that we are not alone, may move us into a better way of living, a better state of being, and improve life on our planet. There are secrets in this book just waiting to be uncovered. There are stories waiting to be discovered. I am excited to share them with you during this amazing time in Earth's history!

An artist's vision of Earth as seen from a 3D-printed Moon base.

Chapter One
Earthrise

"Look again at that dot. That's here. That's home. That's us. On it everyone you love, everyone you know, everyone you ever heard of, every human being who ever was, lived out their lives. The aggregate of our joy and suffering, thousands of confident religions, ideologies, and economic doctrines, every hunter and forager, every hero and coward, every creator and destroyer of civilization, every king and peasant, every young couple in love, every mother and father, hopeful child, inventor and explorer, every teacher of morals, every corrupt politician, every "superstar," every "supreme leader," every saint and sinner in the history of our species lived there—on a mote of dust suspended in a sunbeam."
—Carl Sagan

Since the beginning of history, humans have pondered their place in the universe. They have contemplated such questions as, "Who are we?" "Where did we come from?" "Why are we here?" and "What is our purpose?" In the modern era, we have come a long way in our understanding of the world around us, and our place in it. We have shown great advancements in science and technology, even landing people on a different world. However, we still lack definitive answers to those original, probing questions. Today, there are many theories from scientists, researchers, philosophers, academics, and others that are attempting to answer those questions that have plagued humankind for so long. Some of the theories that have been put forward to answer those questions are profound, others are more fantastical. However, the conversation is moving forward, and one day, hopefully soon, we will have the answers. Due to the divisiveness of this world, there is a good deal of information from history that involves human origins and our place in the universe that most people are not aware of. This is unfortunate because our past holds the key to the questions that have plagued us for so long. Interestingly, the more we search into our past, the more the answers appear to point toward the cosmos. It appears that our origins just may have begun somewhere in the

11

most distant parts of our galaxy and some believe outside of our universe.

Unfortunately, there is a certain amount of fear among people when it comes to questioning our origins. There is fear of the unknown, and fear of what we may learn about ourselves. For the most part, people have been conditioned to live out their lives according to the teachings and the systems put in place. The world appears to simply shut down when new information comes out that is contrary to what people are accustomed to believing. However, it is this author's opinion that for us to move forward, we need to investigate our past, understand who we are, where we came from, and move forward as a more knowledgeable and preferably advanced species in the universe. If not, we may be destined to become that apocalyptic planet that we see so much of in the movies. If we don't learn, grow, and accept our past, then that could very well be the future of Earth.

Earth Origins, What is the Beginning?

Most scientists believe that the Earth was formed approximately 4.5 billion years ago from a solidified cloud of dust and gases that were remnants from the Sun's formation. This they believe, occurred during the same period that the rest of the Solar System was created. Scientists also maintain that life on Earth started over 3.8 billion years ago. Many believe that life evolved from rudimentary microbes that became more complex as time progressed. The question is, how did these initial organisms take form and progress from the "proverbial," primordial soup? Today, scientists are still uncertain when it comes to the origin of life on Earth. There are still ongoing discussions as to exactly how life started here. Amazingly, there are scientists and researchers that are considering whether life originated on Earth at all! Some are in fact looking towards outer space to solve the mystery of the origin of life on Earth. If we open our minds and expand the realm of possibilities, then we may find answers we have never imagined.

Hypothetical Scenarios for Earth Origins

Was the Earth Terraformed?

When it comes to how life came to be on Earth, several hypotheses have been put forward in recent years. Most are extremely unconventional. One such theory is that of the Earth having been terraformed by beings that were highly advanced in the areas of science and technology. If true, then these beings could be eons of years old and have reached, "creator status," meaning that they have the capability to create, maintain and sustain life on other worlds. The term "terraforming" was conceived by author Jack Williamson in his short story *Collision Orbit*, which was published in *Astounding Science Fiction* magazine in 1942. Terraforming is a hypothetical method of transforming an environment that is unsuitable for humans to dwell on, into one that is equipped for human habitation. It is hypothetical of course because we do not yet have the technology to terraform planets. However, this theory is not as unbelievable as it may seem. Scientists today are currently researching terraforming planets, and the various ways that we might one day do so. Interestingly, the idea is not lost on them that this is what may have happened with Earth billions of years ago. Some researchers today are considering the idea that advanced beings may have been responsible for incorporating life on Earth. In fact, it is thought by some researchers that there may have been several alien worlds that had a hand in the preparation, design, and development of life on Earth. It is believed that extraterrestrials could have planned everything from a breathable atmosphere to the creatures that would reside here. It has also been considered that large depositories may have been used for such a task. These depositories have been likened to a futuristic, "Noah's Ark." This means that extraterrestrials may have sent the seeds of life across the universe or universes to plant life on Earth and perhaps other areas of our Solar System as well.

Project Genesis

In my previous book, *The Moon's Galactic History: A Look at the Moon's Extraterrestrial Past and Its Connection to Earth*, I relayed the story of Gene Roddenberry, the creator of *Star Trek*. Some may not take seriously the idea of a science fiction scenario being woven into Earth's history; however, the opportunity presents itself here to briefly tell his story once more, with a focus on Earth. Roddenberry was known to sit in on channeled sessions with a woman named Phyllis Schlemmer who was believed to have received channeled information from benevolent extraterrestrials. If that story isn't strange enough, the information obtained from Ms. Schlemmer stated that the extraterrestrials were on vast ships that roamed the galaxy. According to the information, the beings aboard the ships hailed from different worlds, and had come together on a mission of peace. Roddenberry's idea for *Star Trek* is believed to have come from sitting in on those, and possibly other, extraterrestrial channeling sessions. We do not know all that transpired in those gatherings. However, it is thought that perhaps some of the scripts for *Star Trek* were inspired from information obtained during those meetings. One can only wonder if the following *Star Trek* movie came about because of one of those communications. This could certainly be a case of art imitating life. In this case, it would be *Star Trek* imitating possible real-life events that may have taken place on Earth eons ago.

To start, the information that Roddenberry is said to have received from Schlemmer closely resembles what later became known in the series as "The United Federation of Planets (UFP)," more commonly referred to as "the Federation." According to the *Star Trek Encyclopedia*, the United Federation of Planets was, "An interstellar alliance of planetary governments and colonies, united for mutual trade, exploratory, scientific, cultural, diplomatic, and defensive endeavors." On the *Memory Alpha* website, we are further educated about the UFP. It states that the UFP, "was a supranational interstellar union of multiple planetary nation-states that operated semi-autonomously under a single central government, founded on the principles of liberty, equality, peace, justice, and progress, with the purpose of furthering the universal rights of all sentient life. Federation members exchange knowledge and resources to facilitate peaceful cooperation, scientific development, space exploration, and mutual defense." The question is, could this federation or an extraterrestrial alliance of this type be real? And, if it is, then what else is there about *Star Trek* that may be close to some reality that we are not aware of? Was Gene Roddenberry on to something and we never even knew? Was he trying to tell us something? Most importantly, was he being used as a facilitator between Earth and extraterrestrials? Was he charged with getting the word about them out? Did he use *Star Trek* as the means of doing so?

Interestingly, one of the *Star Trek* movies had a storyline that may be closer to Earth's reality than those that watched it may have understood. In the *Star Trek* movie, *Star Trek II: The Wrath of Khan*, the starship the USS *Reliant* is on a federation mission for a top secret scientific research project known as Project Genesis. Project Genesis focused on developing uninhabitable planets into inhabitable ones, with environments in which humans could live. The USS *Reliant* was on a quest to locate a dead world to experiment on, due to Federation scientists wanting to put Project Genesis to the test. Once an appropriate planet was located, scientists would use the project's "Genesis Device" (a torpedo-like technology that would activate the transforming of the lifeless planet into a live one). Simply put, the Federation developed technology that could terraform a planet.

Even though we know that it is science fiction, and that writers take license to extrapolate and sometimes just plain makeup what we may perceive as facts to create a story, the idea of using a dead planet or moon to become a life-giving entity may not be so farfetched for beings that may be much further advanced than humans. However, we should ask ourselves if this could be possible. Could this have been done eons ago elsewhere in the universe, or even as close as our Solar System? Could it have been done on Earth? Could the Earth have been terraformed? Is this simply science fiction, or is there a chance that an advanced extraterrestrial race developed a technology where they had the ability to terraform planets?

In the movie, during a demonstrative presentation of Project Genesis, scientist Carol Marcus, the head of the project, states the following, "What exactly is Genesis? Put simply, Genesis is life, from lifelessness. It is a process whereby molecular structure is reorganized at the subatomic level into life generating matter of equal mass...It is our intention to introduce the Genesis Device into a preselected area of a lifeless space body, a moon or other dead form. The device is delivered instantaneously causing what we call the Genesis effect. Matter is reorganized with life generating results. Instead of a dead moon, a living breathing planet capable of sustaining whatever life forms we see fit to deposit on it."

Earth, a Failed Experiment?

Ultimately, Project Genesis failed. Something went wrong. All the Federation's hopes and dreams for it died along with the planet and all life on it. Interestingly, this poses a question for us. Could Earth be a failed experiment? Did something go wrong? Are humans a part of a failed experiment in the sense that we live on a planet where everything dies? We are born, become old and die in what is just a few years, as does everything else on Earth. The worldwide life expectancy from birth for women is 75 years old. For men its 70 years old. In the United States the average life expectancy for women is 81 and for men it's 77. Was it meant to be this way from the beginning? Was life here supposed to blossom and then die in just a few years? Also, if it failed, did the beings that may have terraformed this world abandon us? Or have they been here all along watching our progress? Have they been assisting humankind at some points, even giving us upgrades in our bodies and assisting with advancements? Some believe they have. What is more, are they still trying to improve on their creation…their experiment? Is this the reason that some ancient writings talk about the gods wanting to destroy all and everything on Earth? *Were they attempting to start over?* Or are we a failed experiment due to mankind's tendencies towards violence, war and the destruction of resources and life on Earth?

The idea of Earth being terraformed, and humans being placed here is a difficult theory for people to believe. However, we do not know what the cosmos holds. We do not exclusively know who or what is out there. Humankind is still a young race. It is possible that there are beings that are so highly developed in the universe that they may have reached "creator capabilities." This idea is easier to grasp when we look at the magnitude of the numbers. The Milky Way galaxy alone is just one of 2 trillion known galaxies in the universe. It holds 200 billion stars, with the majority of those stars having planets. The chances of there being intelligent, extraterrestrial life elsewhere in the Milky Way or in a different galaxy altogether is extremely high in lieu of those numbers. If they do exist, then some of those potential civilizations may have existed for billions of years. American astrophysicist, radio astronomer and astrobiologist, Frank Drake (1930-2022), approximated that the Milky Way, may hold 10,000 intelligent, technological civilizations. Therefore, there is a very large chance that some of those civilizations would be technologically and scientifically advanced enough to achieve the capability of terraforming other planets and other cosmic entities. Earth may have been one of them. If Earth is a failed experiment, one wonders if *the creators finally achieved success elsewhere.*

Putting the pieces together to the entire story of Earth's past is difficult and fraught with theories. However, it behooves us to ask, "Could extraterrestrials have terraformed our planet?" Are we a product of some great experiment?" Perhaps. Could technology similar to *Star Trek's* Genesis Device have transformed Earth into a flourishing planet? At this point, *anything is possible, and nothing should be ruled out.*

The Boltzmann Brain Concept

The Boltzmann Brain Concept is a fascinating theory that was brought about by Austrian physicist Ludwig Boltzmann (1844-1906). It is the idea that a lifeform exists that has been described as a "single brain," spontaneously formed in a void, seemingly out of nothing, with brain activity, consciousness, but no physical body, existing in space, with the capability to construct realities. Simply put, this Boltzmann Brain would be an all-powerful being that simply appeared and began creating. This theory brings to mind the story of the monotheistic god of Judeo-Christian beliefs. According to that religious belief system, God created everything in the universe, and is believed to exist somewhere in the cosmos. God is thought to be a spiritual, formless being of immense power and intellect. Could this be God? Could God be an all-powerful being that spontaneously appeared? Is God really a being made up strictly of consciousness, free of physicality, and one that would never know death? A being that ultimately chose to experience and sent out particles that became life in which it could experience? Is this the real creator of life? Is this the Alpha and the Omega, the beginning, and the end? Is this the creator of the creators and the planet seeders? *Is this the creator of Earth and humankind?*

Even though the Boltzmann Brain concept sounds particularly unbelievable, we have an occasion here to think way out of the box in examining this whole idea of a formless god in the cosmos; an omnipotent being that is beyond death and the invisible world. One that somehow brought about life. Could it all have begun with an invisible, universal consciousness that exists outside of the universe and time as we know it? It is something to consider as (*again*) we do not know who or what is out there. We are just beginning our journey down this rabbit hole of discovery.

The Panspermia Hypothesis

The panspermia hypothesis is the theory that life did not originally develop on Earth but was inadvertently transported here from elsewhere in the universe via such objects as asteroids, comets, and meteoroids carrying microorganisms. The term panspermia means "seeds." This theory was first introduced by the prominent Greek scientist and philosopher Anaxagoras of

Clazomenae (c.500–428 B.C.E.). Anaxagoras held that panspermia was the origin of life in the universe. However, for people living during that period, the panspermia hypothesis was too advanced for their time and was eventually dismissed. Current research into the origins of humankind, coupled with scientific developments in comprehending the definition of what "life" really means, has reopened the panspermia hypothesis. Interestingly, an alternative version of the panspermia hypothesis has been brought about in more recent times. There are some researchers that maintain that the spread of life throughout the universe was not a natural occurrence but happened as a result of *intelligent beings* purposely planting the "seeds of life" on other worlds. Leading proponents to this theory were Nobel Prize winning English molecular biologist Sir Francis Crick (1916–2004) and chemist Leslie Orgel (1927-2007). The two believed that there was little chance that microorganisms were carried through the universe and placed on Earth randomly, as had been previously hypothesized. In 1973, Crick and Orgel published a paper in the *Icarus* journal. They proposed that life may have reached Earth by means of what would be a variation of the Panspermia Hypothesis; a method they referred to as "Directed Panspermia." The two believed that "Directed Panspermia" could explain how life arrived on Earth. An excerpt from their paper states:

> It now seems unlikely that extraterrestrial living organisms could have reached the earth either as spores driven by the radiation pressure from another star or as living organisms imbedded in a meteorite. As an alternative to these nineteenth-century mechanisms, we have considered Directed Panspermia, the theory that organisms were deliberately transmitted to the earth by intelligent beings on another planet. We conclude that it is possible that life reached the earth in this way, but that the scientific evidence is inadequate at the present time to say anything about the probability. We draw attention to the kinds of evidence that might throw additional light on the topic.

In his book, *Life Itself: Its Origin and Nature* (1981), Crick wrote of a technologically adept, advanced race of beings having engineered Directed Panspermia by providing a craft containing genetic material, along with equipment designed to distribute it on a planet, and kick-start life on the new world. He surmised that a wide variety of microorganisms, that had only a small amount of nutritional requirements, would be able to withstand what would be a lengthy journey across the universe. Crick maintained that the most logical answer would have been to distribute the most elementary life forms on various cosmic bodies such as asteroids, comets, meteoroids, and other entities, with the hope that the microorganisms sent might take hold and develop into intelligent creatures. Even more interesting was Crick's idea that sometime in humankind's future, we too would one day grow to a point where we would be creator beings and distribute seeds of life to other planetary bodies.

The Planet Seeders Hypothesis

One truly fascinating theory that has been put forward on the origin of life is the idea that Earth was intentionally sought out and seeded by beings outside of our universe. In my book titled *The Moon's Galactic History, and its Extraterrestrial Connection to Earth*, I wrote about these possible "planet seeders." These are advanced beings that are believed by some to have seeded many worlds, with varying species including humanoid beings. This may explain the reason there are so many reports of "humanoids" when it comes to those that claim to have had contact with extraterrestrials. The Milky Way galaxy it appears is seeded with several forms of humanoid beings. Some believe that humanoids may even exist on the Moon and Mars (possibly in the past), as well as other cosmic bodies in the Solar System. The most important questions here are, "If there are beings that seeded our galaxy, who are they?" "Where did they come from?" "Did they leave clues behind as to their identity?" I suspect that these planet seeders had the ability to traverse space quickly, or via what I refer to as the "extraterrestrial highway," which I believe includes ways and methods of taking short cuts through space using technologies that humanity has yet to understand. The civilizations of the planet seeders of course would have been around long before humans appeared on Earth. In 1974, famed parapsychological investigator Andrija Puharich famously held channeling sessions in Ossining, New York, where he claims to have been communicating with extraterrestrials. From those sessions he alleged that there were more than twenty extraterrestrial societies involved with the seeding of human beings on Earth. These seeders are said to retain the genetics of humankind, as well as all other life forms on Earth. Exopolitics' Dr. Michael Salla once referred to these seeders as, "the mysterious creators of life." A method of seeding planets may be through the usage of space repositories. It is thought that extraterrestrials stocked a wide variety of genetic material to spread life throughout the galaxy, similar to the *Star Trek* Genesis Project scenario mentioned above.

Prison Planet Hypothesis

Is Earth a prison planet? The basis of the prison theory is that humankind did not begin on Earth but was brought here from somewhere else in the universe, the possible reason being that on another world, there were a group of people that were so violent that they were removed and eventually placed on Earth until they changed their ways. As far out as this hypothesis may seem, it is a theory that has recently been discussed in the search for the origins of humans and a possible connection to other worlds and extraterrestrials. The Prison Planet Hypothesis is similar to the Quarantine Planet Hypothesis, with the exception that these beings were purposely placed here because of their violent tendencies. In a universe predicted to have worlds with peaceable beings (although not entirely), the Prison Planet Hypothesis is based unfortunately on exactly what we see going on in our world today, as humankind is still displaying primitive warring tendencies after the many years of being on Earth. A proponent of this theory is the notable Dr. Ellis Silver, author of the book *Humans are not from Earth: A Scientific Evaluation of the Evidence*. It is Ellis' contention that humans did not originate on Earth but were either brought here due to their violent tendencies, and exiled. According to an article on the *Alien UFO Sightings* website titled "Expert Says Humans are Aliens—and We Were Brought to Earth Hundreds of Thousands of Years Ago," Ellis is quoted as stating, "mankind may have evolved on a different planet, and we may have been brought here as a highly developed species. One reason for this...is that the Earth might be a prison planet since we seem to be a naturally violent species and we're here until we learn to behave ourselves."

The Zoo Hypothesis

When it comes to extraterrestrials, there are those that are eagerly awaiting "first contact." They imagine a scenario along the lines of aliens landing on the White House lawn and demanding, "Take me to your leader." Others are awaiting the day of "disclosure," a time when the governments of the world will share what they know about extraterrestrials and life in outer space. The question is, why hasn't this happened yet? If extraterrestrials exist, and if we are being visited, then, "Why haven't we *officially* met extraterrestrials on a public scale? If they exist then why all the secrecy?" "Why the mystery?" The theory is that extraterrestrials are waiting for humankind to mature and become more "seasoned" before they make their presence known. It is thought by some researchers that we may be living in a zoo-like scenario where extraterrestrials are observing us, but we cannot interact with them, or even know that they are watching. It is also believed that they are not allowed to interfere in our development. This is very much like *Star Trek's* "prime directive" of *noninterference* with the natural development of alien civilizations, and it makes sense. Until the time comes that humans mature and reach a more advanced level of thinking, they just may be keeping their distance, all the while allowing us to forge our own path and be the masters of our own destiny. When it comes to the subjects of "first contact" and "disclosure," there just may be extraterrestrials that are in charge of deciding when humankind will be informed of their existence on a mass scale. We just may live in a universe with a hierarchy that has rules, and laws put in place by advanced beings that are in charge. There may be consequences to other worlds breaking certain laws, one being that of contact with newly developing worlds. Therefore, first contact may not be permitted yet by beings that have the last word on when it happens. This may be the reason that we have not had the *big reveal*. Perhaps this is the case with all new civilizations across the galaxy. In *Star Trek*, the Federation was informed when a civilization was ready for first contact. This occurred when the people of a new world reached warp drive capability. Before warping into space, the Federation wanted them to understand that they were not alone in the universe, and that they may encounter beings from other worlds as they explored the stars. In the *Star Trek* universe, it took a certain level of science and technology before a world reached that point. Once a world reached warp drive abilities, it was thought that the people might be ready for the truth about the universe and their place in it.

There are those that maintain that extraterrestrials are subtly preparing humankind for first contact. One of the ways suggested is through our media. This includes using movies, books, social media and other means to slowly introduce the idea that there is other life in the universe. I have stated that Gene Roddenberry's *Star Trek* may be one of the means that is used to disseminate this information. Along those lines, I recall *Star Trek the Next Generation,* Season 4, episode 15 titled "First Contact." This episode is thought-provoking in that it gives a good example of what may be happening in the Zoo Hypothesis. In this episode, Captain Picard and his counselor, Deanna Troy, visit a scientist on a distant world that has newly reached warp capability. Picard explains to the scientist the reason for their visit stating, "We have been monitoring your progress toward warp drive capability. When a society reaches your level of technology and is clearly about to initiate warp travel, we feel the time is right for first contact. We prefer meeting like this rather than a random confrontation in deep space."

Another scenario that falls under the Zoo Hypothesis is the possibility that extraterrestrials may be visiting the Earth in disguise. This may be a way to observe humankind without disrupting our world view. It may also be a way that they quietly pass information to us for thought and consideration for our development, and in anticipation of them eventually making contact. Secret surveillance activity by extraterrestrials may have been going on for ages, without us even being aware that they are here. For whatever reason extraterrestrials may be observing us, for now they have chosen not to reveal themselves to humankind on a mass scale.

Another possibility involving the Zoo Hypothesis is the idea that we are being shielded from locating life in outer space because they believe that we are not ready. Modern day astronomers, astrophysicists and others have been searching for life in the universe for many years now, as well as various organizations. SETI for example has been searching for life for years. Is it possible that we are not locating other worldly beings or even definitive signals due to them simply blocking us from doing so? Are we being shielded from regular extraterrestrial broadcasts, signals, and transmissions? As stated before, perhaps they are in charge when it comes to how much we are actually allowed to know about extraterrestrials and our place in the cosmos. Scientists have allegedly picked up signals from space that indicate that someone or something intelligent is out there. However, these signals are few and far between. Were these signals that slipped through? I discuss this further in Chapter Seven, Signs, Symbols, Messages and Clues later in the book. What is even more puzzling is the fact that UFOs have been seen around the world for centuries, but there is nothing definitive enough to call *first contact*. Why would this be, unless again, we are being prevented from this knowledge on a mass scale.

Is this also the case with the Moon and Mars? Are we also being shielded from knowing that extraterrestrials exist on both of these worlds? How is it possible for us to find what many believe to be structures on the Moon, observe strange lights and objects moving on the Moon, and not locate those responsible for them, unless they have been told not to reveal themselves. When it comes to the Moon (an area that I have written two books on and speak publicly about regularly), how is it that there is so much obvious evidence of someone being up there and us not locating them, unless they simply did not want to be found? The same applies to Mars. There have been several photographs with evidence that there is life there. There are pictures again with anomalous constructions and strange lights on the planet, yet mysteriously, those responsible are nowhere to be found, leaving researchers questioning their own eyes! We may be dealing with extraterrestrials with a plan of their own, and with science and technology so advanced that they can easily hide from us and block us from fully discovering them. This just may be the reason that the masses do not believe in their existence. It may be by design. *For now.* If they are there, and observing us, then they know the level of our understanding. As a researcher once told me about the possibility of there being extraterrestrials on the Moon, "If they want to hide, all they have to do is turn off the lights."

Perhaps at the right time, the proverbial veil will be lifted, and we will be able to meet our cosmic family and take our place in the galactic, even universal community. However, there may come a time when the people of Earth may demand answers and insist that the extraterrestrials reveal themselves. If there were a public plea or outcry from the masses, would they oblige us? Would they make themselves known if we as a world understood that we are not alone in the universe, and let them know that we are ready? Perhaps this is what is happening now with the governments revealing classified information on UAPs (UFOs) to the public.

Once we know and understand they are there, perhaps they will finally introduce themselves. Then perhaps the many spaceships seen in the sky today *will land*. But for now, it appears that when it comes to Earth and extraterrestrials, it's lights out!

Quarantine Planet Hypothesis

There is a theory that Earth was placed under quarantine ages ago by advanced beings, and that this may be the reason that we have not yet made contact with extraterrestrials on a global basis. Again, they just may be keeping us at bay. However, the reasons are different than those given under the Zoo Hypothesis." If this theory is correct, then what would the reason for a quarantine be? It could be that humans are not viewed as peaceable beings. According to some ufologists, and those that claim to have had contact with extraterrestrials (yes there are those that allegedly have, I cover that in Chapter Seven), the universe is made up of mostly peaceful civilizations. Therefore, it has been speculated that advanced extraterrestrials have placed Earth in a "quarantine status" due to the position taken by humans on the issues of war and nuclear weaponry. What the extraterrestrials perceive as a warlike, even primitive nature in their eyes, may make us appear not yet ready to interact with those from nonviolent worlds. They possibly do not want us taking this kind of mindset into outer space and possibly affecting other worlds. Interestingly, there are reports that extraterrestrials have met with government officials, requesting them to do away with nuclear weapons, with earthly governments saying no to the request, even though the extraterrestrials offered superior technology in trade for them agreeing to do so. According to accounts, the extraterrestrials are concerned that life on Earth will be destroyed and have suggested that they will not allow that to happen. They have also stated, according to sources, that the usage of nuclear weapons can have a ripple effect on other worlds in the galaxy. If the stories are true, and extraterrestrials did visit Earth's governments, then they are very alarmed at the possibility of humans using this type of defense system. There have also been mysterious accounts of nuclear bombs being disabled and other strange events surrounding nuclear sites that are believed to have been extraterrestrial related.

Besides the warring tendencies of humanity, there may be other areas that extraterrestrials find troubling such as how humankind treats one another as a whole. There are such issues as crime, prejudice, nationalism, egoism, materialism and so forth that make Earth appear to be a place to avoid. One report stated that they are concerned with how humans treat each other, as well as animals. Even the governments of this world have "status pages" when it comes to citizens traveling to other countries, warning people of countries to avoid. Why would this be any different with extraterrestrials if we are living within a galactic community? It has also been said that the astronauts were warned off the Moon. After some speculation about this, it has been suggested that the reason for this rather shocking warning is that the astronauts were from Earth, and they did not want us there due to the idea of Earth being a warring civilization. *Very interesting!*

Could it be that humans behave so despicably in the eyes of extraterrestrials, that it deters them when it comes to the idea of making contact? It is possible that some of these groups of extraterrestrials have had experience with new worlds containing young species of beings such as humans? They may recognize the signs of a troubled world and avoid them. They may already know that for a species to evolve, it takes time. It could be that other worlds began in the same manner and eventually changed their ways and perspective on these issues over time. Perhaps now is not the time for humanity to connect to other worldly civilizations for this very reason. In his book *Exopolitics: Politics, Government, and Law in the Universe* (page 13), author Alfred Lambremont Webre writes of Earth being a quarantined planet stating, "Universe society does not want us to export war or violence into interstellar or inter-dimensional space." Still, Webre gives us hope stating, "It is possible that Earth may be permitted to rejoin Universe society, under certain conditions, at a future time." We can only hope that will be the case.

The Simulation Hypothesis

Are we the avatars of advanced beings in a simulated game? Are we asleep while playing a role in a simulated reality? If so, will we one day awaken to a false existence? The Simulation Hypothesis proposes that humans exist in a highly advanced, technological, brilliantly executed computer program virtual reality. It is essentially a simulated universe. The 1999 science fiction film the *Matrix* has been used as an example of this theory. The film portrays a dystopian future where humankind is unknowingly ensnared within a simulated world created by intelligent machines. Humans are attached to machinery and exist in a sleep-like state where they believe they are living regular lives, in a normal world. They are unaware that their physical bodies are attached to machines and that they are being used as a power source for AIs. The Simulation Hypothesis, was first introduced by Professor Nick Bostrom, an Oxford University philosopher. In 2003, Bostrom published a paper titled "The Simulation Hypothesis." However, versions of such an idea can also be found in ancient writings. In Hinduism and Buddhism, we find the idea that the world is *Maya*, which means "illusion." The difference here is that both Buddhism and Hinduism understand and acknowledge that the world is *not real*, and that we exist in something akin to a dream. If our world really is a simulation, and humankind is asleep, do we have rescuers coming to help? Might this explain the many people that claim to be "awakening," to who they really are, often stating that they are from elsewhere in the universe and have come to help the people of Earth during this time? Are they here to help us to awaken from a sleep-like systematic state similar to a simulated world? Is humankind trapped? Does this explain the idea behind the reincarnation process? Are there those here to help us to break free of what can only be referred to as a complicated soul cycle? Again, we can only hope.

Chapter Two
Human Origins

"Man must learn to think for himself, rather than follow
blindly what he has been taught."
—Buckminster Fuller

Most people grew up with some idea of a creation story that explained how humans came to be on Earth. The most prominent one is that of a god that created the first man and woman. Versions of this story can be found around the world, with the most far-reaching account being that of Judeo-Christian beliefs. Whereas, once it was the norm to accept this creation tale of how humankind came to be, there is now skepticism and questioning. This explanation of how humans arrived on Earth is no longer satisfying to a great number of people. Today, many have set out to find answers, often leaving religious traditions behind. What people are learning is that there is more to our origins than we could ever have imagined.

We are living in a time of an information explosion when it comes to the topic of our ancient past. It is almost as if this knowledge was meant to remain dormant until the right time in Earth's history when people would become aware of us having a connection to the stars. Today, people from various backgrounds, professions, spiritual beliefs and more, are questioning how humans came to exist. Many are examining the idea of there having been extraterrestrial intervention. Fascinating news that has come about from a variety of sources is that humans may indeed have a connection to advanced extraterrestrials when it comes to our origins. Some of the theories being tossed around are truly mind-boggling. I imagine that any intelligent, otherworldly beings in the universe may have asked and pursued the same questions at some point in their advancement. If they exist (and I believe they do), then they may have been down this same journey of discovery as they sought answers as to how they came to be in this vast universe. They too may have had religious and mythological tales of gods and creation before they eventually discovered the ultimate truths. I use the word, "truths" because there may be more than one aspect to the creation of our species. The making of humans may be far more complex than we could ever have imagined.

Human Origin Hypotheses

For millions of years humanity has believed that we are the center of the universe. Much of human history is dependent upon this idea, underlying everything we believe about ourselves, God, the universe, even the afterlife. But that belief system is now being questioned by researchers, archaeologists, scientists, anthropologists, astrophysicists, and people from all walks of life. Additionally, due to the sheer fact that we have no definite answers to how the Solar System was created, nor how life began on Earth, our belief systems are being eroded. Today more and more people are questioning much of what we have been taught by way of our spirituality, history, thoughts on the cosmos, and even some scientific beliefs.

Scientists have said that determining how life formed on Earth is a problem for them; they do not know definitively how life started. In an article from the *Scientific American* by John Horgan, titled "Pssst! Don't tell the creationists, but scientists don't have a clue how life began," Horgan writes, "Dennis Overbye just wrote a status report for *The New York Times* on research into life's origin, based on a conference on the topic at Arizona State University. Geologists, chemists, astronomers, and biologists are as stumped as ever by the riddle of life." Even the origin of the Moon is still unknown. With all the time, energy, effort, money—and most importantly lives—lost during the time of the Apollo missions, we are no closer to understanding where the Moon came from than before the Apollo missions began, with the latest proposal being the "Giant Impact Theory," which has been discarded by scientists. In his popular book *Origin of the Moon*, the famed planetary scientist William Hartmann stated, "neither the Apollo astronauts, the Luna vehicles, nor all the king's horses and all the king's men could assemble enough data to explain the circumstances of the moon's birth." It seems that analogy can be applied to human origins as well. We simply do not know the answers, after all this time, to how humans came to be on Earth in the first place. This author believes it is important to keep our minds open, and the conversations going unless we want to remain a world society that exists with limited knowledge and information about our own world, about ourselves, and about our place in the universe. The following are some of the hypotheses that have come about in recent years, as people attempt to better understand human origins.

Colonization from Another World Hypothesis 1

Did humans come to Earth from a different world? Are we extraterrestrials that came from another world to live on Earth, for reasons we do not remember or understand? The "Colonization from Another World Hypothesis" is the theory that our ancestors originally came from somewhere else in the universe (or even in a different universe altogether). They may have come as explorers colonizing other planets. They may have brought a variety of people in specialized areas to start a colony such as scientists, engineers, intellectuals, and others to colonize Earth, just as our scientists are planning to do on Mars in the future. Some have speculated that there may have even been more than one race of beings involved in the founding of this new civilization. If true, then it appears that people from other worlds and star systems that are far more advanced than humans have already achieved what we are only just beginning to plan. Life on Earth today just may be the result of colonization from beings that were seeking to spread their race through the cosmos. These extraterrestrial-human pioneers would have been trained and educated on how to succeed in a new world. They would have come equipped with everything needed to jump-start this new civilization. The theory is that somewhere along the line, something went wrong; that as these first colonists were left on their own to thrive, they appear to have lost touch with their origins and forgot who they were, and from where they came. Are we the offspring of extraterrestrial ancestors that came to a new world to colonize and we have forgotten who we are? Is this the reason that we lack definitive answers about the creation of life on Earth and in the universe? Did we once have these answers? Surely, the first humans on Earth coming from an advanced race would have been educated in the making and workings of the universe. They may also have had detailed records of their home world, their travel to Earth, and records of the first civilization.

Colonization from Another World Hypothesis 2

Here we entertain a "slightly" different version of the "Colonization from Another World Hypothesis." We just may not be who we thought we were, which would be the original humans on Earth. There is a theory that we were fully developed *Homo sapiens* that were created on another world and were transported here. According to this theory, humankind originated on a world that was better suited for us, but for some reason had to abandon it, and travelled across the universe to Earth. What is most interesting about this summation is that it would make *us* the aliens! We may just be guests on Earth. Could humans have been added to the life that already existed on Earth? In other words, was this a fully functioning planet before we arrived? It would appear so, as it does seem that humans do not belong here. Earth also seems to have suffered from the existence of humans living here. Humans seem completely foreign to Earth. If we can imagine a time before humans, we can visualize a lush world, full of exotic plants and vegetation that grew as far and wide as the eyes can see. Imagine no roads, highways, or buildings; just a world rich in nature and the original animals that existed here. It seems obvious that the addition of humans changed all of that. The introduction of humans into Earth's environment has nearly destroyed it. In this theory, we are not talking about planet seeders, or panspermia. This is about a group of humanoid people that purposely left their home world, and for reasons unknown, felt compelled to come and live on Earth. Perhaps there was a threat to their world. Rather than allowing their species to be wiped out, they went searching for a planet similar to their own that they could escape safely to. The universe is volatile. Meteorites smash into planets, suns explode, there may even be wars and political uproars of other civilizations in space. The possibilities as to why a group of people would leave their home world are endless.

Dr. Ellis Silver, a chief environmentalist and ecologist, wrote extensively about humans not being from Earth in his book aptly titled, *Humans are not from Earth: a scientific evaluation of the evidence.* In his book, Silver enumerates various ways in which humans struggle on Earth. He surmises that we are from elsewhere in the universe. Silver points out that humans are the most advanced species on the planet. Even so, we struggle to physically exist here, whereas the animal world around us lives quite easily. Dr. Silver believes that humans did not develop along with other animals and living organisms on Earth. One of the problems that Silver points out is that humans are shockingly incompatible with and unequipped for life on Earth, and the various environments located here. He points out that for the most part, humans generally have difficulties living in most of them. Silver cites such things as human difficulty with sunlight, high rates of disease and maladies, problems during birth, as well as severe back ailments. These issues, he maintains, are not problems seen often in the animal kingdom. Dr. Ellis concludes that humans developed on a different world, then were later brought here sometime during the last 60,000 to 200,000 years.

In both of the colonization from another world hypotheses (shown above), the work of prominent researcher and author Lloyd Pye (1946–2013) comes to mind. Pye was recognized for his distinctive version of the "Intervention Theory." It was the hypothesis that extraterrestrials had a role in the establishment of human life on Earth. In his book titled *Everything You Know is Still Wrong*, Pye expounded upon his belief that life on Earth did not evolve but appeared here. He commented that after Earth-wide catastrophes, there was no evidence that anything had evolved, but that the various forms of life on Earth appeared here fully developed and ready to procreate. He writes, "Although there are modifications within species, nothing transforms into anything 'higher'; it all simply appears, somehow, as fully functioning sexual units of males and females…ready to live and procreate." In his book he even quoted renowned biologist Richard Dawkins as stating: "It is as though they were just planted here without any evolutionary history." *Amazing!* Pye also wrote: "After a typical sudden appearance, neither plants nor animals will show significant morphological (fundamental physical) change." He later states, "There is no way around it, we are talking about aliens…We humans have contemplated future colonization of the Moon or even Mars, so how can it be ridiculous to think that other advanced life might have had the same idea?"

Are Humans a form of AI?

Were humans engineered? Are we artificially intelligent beings (AIs)? There is a theory that humans were created by advanced extraterrestrial engineers that hold complex, artificial intelligence technology, and the capability of tissue cloning, or some other science that is outside of the present human level of understanding. An even more amazing question is, could humans have been AIs that became self-aware and were later given free will? The AI scenario, and the question as to whether AIs are sentient and therefore should be free, was played out in a remarkable *Star Trek* episode. In *Star Trek: The Next Generation*, there was a popular character that was an android named Data. Data was a male artificial life form with superior intelligence and strength. He was self-aware and conscious. He served as the second officer and chief operations officer aboard the Federation Starship, USS *Enterprise-D* and later the USS *Enterprise-E*. He was well known for his positronic brain which gave him extraordinary computational skills. In one episode, titled "The Measure of a Man," a formal hearing is convened to determine whether Data is the property of Starfleet. It had to be determined if Data was only an AI without any rights or if he was a sentient being with free will. The situation was presented in court to the Starfleet Judge Advocate General, who was to make a ruling which would determine Data's status and future. After hearing the evidence, the Judge makes the following statement:

> It [Data] sits there looking at me, and I don't know what it is. This case has dealt with metaphysics, with questions best left to saints and philosophers. I'm neither competent nor qualified to answer those. I've got to make a ruling, to try to speak to the future. *Is Data a machine? Yes. Is he the property of Starfleet? No.* We have all been dancing around the basic issue. Does Data have a soul? I don't know that he has. I don't know that I have. But I have got to give him the freedom to explore that question himself. It is the ruling of this court that Lieutenant Commander Data has the freedom to choose.

Today, so far into the future from the beginning of human history, we would not recognize that we could be a form of AI. If we are, then *this might explain the possible extraterrestrial* presence on Earth, and all the UFOs in the skies. They may be observing our progress and keeping an eye on their AIs. Over time, it is possible that they have been giving us upgrades such as extending our memories, lengthening our lives, introducing us to breakthroughs in medicine and science. In the quest for determining our origins, the idea of humanity being a form of biological AIs that became sentient and given the freedom to chose our own path is one of the most fascinating.

Gene Roddenberry, the creator of *Star Trek*.

From Different Suns

It is believed by some researchers and ufologists that humans (or humanoids) throughout the universe may have been an experiment for the seeding of worlds and the expansion of humanoid life. It is also believed that it is not just one group of extraterrestrial races that had a hand in the seeding of worlds with humanoids, but that it was a plan that included several extraterrestrial races in this life-giving project. It is also believed that it was benevolent humanoid extraterrestrials that provided the genetic material to create the human race on Earth. These days, information is coming from a variety of sources pertaining to our ancient origins. Is this what humanity has been missing all along in their quest for answers to our purpose here, our reason for being, and where we came from? Some have hypothesized that our DNA has a program, one that is designed for us to awaken at a certain point and realize that our heritage goes far beyond Earth, with the understanding that we come from somewhere else in the universe. Some speculate that it may be connected to this time in history. *If so, then we are all living in a very special time!* Once the questions have finally been answered, then what? Will Earth finally be at peace, and will we have what I refer to as a *Star Trek* future: one where it is humanity's turn to travel the stars and establish worlds? We can dream.

What would the repercussions be if we learned that we did not originate on Earth? Most certainly humankind would have to reevaluate their beliefs. Given all the different belief systems of this world, and the warring over religious dogma, perhaps this would not be a bad thing for humanity. For once, they would be united in understanding *that we are one world.*

Not only is there a possibility that humanity was created elsewhere and brought here, but there is also a possibility that we are a combination of worlds, and different groups of humanoid beings. There is a possibility that there are beings from several worlds involved in placing humanity on Earth, or in the creation of humanity. We just may be a rather grand experiment. We may be the result of scientists from otherworldly civilizations working together and for whatever reason, creating humanity. We may have cousins (so to speak) on other planets that are working toward understanding their origins and planning their sojourns into space just as we are. This may also be who we see visiting our skies, operating the UFOs and the many reports of humanoid beings allegedly encountered around the planet. These planets, these worlds may be traveling around different suns, their lives similar yet different from ours. The one thing that I believe is universal is the desire to live our lives, wherever that is and however long, in a productive way. We can only wonder about otherworldly civilizations. Do their children go to school? Do they worship a god? How about their home and shelter and travel? Are they culturally like us in any way? Once we finally achieve space travel, I believe we will meet these people from different suns, on different worlds, and learn that there is good and bad out there and they all have the same goal of trying to live out their lives in a satisfying manner.

What We Know

Looking at what has been told to us, what has been handed down to us throughout history, and in some cases what is being presented today, we have been visited by otherworldly beings from the beginning of our history. Our ancient ancestors left us records so that we would have this information. According to ancient records, humanity has been visited by extraterrestrials throughout history. The Assyrians, Aztecs, Babylonians, Chaldeans, Egyptians, Greeks, Hebrews, Hindus, Mayans, Phoenicians, Sumerians, Tibetans and others, all kept records in some form of their interactions with beings from other worlds. According to the stories, many of these beings taught humanity how to live and thrive on Earth, and how to establish and maintain their civilizations. Perhaps this was because of humanity being a new race of people, one they hoped would eventually become a part of the galactic community…far into the future. It may have also been that these beings were our creators, and therefore acted as our guides, teachers, nurturers, and protectors. If the ancient extraterrestrial visitors were the "seeders of planets," they may have had the same agenda for all the worlds where they established life. One wonders if this is something that is done with all civilizations that developed within the Milky Way galaxy. Might there be beings assigned to assist new worlds, and then leave them at some point in the process to watch them develop, being careful not to interfere in their free will?

If the Earth was terraformed (as discussed in Chapter One), and then seeded by advanced beings that sent a hypothetical Genesis-type technology through the galaxy in hopes of seeding planets with intelligent life, we must question whether these seeders were different from those that physically came to Earth and helped humanity to establish civilization. In other words, are there two separate groups? Did the seeders come first (in whatever capacity they were seeding worlds), and then later came the extraterrestrial teachers? One wonders. Perhaps, the seeders were in a form such that they could not visit the planets they seeded with life. I imagine that these beings were considerably advanced and far beyond visiting planets. Maybe they were so advanced that they simply planted the seeds of life and moved on, while watching the outcome from a distance, but never interacting with their "seedlings." This also could have been their one and only task in the universe, which is to seed planets and then leave. Therefore, after the seeding of Earth, could it be that otherworldly beings caught sight of Earth, and came here with their own agenda? In other words, were the ancient extraterrestrials that visited Earth, a different race from the original planet seeders and or the terraformers? Or are they the same beings? One wonders too if they were from the same universe as ours. Were they humanoid? The scenarios and questions are endless. But they are a start in attempting to understand our origins and what happened on Earth at the beginning of history.

Earth Was the Strange New World

Many of us are familiar with the introductory words as spoken by William Shatner as Captain James T. Kirk at the beginning of each episode of the original *Star Trek* series in the 1960s, where he stated, "Space, the final frontier. These are the voyages of the

The *Enterprise* of *Star Trek*.

starship Enterprise. Its five-year mission: to explore strange new worlds. To seek out new life and new civilizations. To boldly go where no man has gone before!" Today, many dream of humankind one day traveling to the stars to explore new worlds. However, most have not considered the idea that our dream may have been that of others in the universe as well. While many on Earth are still contemplating whether extraterrestrials exist, there may be extraterrestrials out there that are already traveling the universe as explorers. It could well be that Earth is one of the strange new worlds they discovered while we were still in our infancy on this planet, just as the crew of the *Enterprise* did on many occasions. In our arrogance, we have always fancied ourselves as the center of the universe. We have been led to believe that we are. We believe that we are technologically advanced, and that we can travel to the stars and lay claim to other planetary bodies (such as the Moon and Mars for example). We never stop to consider that there are others out there that have been around longer, and that are more advanced than we are. Research shows that in the beginning of its history, Earth was the "strange new world" that was discovered. It was humans that mistook spaceships in the sky, and the people inside of them as gods. It was humans that set about worshipping them. That was who we were. That it seems is what happened in our ancient past.

In fact, there may be not one, but several spacefaring races that were far ahead of us in their science and technological achievements, and were ready, willing, and able to cross the universe and start their exploration of the stars. It appears that we may not be the only race in the cosmos with this ambition. We just may be as they say, "late for the party." Some of these groups appear to have already visited Earth and may even have started colonies on Earth and elsewhere before humanity ever arrived on the scene. *That's right.* It may also be that once we arrived here, we were visited by not just one, but several races of extraterrestrial beings. Some may have come for exploration, others scientific purposes, others to mine for resources, while others may have been experimenting with creating life, and perhaps—according to some accounts—may have created humanity. There may have been an agreement between world allies or groups of allies to visit different parts of the galaxy, to explore the planets and worlds, with Earth being one of them. These are ideas that I believe should be considered when looking at our enigmatic past where so much does not add up in our history. Scientists, historians, and religious groups have been looking at just one path that humanity has been traveling on, when really there may be more than one scenario.

"We are not alone, and we never were." That has become my motto. I find myself repeating it to people that I am engaged with in conversation, and on podcasts, radio shows and in my books. For as many people out there that believe this to be a fact, there are millions that are unaware that extraterrestrials exist and have been visiting Earth since the beginning of history. As we continue to examine the Earth's galactic history and its extraterrestrial connections, we need to recognize that in all probability, advanced otherworldly beings had a hand in our creation, establishing our civilizations and guiding us, and have remained interested in our progress. That would explain the many mysteries of the past which we will soon delve into in this chapter. Many reading this book may be well versed in some of the information about our ancient past regarding extraterrestrials. However, for those seeking knowledge on our extraterrestrial connection, who are hearing this information for the first time, you will be surprised.

I believe that humanity has come to a pivotal point in history, one that will decide which direction we will take. Although we are still seeking answers about our past, in our journey up to this point, we have amassed enough information to know that our past is not what we have been taught. We have also grown enough to understand that we are the masters of our own destiny; we have become open enough to now be aware that what we understood, and much of what we believed about ourselves and our history is incorrect. We now understand that our knowledge about our origins and our place in the universe is not what we thought. All races, species and civilizations must grow. Therefore, as a world society, we are finally at the stage where more knowledge about our past is slowly opening up to us. This is a time where our belief systems are being challenged. We are now at a point in our existence where the idea of extraterrestrials being a reality is no longer just a theory or speculation, it is being proven as a fact. There is just too much evidence to ignore. We can no longer shrug it off or sweep it under the carpet.

Still, there will be some that will not be ready for this information. I once read a warning from a researcher/writer by the name of Steve Omar, who authored many in-depth articles about extraterrestrials, UFOs, and space mysteries. In one article he talked about the idea of disseminating information on these topics stating, "Use common sense, wisdom, discretion in spreading this information, while avoiding skeptics, paranoid types, religious fanatics, and the emotionally unstable." He wrote this many years ago, and apparently did not believe that some were ready for this knowledge. He wrote this during a period when this information was more secretive and not taken seriously. It is my hope that we have now moved past this period and that people are more aware (and interested) in learning the information provided to us from the past by so many researchers, writers, historians, experiencers, and others that have struggled for so long to bring the truth about our reality to the world.

The Human Extraterrestrial Connection, The Starting Point

After years of painstaking research by pioneers in the fields of ufology, archeology, ancient history, anthropology, and various other sciences, we have evidence that not only are we *not* alone in the universe, but that there has been extraterrestrial interaction with humans from the beginning. We have enough evidence from our ancient past by way of artifacts, ancient writings, ancient art, eyewitness accounts and more, depicting extraterrestrials and spacecraft that we can deduce that Earth was visited, early on, by intelligent, sophisticated visitors from outer space. Some of the clearest and most startling evidence that we were visited in ancient times involves some very startling tales, leaving little doubt that something huge involving extraterrestrials occurred back then, leading to the conclusion that we were not only visited, but we were led, taught, and helped by these advanced people. They brought us knowledge and they helped our civilizations to thrive. They taught us how to live and helped us to grow. In the end, it appears that whatever hierarchy is in charge out there put in place a kind of "prime directive" (yes the kind in *Star Trek*) to leave us alone and let us thrive on our own. I say this because at some point, direct contact with extraterrestrials stopped occurring on a large scale. They appear to have removed themselves for the most part, physically, on a mass scale, from our presence. *At least for a period of time.* Since that time, they have been waiting and watching for us to mature, as is most likely done in all new developing civilizations in the universe.

Whether or not we are alone in the universe is one of humanity's most pressing questions. Our Milky Way galaxy is so vast, with so many different types of stars with planets orbiting them, that we now understand that it is statistically possible for life to have arisen on another planet eons ago. We would not be the first intelligent life to form in the galaxy. Therefore, it is not so much of a stretch to suggest that extraterrestrials may have come here from a distant world and colonized Earth long ago. These beings would have been further along than humankind by way of science and technology. Eons ago they may have accomplished what humans are just beginning to experiment with by way of space travel, science, and technology. Most likely, there are many extraterrestrial civilizations that had perfected space travel and were already exploring the cosmos when humans first appeared on Earth. By then they may have already perfected AI technology, EBEs, and as mentioned in Chapter One, some may even have found the means to terraform worlds. Where humans are just beginning to experiment with cloning individuals, they may already be creating armies of cloned beings. Where we now have artificial insemination, there may be worlds where this is the only means of reproduction. Where we are still a warring species on a planet filled with strife, many may have already been living in a peaceful state or even a utopian world for millennia. These beings may have reached a point where they are fully capable of being creators of life, and many today believe that this just may be what happened with humans on Earth.

Therefore, we should ask, "Did we come from the stars?" Did the very beings that may have created humans continue their work by visiting Earth and assisting humanity to thrive? Is it possible that there is more to humankind's history than we can possibly have imagined? Could we have forgotten our past? Did we *originally* understand where we came from? Perhaps in the beginning it was not a mystery. Perhaps interactions with extraterrestrials were once well known to us, and it was accepted and understood that we were a part of them, and perhaps even recognized that humans were their creation, and if not their creation at least their prodigies, and maybe even their hybrid children. Or could it have been that we are them? Could there have been a group of humanoid beings that colonized Earth and *we* are them? We may have known in our remote past about our origins, and what occurred with us in the beginning of human history. We may also have once known the history of the universe. We may have been taught and educated in all things before something went wrong...before our history went off course and we forgot. *Could we be gods that have lost our way?*

It is due to our naïve state that most of us do not recognize this possibility, although there are some cultures that have always been aware of this connection. There are people around the world that have had stories handed down to them from the beginning of their culture that told of visitors from the stars. Those cultures always knew. They always believed this to be true. For most of the world, this information is just coming to light in our modern era... albeit *slowly*. Many are now becoming awake to this idea. Over the last fifty years there has been a greater interest in our ancient past, human development, and how it all began. The first seeds appear to have been planted by researcher and author Erich von Daniken in his book *Chariots of the Gods*, which was published in 1968. *Chariots of the Gods* implies that the technologies and religions of several ancient civilizations were given to them by extraterrestrials that were welcomed as gods. They are referred to today as ancient astronauts and ancient aliens. There are those that take issue with the idea that ancient civilizations were jump-started by beings from other worlds, believing that any credit for human progress is owed to humanity only. However, as much as we would like to believe this, evidence shows that this is not the case. *We had help.*

Finally...

If we really do have an extraterrestrial connection when it

comes to our origins, then Earth may have a problem, at least for a while. Why? There *may* be complications in our world society because this would challenge many people's beliefs. To deviate from the two main ideas of how humankind came to be, which involve religious ideas of creation and the process of evolution, means that many people's belief systems will have to be reevaluated. This new reality would upend conventional teachings. A reeducation program may be needed when it comes to our history and science, the understanding of Earth, the cosmos and more. It is also because we live in a world of myth and dogma that most do not question. Due to their belief systems, many are not concerned about otherworldly activities that are going on in the universe. Many still believe that no one can travel the vast universe. This is not necessarily true as advanced beings may have the means and ways that we do not yet understand. (See Chapter Seven: The Cosmic Freeway: Stargates, Portals and Wormholes)

However, more and more people are becoming interested in new ideas pertaining to humanity's origins and our place in the universe. These thinkers of the world are out to make a change here on Earth for the betterment of Earth. They are finding that the more they search, the more they discover the cosmic connection to Earth. This author predicts that soon we will encounter knowledgeable beings that will inform us of what transpired in the beginning of humanity's history. A very interesting thought was once suggested by Al Chop, a former U.S. Department of Defense and National Aeronautics and Space Administration official. Chop stated in an interview with the *Desert Sun* newspaper, number 287, on July 13, 1981, that he believed that sometime in the future, humans will time travel back to our past. He proposed that we would one day enter a time traveling vehicle, that would enable us to travel back in time to learn about human origins. He also speculated that the UFOs seen today, may be time travel vehicles allowing extraterrestrials to travel through time and observe us. He was quoted as saying, "I believe they're interplanetary vehicles."

Once we move past the theories of how life on Earth came to be, we begin to look at the universe in a different way. Once we understand just how vast the universe is, we can see that the chances of us being alone are nonexistent. Not only are we not alone, but the chances of there being advanced civilizations out there that have been around for eons are incredibly high. It appears that humanity is very young in comparison to what and who is out

41

there. Not only is there a chance that we may have been created by advanced extraterrestrials, but there is a very good chance that the first civilization on Earth was established by highly advanced beings as well. The idea of them living among humans is also plausible as they may have come to pass on knowledge to us. In other words, there may have been technologically advanced extraterrestrials that at the beginning of time established civilization here, or at the very least helped humans along. These same helpers may have been the seeders of Earth. If so, one wonders if the Earth is owned by someone in the cosmos; and if these beings could be living among us today. Perhaps they have always been here, hidden away from the mainstream populace. This could explain so many of the strange and anomalous supernatural activities on Earth that have been recorded through the ages.

The Earth rising from the Moon.. (NASA)

Chapter Three
Extraterrestrials and the Ancient Past

"Given the millions of billions of Earth-like planets, life elsewhere in the Universe without a doubt, does exist. In the vastness of the Universe we are not alone."
— Albert Einstein

Did beings from other worlds visit Earth in the beginning of human history? Evidence has been uncovered that indicates that they did. If true, then this presents a plethora of questions such as, "When did this visitation begin?" "Who were they?" "What was their purpose for visiting Earth?" One thing that we know for certain is there are ancient accounts of beings that came from the stars and interacted with humans. These narratives are found all over the world in various forms of ancient writings, oral tales, and historical records from several civilizations. For many cultures, these stories are sacred and celebrated with great fanfare. From this information, we know that something happened in Earth's past from which we are still experiencing the ramifications today. While many people are seeking disclosure from governments about extraterrestrial visitation today others are searching for answers about an extraterrestrial connection to our ancient past. Answers are being sought to such questions as, "What is our connection to cosmos?" "Did extraterrestrials visit Earth in ancient times?" "Did we come from the stars?" These are just a few of the questions that are being asked today, and the answers are truly *astounding*!

The Ancient Extraterrestrial Visitors

Just who were these ancient visitors and what was their purpose in coming to Earth? We understand from the information of our past that advanced extraterrestrials came to Earth and elevated the living conditions of humans. Some researchers believe that these visitors were seeking to use the human race for their own selfish reasons. Still others maintain that these beings came to Earth with the idea of helping humanity and were mistaken for gods due to their technology. Another possibility is that they may have been the same beings that placed humans on Earth in the first place, and later returned to assist. In the end, it appears that humanity was eventually left to its own devices, as it seems that the extraterrestrials either left or faded into the background. They may have been watching humanity this entire time, discreetly helping us to progress.

It was well known to many cultures in ancient times that these "gods" or "star people" were not from Earth. It was common knowledge that humans were connected to the cosmos, and that our creators were from the stars. They may even have known the names of these beings, and of their home worlds. They may have been told the story of Earth and humanity's past. Some attempted to salvage the knowledge by writing it down or passing the information through oral accounts to their descendants. In some cultures, that was the responsibility of one individual. It was their job to recount the history and pass it on. As a result, this knowledge was in humankind's consciousness for thousands of years, until it was either diluted over time, or a catastrophe occurred erasing the memory of our history due to people perishing on a large scale. Either way, that part of our past has come to be seen as a forgotten history. We have forgotten who we are, where we came from, and how we came to be. Perhaps if we delve into researching our past, and examining the information that we have, then we can form a better understanding of what occurred in the beginning of human history. This research is important to all of humankind. Therefore, researchers, ufologists, scientists, astrophysicists, archeologists, and many others continue to attempt to understand the information that we have about our past.

Extraterrestrials on Earth in Ancient Times

As we investigate our past and our connection to the stars, we learn that there is an abundance of information that supports the idea of extraterrestrial visitation on Earth in ancient times. So much so that it has come to the point where the idea of extraterrestrial visitation on Earth during that time is no longer just a theory, it has become an accepted fact among many researchers. After years of painstaking research by pioneers in the field of ufology, archeology, ancient history, anthropology, and various sciences, we have evidence that beings from elsewhere once visited Earth and interacted with humans. The reasons these beings came and then left is a great mystery. Even more importantly, *did they ever leave?* It also appears that there has been more than one group of beings that have come to Earth over the millennia.

In 1968 author, researcher Erich von Daniken published his best-selling book, *Chariots of the Gods*, in which he referred to these spacefaring beings as "ancient astronauts." The idea of ancient astronauts intrigued people as this was during the time that the Apollo Program (1968-1972) was preparing for landing the first people on the Moon. During this period, some questioned if extraterrestrials had visited Earth, seeing a parallel with what we were doing by landing people on the Moon. In order to make sense of the idea of extraterrestrial visitation to Earth's ancient past, we need to look at some of the purported evidence that have brought so many reputable people to this startling conclusion.

Who Were the Ancient Astronauts?

The people of the ancient world more than likely viewed the world much differently than how we imagine they did. For one thing, it appears that several cultures witnessed aerial craft in the skies. They most certainly knew about space travel, as some have recalled tales of the gods leaving the Earth on ships and travelling to the stars. Unlike modern humans with our cameras, television, social media and more, where we can easily document and recount what we are seeing on practically a minute-by-minute basis, our ancestors had no such technologies. However, this did not prevent them from documenting as much as they could about strange phenomena. One difference is that they seemed less fearful in their tales. Extraterrestrials seemed more familiar to them, and they accepted their associations with otherworldly beings and the role they played in their lives. The research into the past tells us that throughout history, there have been several cultures that recounted tales of beings that came from the stars, giving them knowledge of how to improve their lives. These accounts portray what appear to have been powerful, almost supernatural people that came from space. Plainly stated, they taught primitive humankind how to live safely, comfortably, and healthy on Earth. They taught humanity how to thrive. *And we did*.

There is tangible proof of extraterrestrial visitation all over the world. We see it today in such areas as architectural wonders, ruins, structures, writings, and the cosmological information they bestowed upon early humans. Proponents of the ancient astronaut theory maintain that many of the ruins and structures of antiquity were designed and built by these otherworldly beings, or in some cases they enlisted human assistance to construct them. Another argument for this theory is the jumps or gaps in humanity's knowledge of technology. This is shown especially in out-of-place artifacts and in some areas that were only discovered by humankind in our modern era. It should be noted too that these extraterrestrial visits were not just a one-time occurrence in Earth's past. This has been ongoing throughout history.

Hypothetical Reasons Extraterrestrials Visited Ancient Earth

Why would people from other worlds visit Earth? We have speculated above that they came to Earth to help humankind; that they saw a fledgling world that needed help. That of course would have been a noble reason. But is that the only reason? The following are theories that have been considered as to their reasons for coming. They are interesting to contemplate, and some may point us toward the truth as we attempt to unravel our galactic origins.

The Ownership of Earth Hypothesis

One of the most interesting hypotheses falls under the category of ownership. Is it possible that there may be real estate in the cosmos and there are those that own sectors of the galaxy? If so, is this something that could be part of a universal way of operating? Or, to put it another way, are there areas of the galaxy that are being run by certain groups, and Earth (unbeknownst to us) falls under this category? Could it be that the Earth belongs to someone else? This is the same scenario that humans are working out today. Governments are currently vying for certain areas of the Moon. They are also preparing to colonize Mars. This may be what happened with Earth. There may have been in the ancient past (or even now) extraterrestrial ambitions when it came to our planet. Our world may be owned by others. We may be a colony that was placed here. This may be the reason for so many UFO sightings on Earth today.

The Experiment Hypothesis

Astronaut Jim Lovell, the Command Module pilot of *Apollo 8*, once commented, "The Earth from here is a grand oasis in the big vastness of space." Earth is known for its magnificence. From space the astronauts talked about how it resembled a beautiful jewel or marble in space. Earth stands out as the prominent place in the Solar System when it comes to beauty and life; it is a world unlike any other in this vicinity of the galaxy. So why wouldn't there be those out there that would notice our world?

If we consider the idea that there may be beings in the universe with abilities that far surpass our own, then it is very possible that extraterrestrials know we are here. It is also possible that probes were sent out by extraterrestrials to follow the progress of Earth. It is possible too that they had ambitions to populate the galaxy, or to learn of other worlds, and that they placed a colony here as an experiment to see how life would thrive here, and to see if they could exist here. Humanity may have been the very first experiment of this kind. Humans may be the beginning of a colony that has been watched. We could be watched with extraterrestrials recording the results. Interestingly, there are some that believe that is partially what is happening on the Moon. There is a theory that beings are observing Earth from the Moon, keeping track of our progress, and reporting back to the galaxy's higher echelons on humanity's progress. *If we are an experiment, did we pass or fail?*

Following up on the Terraforming of Earth Hypothesis

In Chapter One: Earthrise, I wrote about the possibility that the Earth was terraformed. If the Earth were terraformed, could it be that extraterrestrials visited in ancient times to follow up on this progress? We can assume that such an undertaking, the creation of a new world, would have come at great cost, and they would not have abandoned the project. They may have returned after the terraforming of Earth to observe the status of the planet, remaining here for some time before returning to their home world.

The Seeders of Life are Watching Their Creations Hypothesis

Returning to the Panspermia Hypothesis there is the idea that the seeders of life on Earth came to experience their creation firsthand. As in the terraforming of Earth theory, these beings may have traveled to Earth to check the progress of their work. They may have come for a progress report, checking on whether intelligent life had taken hold. They may have been physical beings or etheric with the capability of taking form, such as the extraterrestrial group called "the Clarions," believed by some to be the original Master race of our universe. They may have sent emissaries that remained on Earth for a period time, perfecting and even upgrading their project. They may have stayed on Earth for a period, in similar fashion to a parent checking on their children, and assisted them in establishing civilizations, and later returned to their home in the cosmos.

Resources Hypothesis

Some researchers theorize that extraterrestrials came here in the past for Earth's resources. They think that coming to Earth was purely a business venture. Many feel that Earth is a prime place for resources, much as the governments of the world are viewing the Moon. Why would we believe for a moment that if there are others out there, that they would not recognize Earth as a great resource for a variety of materials? That is what many researchers think would be the attraction for some otherworldly beings. Some believe that in ancient times the Earth was mined for its resources, especially the metals, with gold being the most important. Some, it is believed, are attracted to our large bodies of water. Others, it is thought, were trying to save themselves and continue their species through a hybrid program. If you look at the tales of the gods, there was a lot going on with the intimate interactions between the gods and humans. Just imagine what else may have gone on, that we have no record of.

These are just some of the hypotheses for why extraterrestrials may have first come to Earth in our remote past. Why they are here now, may be a different story altogether, and are covered in Chapter Eight: From Elsewhere: Extraterrestrials Among Us.

Extraterrestrials, Ancient Earth, and the Moon

I noticed just how much of our past had been forgotten when I was writing the book *The Moon's Galactic History: A Look at the Moon's Extraterrestrial Past and Its Connection to Earth*. There I gave accounts of writings from people that talked about a time when it is said that there was no Moon in the sky, a time of a pre-lunar Earth. This information was written down by people that were alive at the beginning of humanity's early civilizations. They wrote about a time that even preceded them. We have lost a great deal of information over the eons about our past, so it is important to at least consider the information that we have access to from so long ago. The information about there being a possible time without a moon was surprising if not shocking to most people that heard this information for the first time. It made me wonder that if this is true, and the Moon was not there in the beginning, then why is it here now? Where are those beings now, that allegedly helped Earth by bringing in the Moon? One of the theories as to why the Moon is here is that it was brought and purposely placed in orbit to aid Earth in some way.

It occurred to me as I was writing the aforementioned book that there was a good deal of information that humankind may be missing, or, has forgotten, about our past. The writings about a pre-lunar Earth, as told to us by some of the most prominent philosophers and writers from the ancient world, takes us far back in time... to a time before our first civilizations; a time before Mesopotamia, Sumer, and ancient Egypt, which were there at the cradle of civilization. The ancients that wrote about a time without a moon had access to this history. During that period the information was new, written down and not forgotten or lost. The writers were reputable, upstanding men during their time, and we still hold them in high regard today. They include the renowned Greek philosopher Anaxagoras of Clazomenae (c. 500-c. 428 BC); the great Greek philosopher and scientist, Aristotle (384 BC-322 BC); Italian philosopher, cosmologist, and theorist Giordano Bruno (1548-1600); the famous third century Roman grammarian and author Censorinus (unknown birth and death dates); Greek philosopher Democritus (460-370 BC); author Dionysius Chalcidensis (aprox. 399-100 BC); the noted theologian and ecclesiastical writer Hippolytus of Rome (160 AD-236 AD); the notable satirist and author Lucian of Samosata (120 AD-180 AD prominent Greek historian Mnaseas of Patrae (late 3rd century); the eminent Greek philosopher, biographer and essayist Plutarch (ca. 45-120 AD); noted poet Ovid (43 BC-17 AD); and the distinguished mathematician Theodorus of Cyrene (465 BC-398 BC).

All of these men wrote about a time without the Moon. It was Ovid's accounting of that era that was the most telling when it comes to information about a time with no Moon, information that many are not aware of. Ovid wrote:

The Arcadians are said to have possessed their land

49

before the birth of Jove (the god Jupiter), and their race is older than the Moon. They lived like beasts, lives spent to no purpose: The common people were crude as yet, without arts. They built houses from leafy branches, grass their crops, water, scooped in their palms, was nectar to them. No bull panted yoked to the curved ploughshare. No soil was under the command of the farmer. Horses were not used, all carried their own burdens. The sheep went about still clothed in their wool. People lived in the open and went about nude, inured to heaven downpours from rain-filled winds. To this day the naked priests recall the memory of old customs and testify to those ancient ways. (Fasti, Book II).

Ovid's description is so detailed, so precise, that we can easily imagine that time without a moon, where humans were uncultured and feral.

If true, and there was a time when there was no moon in the sky, the question is how did it get here? The theory is that an extraterrestrial group brought the Moon here and placed it in Earth's vicinity as a means of helping the Earth to stabilize, and helping life to thrive. We have no idea as to what the ramifications may have been for the rest of the galaxy if Earth continued without the stabilizing Moon. It is my understanding that when something occurs with one planetary body, the rest of the galaxy is affected in a domino effect.

Interestingly, this time without a moon is talked about on the ancient Sun Gate at Tiahuanaco, located in the ancient city of Tiahuanaco in Bolivia. The Sun Gate is a large, rock-solid, ancient megalithic stone structure. It is roughly three meters tall and is carved from a block of stone that weighs 10 tons. On it are found mysterious symbols and figures that have astronomical meanings. According to the symbols, the Moon arrived in our Solar System around 12,000 years ago, and in the process caused chaos on Earth. This conclusion was reached in 1956 by researcher and author Hans Schindler Bellamy, who examined the Sun Gate and later wrote a book about it titled *The Calendar of Tiahuanaco*. It is in cases like this that we understand that there is knowledge pertaining to the galaxy and Earth that has been either lost or forgotten. Unfortunately, there is no other information to be learned here. We do not know the reason for the Moon being brought in, the state of Earth at that time in the galaxy, nor what group of extraterrestrials placed the Moon where it is. As we search for answers involving Earth's galactic history, I believe that this is pertinent information to consider when attempting to put the pieces together. To summarize, if there really was no moon in the sky, and it was brought in as the Sun Gate says, then who are the extraterrestrials that brought it here, and why?

Earth Seeded by Extraterrestrials More than Once Hypothesis

Could it be that humans were not the first intelligent beings on Earth? Might there have been intelligent beings that we know nothing about that were placed here by extraterrestrials that eventually died off, and then the earth was seeded again? That may just explain the out-of-place artifacts, relics, odd shaped skeletons, giant skeletons, unknown metals and other items that scientists are continuing to uncover today. With this theory, our history, our past, comes into question, and this may be why some museums of the world are allegedly hiding anomalous artifacts, and others are destroying them. Has humanity finally reached a time in our history when we are beginning to understand these possibilities? We can see why some of the science may not add up. Have we finally reached a time on Earth where we can "see" the possible truths of our origins? Are we finally waking up to who we are? *Once the extraterrestrials understand that we are awakening, will they finally introduce themselves? Will some return? Will they tell us the story of our history?*

Earth's Forgotten Galactic Origins and Extraterrestrial Past

Has humankind forgotten its galactic extraterrestrial past? It appears that for the most part, *yes*. During an interview on October 21, 2021 on the *Theories of Everything* podcast with Curt Jaimungal, former U.S. Army Counterintelligence Special Agent Luis Elizondo stated, "Most of our history we have no idea about. It's like spending an entire day and having amnesia, except for the last five minutes before you go to bed." Indeed. There is a lot of information that has been either lost or forgotten. In fact, it appears that nearly the complete knowledge of UFOs and extraterrestrials from our ancient past is lost to humanity. As a researcher, I am grateful for the information we do have. How did this situation come about? How did we "forget" or "lose" most of this knowledge in the first place? It's complicated. Some information has been kept from us due to religious doctrine and manipulation. In some cases, knowledge was kept from humanity, purposely hidden, distorted and sometimes destroyed either purposely or by accident. Some knowledge was lost during worldwide disasters and other information just became lost through the long windings of time. Yet still, certain information was merged with cultural traditions and is now regarded as myth.

Today, the responsibility lies with us to uncover the truth by putting the pieces of the puzzle together, as best we can. Other potential reasons that we have forgotten or lost our galactic historical knowledge relating to extraterrestrials are as follows:

Deliberate Destruction of Knowledge

In history, there are those that have attempted to manipulate people through doctrine and religion. For this reason, some with nefarious intentions may have destroyed records (or hidden them) with information about our extraterrestrial connections. This information may have told us about our true origins. However, it would not have served the purpose of those that wanted to control masses of people.

Natural Disasters, Destructions and Catastrophes

The occurrence of natural disasters and worldwide calamities where most of life on Earth was destroyed is believed to be one of the reasons that we do not have a complete accounting of our galactic history and connections with otherworldly beings. Earth has suffered from several global disasters. Much of the knowledge of humanity's past may have been wiped away during these events. Although some information appears to have been salvaged after the fact, other information is long gone, or perhaps lies at the bottom of the oceans, or covered under earth and sands in the deserts. We know of such events as the "great flood," and tales of entire civilizations being wiped out due to other huge devastating events. If we were once openly connected to extraterrestrials, there is speculation that after the last life-altering catastrophe, that space communications with extraterrestrials may have been terminated, and the afflicted survivors on Earth left abandoned and having to rebuild civilization on Earth alone. After so long, the knowledge of Earth's past and its extraterrestrial connection would have been forgotten.

With that said, there is still some salvaged information. For example, some stories from the tribes of northern Canada state that in their ancient tales, their ancestors resided in a warm country. However, they state that the "sky fell down" and the survivors of this devastating event were relocated to the Arctic. This sounds like perhaps a cosmic catastrophe that took place in the skies. Whatever it was, it brought destruction. However, there were survivors that had to start over, it appears in the area of the Arctic Circle. In the Yucatan, it is believed from their ancient teachings that following four worldwide disasters, humanity had to begin its progression again. If any of this information is true, then a great deal of knowledge and pertinent information about our history was lost.

In addition, knowledge may have been lost due to the many thousands of wars fought around the planet, as well as conquerors who either didn't care about history when it came to the destruction of relics and artifacts, such as Nero allegedly setting Rome on fire, or the destruction of libraries including the great Library of Alexandria. The Library of Alexandria and others that were destroyed are believed by some historians to have contained knowledge of our origins, our past and our extraterrestrial connections. In our own time we have witnessed sacred artifacts being destroyed in Iraq. This could have happened before, perhaps more than once in our history.

Finally, there is thought that some of the past catastrophes were orchestrated purposely by beings to keep us in a state of ignorance; meaning that if Earth is owned, there may be someone out there powerful enough to control our weather, population, conditions on Earth and our knowledge. As I stated before, it could well be that there are extraterrestrials out there that do not want us to know our origins. *Yet*.

Authors Thoughts: It has been conveyed in narratives from extraterrestrials that in their opinion, humans have a warring nature. Perhaps these extraterrestrials are concerned that if we are aware of who we are, and that we are connected to beings out in space somewhere, then we may reach a point where we may actually pose a threat to the galaxy. They may be anxious about this aspect of humanity. They might be worried that once we achieve space traveling capabilities, that this knowledge of who we are and where we came from may make humanity more ambitious and dangerous. There is the fear that humanity's warring nature might spew out into the galaxy as we attempt to colonize planets and explore the universe. The alien race known as the Dracos (see Chapter Eight: From Elsewhere: Extraterrestrials Among Us) are said to be concerned about humans advancing to a point that we may even be an eventual competitor. According to sources the Dracos are a powerful, malevolent race of beings. They are said to be concerned that eventually, humanity will be vying for control of certain sectors of the galaxy. The Dracos themselves believe they are privy to Earth and other areas of the universe and play a role in a number of negative scenarios in the galaxy. This is certainly interesting information to consider when thinking about humanity's loss of knowledge, the violent wars on Earth, disasters, the confusion on Earth, and humanity's seemingly general bad luck! One wonders if this is all by design to keep us in the dark.

Real Life Events Relegated to Myths

Many researchers today that are investigating Earth's galactic history have come to the conclusion that some of our mythological tales of gods interacting with humans are true. They maintain that these so-called "gods" were actually people from other worlds that came to Earth and were mistaken as superior beings. Today, many of these accounts, such as the tales of ancient Egypt, Rome, Greece, and others are now relegated to mythical stories. If there is any truth in this theory, then some of the answers to our extraterrestrial history have been in front of us all along. What we perceive today as mythology may be priceless information that has been distorted. Some argue that several of the gods portrayed in myth are not fully human, and therefore were mythical beings. This may be a grave mistake in our thinking. There are numerous amounts of artifacts from ancient times depicting different types of beings, such as birdlike humanoids, flying humans, cat people, small beings with large heads, reptilian type beings, humans with elongated skulls, and others. Who is to say that these were not depictions of extraterrestrials, or even creatures from Earth that were around during that time? This tells us that there were others here of non-human origin living among humanity. There is a chance, given the research, that humans may have lived side by side with extraterrestrials of different forms that either came to Earth or were seeded here as we were; and that those species may have been wiped out or left Earth all together. Or not, as there are numerous sightings of strange beings today, and we do not know where they come from. That of course is another book.

Natural Elements

Many items, artifacts or constructions either brought here or built here by extraterrestrials in the past may not have withstood time. Although we have such structures as the pyramids of Giza and Stonehenge and others that have remained, many others may not have survived the natural elements over millions of years. There may have been several lost artifacts that further show our interactions with extraterrestrials. There are items being discovered today that show they were made with advanced technology and scientists are baffled by them. These items (covered below) are objects from our ancient past that should not exist.

The Destruction of the Library of Alexandria

The Library of Alexandria was located in Alexandria, Egypt. It was one of the largest and most important libraries of the ancient world. It has been referred to as, "the cradle of world knowledge." It housed millions of papyri, scrolls, ancient texts, writings, and manuscripts containing information from civilizations from around the known world during its time. Because it held such early knowledge, and a great deal of information about our history, some researchers wonder whether there was information about extraterrestrials kept there. This author suspects that there was plenty of information on this topic to be found on the numerous shelves that filled this great place. While the Library of Alexandria suffered several losses of information during its time due to several wars and other occurrences during its existence, it was during the Ptolemaic siege in 48 BC that sealed its fate. At that time the library sustained devastating damage. Its tragic end is considered an immense loss for humanity. Ancient historical reports tell of its unfortunate end, and about the enormous amount of significant of information about our world that was destroyed. Just imagine the encounters with otherworldly beings that had been written down and placed in that library. Some believe that it may have held the answers to our origins and many other questions that remain a mystery to this day.

Ancient Civilizations and Evidence of ET Contact

Throughout my research on our early galactic history, one thing is abundantly clear: there were extraterrestrials all over the ancient world. Even with the loss of knowledge, there is still ample evidence that several ancient civilizations had direct interactions with extraterrestrials. In fact, there are several civilizations that documented visitations of celestial beings that they said came from outer space. These visitors are usually described as having great power, came from other worlds, and gave them knowledge and technology that helped them to progress. Let us revisit our past and examine extraterrestrial roots.

Ancient Egypt

Egypt historically has been a favorite among many researchers when it comes to the study of humanity's ancient past. It is one of the most important places to visit when looking at Earth's galactic history and its extraterrestrial connection. There has always been something very special and different about ancient Egypt. We know it to be one of the most enigmatic civilizations in history, leaving behind evidence of a sophisticated infrastructure as well as technology that was advanced for that time. It was a beautiful, powerful empire, and one that many believe was directly connected to the cosmos and extraterrestrials. Some researchers maintain that the ancient Egyptian society was created by advanced beings from another world, and that some of its residents may have come directly from another world in the galaxy.

Evidence shows that Egypt was much more than has been portrayed in pictures. Today, all that we see of Egypt are the pyramids and sphinx looking rather weathered and eroded. However, in its heyday, ancient Egypt was a civilization that was state of the art. The pyramids did not show the dull stones that we see today. During that time, they were encased in smooth, white marble! At night Egypt may have been lit up, as they possibly had electricity (see below). In the skies sophisticated aircraft were seen. In the ocean there were brightly lit vessels. Research shows that they were advanced in such areas as architecture, mathematics, medicine, and several other fields. When researching and examining this culture, one understands that there is something very otherworldly about it.

The story of the ancient Egyptian society begins in approximately 3,000 BCE. The ancient Egyptians had treasures, mysterious deities, and an engineering competency that amazed the people of other societies in the ancient world. The Egyptians possessed a complicated hieroglyphic system of writing, a highly developed method of mummification, and crafted remarkable immense edifices. Many have asked how this ancient civilization achieved such great feats and accomplishments during a time of limited knowledge in the areas of science and technology. In fact, today's science is still unable to explain the remarkable accomplishments of ancient Egypt. Scientists have no idea how they had such complex achievements with the limited technological understanding of their day. Their progress and advancement were so extraordinary that several researchers and ancient astronaut proponents believe that the ancient Egyptians may have been under the control of an advanced otherworldly civilization. Some maintain that conclusive evidence that extraterrestrials existed in ancient Egypt may be concealed by Earth's governments, some religious groups and various organization today, as not to interrupt the status quo.

The Great Pyramid of Giza, The Workmanship of Extraterrestrials?

The great Pyramid of Giza (also known as the Pyramid of Khufu) is one of the world's most famous structures. It has been shrouded by mystery and intrigue for millennia. This is due to it being one of the world's most amazing engineering feats. Some

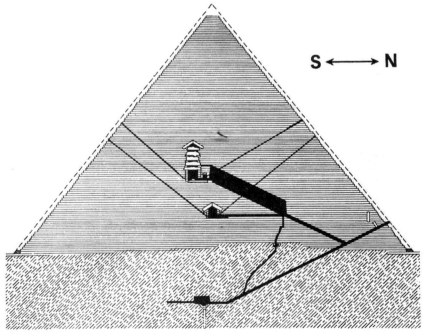

A diagram of the inner chambers and tunnels of the Great Pyramid of Giza.

believe that it was created to harness and transmit energy on an unparalleled and unmatched scale. It is one of the most intricately made and complex monuments ever erected. It is the oldest, and the last of the Seven Wonders of the ancient world. Supposedly built around 2500 BC, no one can explain how it was created. Standing more than 450 feet high, it comprises a staggering 2,300,000 granite blocks, with each weighing between 12 and 70 tons. Scientists have always had a difficult time explaining how the Great Pyramid of Giza (and those near it) were built. This is due to the weight and the number of blocks used for it, which would have been a challenging feat at that time, and in our modern era as well. As a result, scientists and historians cannot tell us precisely how the ancient Egyptians made the Great Pyramid of Giza. When attempting to determine how it was constructed, they have questioned how the Egyptians purposefully positioned so many enormous blocks together, especially as the pyramid became elevated. Equally convoluted are the three primary chambers. Each of these rooms contain an intricately made aeration system. *No explanation*. Additionally, its walls are perfectly positioned to correspond with the four cardinal points of the compass. In our modern era, we have placed men on the Moon, yet we still cannot explain how the Great Pyramid of Giza was made, and we cannot duplicate this feat today! Given what we have just learned about Egypt's potential connection with extraterrestrials, the chances of it having been constructed by a powerful, technologically advanced group seems plausible. There is a theory that these mysterious beings used a method of levitating the blocks into place.

It is also believed that each of the Egyptian pyramids have a purpose behind them that is unknown to us. The reason they were placed there may be of great importance—perhaps more than we may ever know. Why else would anyone go through the trouble of erecting these monuments if not for some grand important reason? One that is certainly more than that of a tomb for a pharaoh as has been hypothesized. We cannot know what the pyramid builders had in mind, but many are attempting to sort out the riddle as to why they are there, what they mean, and who built them.

To better understand why it is believed that ancient Egypt had an extraterrestrial connection, and what convinced researchers that this is a possibility, one must look closer at the data.

•Pyramids Construction (more). The mysterious

accuracy as well as the meticulous engineering achievements of the pyramids continue to challenge all conventional reasonings and rationalizations. Without wheels, they somehow transported over great distances stones weighing several tons, joining them together seamlessly, one by one, without the use of mortar. This alone demonstrates the level of skill, expertise, and ability that they had access to, and that are unmatched today. Nothing compares to them. After all these years, there is still no definitive answer as to how this was accomplished.

•*The Configuration.* The pyramids are aligned with certain stars including those of Orion's Belt. This exhibits a degree of astronomical understanding that was far superior to others living during that period.

•*Pyramids Discovered on Other Planetary Bodies.* Pyramids have been located on Earth, Mars, Venus, the Moon, and the dwarf star Ceres. This shows that there just may be an extraterrestrial element at play here connecting ancient Egypt to the stars.

•*No Hieroglyphics.* One interesting piece of information is that there are no hieroglyphics in Egypt that portray the building of the pyramids. In a culture that kept meticulous records of what they saw, this is not shown, which for some researchers lends credence to the idea that they were built by extraterrestrials, and perhaps sometime before humans took up residence there. Perhaps the pyramids were in place because of the energy component before the Egyptians arrived.

•*Hieroglyphs and the Temple of Abydos.* Abydos is one of Egypt's most prominent, scared, ancient cities. Located in upper Egypt near modern El Araba El Madfuna, it is considered a place of great archaeological importance as it was once a necropolis for early Egyptian royalty. It later became a pilgrimage center for the worship of Osiris (god of the Underworld). Within the city are the ruins of temples created by Seti I, during the 19th dynasty, and by Ramses II. Carved tablets discovered there (now located in the British Museum) are amongst the main sources of Egyptian history from 4700 BC forward. Hieroglyphs found in the Temple of Seti portray mysterious images that appear to be advanced aircraft, including a jet airliner, a helicopter, and a spaceship. There is also what looks like a submarine. The meaning of the hieroglyphs remains unknown. Do these hieroglyphs link the Egyptians to extraterrestrials? They tell us that the ancient Egyptians had far more experience with technology than we originally understood. These hieroglyphs also suggests that the speculation that the pyramids of Egypt were designed and built by advanced beings visiting Earth is true.

The Use of Electricity

There are researchers that believe that the ancient Egyptians had access to electricity. This is perhaps one of the most fascinating pieces of evidence of extraterrestrial interactions with ancient Egypt that has been found. The idea that they had electricity is simply astounding. On the walls of Egypt's Dendera Temple complex there are depictions of what appear to be light bulbs. Archeologists have variously referred to the items in the images as "light bulbs," "bulbs," "batteries," "electric lights," and in the case of one large depiction of one of the objects, "the Dendera Light." This may indicate that ancient Egyptians used electricity. In the most prominent image of the "Dendera light," a priest is portrayed lifting the light upwards; underneath the light, there are people sitting. This depiction of a light was made 3,000 years before Thomas Edison invented the light bulb. Many researchers are left

Egyptian light bulbs featured at the Temple of Hathor.

with the idea that, along with many other things in the ancient Egyptian culture, the usage of electricity was given to them by advanced beings, perhaps from another world that they were in contact with.

Egyptian Mythology

In Egyptian mythology, we find gods and goddesses that are different from other pantheons of gods found during that era. The gods of Rome and Greece were completely human in appearance. However, those of the Egyptians were vastly different. Several of the gods and goddesses of the Egyptian pantheon had animal heads and human bodies. These included Anubis who had the head of a canine, Bastet who is depicted with the head of a feline, and Horus who had the head of a falcon or bird. It has been suggested that these were hybrid beings created via genetic engineering by extraterrestrials in some type of experimentation that was happening in the ancient world among extraterrestrials. Others believe that these were extraterrestrials that were ruling the people, and this was their true form. This last thought is not as far-fetched as it may seem given what we are learning about extraterrestrial history through documentation, channelers, experiences

A Djed column with ankh and orb.

and others. As you will see in Chapter Eight there have been extraterrestrials from our galaxy that have been described with some of these very same features.

The Turin Royal Canon (or the Turin King List)

The Turin Royal Canon is an ancient Egyptian hieratic papyrus thought to date from the reign of Pharaoh Ramesses II. It proves that gods (extraterrestrials) ruled ancient Egypt. The last two lines of the Turin Royal Canon supports this idea, stating, "…Pharaoh Shemsu-Khor ruled for 13,420 years; pharaoh before Shemsu-Hor, 23,200 years." According to this, the pharaohs ruled for a total of 36,620 years. Some wonder how it is that the lifespans of these god-like rulers were so long… unless they were not human, and as a result had the means to live for those long periods of time.

The Disk of Sabu

The Disk of Sabu is one of the greatest mysteries, and dare I say strongest evidences of extraterrestrial assistance and influence in ancient Egypt. It has been the focus of much discussion and speculation for decades regarding its purpose, and how it was made. This enigmatic object has been described as "an object like no other." Located in the Cairo Museum, in Egypt, it is similar in shape to a discus. It measures 24 inches (610 millimeters) in diameter and nearly 4 inches (104 millimeters) in height.

The Disk of Sabu was unearthed in 1936 by renowned Egyptologist Walter Bryan Emery while on an excavation in Saqqara, Egypt. Emery located the disc while excavating the tomb of Prince Sabu, who was the son of the famous Pharaoh Anedjib. It is estimated to be at least 5,000 years old. There are two mysteries that center around the disk. The first mystery involves how this disc, that was so intricately carved, was made. The disc was fashioned from a brittle stone known as *schist*. Schist is a porous, delicate, rock. It has the tendency to flake when worked with and crumples easily. It would have been impossible to carve without destroying it. To do this work, one would have to have highly sophisticated tools. In fact, the tools in those days were created from copper and stone. This would have made fine workmanship unattainable on schist stone in ancient times. The Disc of Sabu is an example of the kind of sophisticated, even state of the art resources the Egyptians had available to them. Just what was the Disc of Sabu used for? The attribution card in the Cairo Museum states, "Vase of schist, of unique form, intended to be mounted on a post, and possibly intended to hold lotus flowers. First dynasty. Saqqara. Tomb of Sabu. Emery, 1937."

Examiners of the disc speculate that the information on the attribution card is incorrect. They believe that the disc was from a piece of machinery.

The Enigmatic Tulli Papyrus

The Tulli Papyrus is a copy of an ancient document purportedly dating from the time of Thutmose III. It has been described as the first written account of a UFO sighting, which if true is more evidence of UFO activity in the ancient world. The document

The Tulli Papyrus which speaks about a UFO in ancient Egypt.

shows flying fiery disks as described by one of the pharaohs. It was discovered in an antique shop in Cairo, Egypt by Alberto Tulli who was the director of the Vatican museum's Egyptian studies division. The document is named after him. The text gives a startling account of people crossing ancient Egypt's deserts approximately 3,500 years ago. It tells an amazing tale that some believe could alter the way we perceive history.

According to the account, it was approximately 1480 BC when a massive UFO sighting occurred. Thutmose III was the Pharaoh of Egypt during that period. This incredible sighting was recorded in Egyptian history as one of great importance. It was recorded by the Egyptians as a day when something inconceivable took place. The following is a translation of the text according to anthropologist, and author R. Cedric Leonard (1934—2022):

> In the year 22, in the 3rd month of winter, in the sixth hour of the day, the scribes of House of Life noticed a circle of fire that was coming from the sky. From the mouth it emitted a foul breath. It had no head. Its body was one rod long and one rod wide. It had no voice. And from that the hearts of the scribes became confused and they threw themselves down on their bellies, then they reported the thing to the Pharaoh. His majesty ordered [...] and he was meditating on what had happened, that it was recorded in the scrolls of the House of Life.
>
> Now after some days had passed, these things became

more and more numerous in the skies. Their splendour exceeded that of the sun and extended to the limits of the four angles of the sky. High and wide in the sky was the position from which these fire circles came and went. The army of the Pharaoh looked on with him in their midst. It was after supper. Then these fire circles ascended higher into the sky and they headed toward the south. Fish and birds then fell from the sky. A marvel never before known since the foundation of their land. And Pharaoh caused incense to be brought to make peace with Earth, and what happened was ordered to be written in the Annals of the House of Life so that it be remembered for all time forward.

Although there is no indication in the text as to whether the Egyptians actually met the visitors, one wonders who was flying these ships and what was their purpose. These are the same questions that we are asking today as we too look into the skies and see what are essentially spaceships.

*Mysterious Medicine

Not only did the Egyptians have advanced stone working technology at their disposal, but there were other areas in which they excelled as well, such as medical procedures. I would like to discuss the subject of artificial organs, one case in particular, involving a heart. The incomparable Erich von Daniken, shared information that he obtained on that very subject that took place in ancient Egypt. In his book *Impossible Truths: Amazing Evidence of Extraterrestrial Contact* (pages 126-129), von Daniken wrote about the mummy of a male child of around six years old. According to the account, after examining the body of the mummified child, archeologists determined that the child had a false heart installed that allowed him to live for a longer period of time. Where did the Egyptians obtain this advanced medical information in those days? It is believed by some that this may have been the science of advanced extraterrestrials.

*The Saqqara Bird

The Saqqara Bird is a mysterious bird-shaped artifact that was unearthed in 1898 during an excavation of the Pa-di-lmen tomb in Saqqara, Egypt. Made of sycamore wood, it is believed that the Saqqara Bird does not represent a bird at all, but is a replica of an ancient aircraft. It's estimated to be approximately 2,200 years old.

A photograph of the Saqqara Bird.

The replica is small, with a 7-inch wingspan. After examining the artifact in 1969, prominent Egyptian physician and archeologist Dr. Khalil Messiha determined that the ancient Egyptians produced the first airplanes. Modern technology has shown that at full size the Saqqara Bird could have traversed the skies of ancient Egypt and beyond. Dr. John H. Lienhard, in an article from the University of Houston Cullen College of Engineering, titled, "The Engines of Our Ingenuity, An Egyptian Model Airplane," states, "No one could have come this close to the real shape of flight without working on a larger scale. This little wooden model could hardly exist unless someone had worked with large, light models, or even with man-carrying versions." Today, the Saqqara Bird is housed in the Egyptian Museum in Cairo.

*The Alien Coins

The alien coins are a fairly new discovery that, as of this writing, has not yet been authenticated. It is *one strange* tale. If true, then this would change the way we look at ancient Egyptian history and the ancient world in general. It would also be more proof that extraterrestrials lived among the people in the ancient world. According to the account, U.S. archeologists have discovered two ancient coins in Egypt. One of the coins is engraved with the image of what looks like an alien, showing the head and shoulders of the being. The second coin has a UFO (spaceship) engraved on it. The coins were discovered when a group of people were renovating a house in southern Egypt. On the back of one of the coins is an engraving that states, "Opportvnvs Adest." In Latin this means, "for it's here in due time." We may never know if this story is true or not, as there is said to be a cover-up involving the coins. If the story is fabricated, then someone has gone through a great deal of trouble to create images on coins and include an inscription for an rather elaborate hoax.

*The Sphinx

The famous Sphinx is viewed as a part of ancient Egypt's past, a desert enigma, standing guard over its people. It has withstood the sands of time, with literally millions of people journeying from all over the world to see it. However, there may be more to the Sphinx than we know. There is evidence that the Sphinx was built before the ancient Egyptian civilization. It is believed by some archeologists to antedate the Egyptian civilization by thousands of years. In other words, the Egyptians may not have created this iconic monument. Simply put, there is a chance that the Sphinx was built by a civilization that predates ancient Egypt. Furthermore, duplicates of the structure are believed to exist on the Moon, Mars, and Venus. Therefore, it appears that the Sphinx may have a galactic connection. If the Sphinx is older than we thought by a thousand years, then the ancient Egyptians may very well have come from a pre-history civilization that some researchers believe were extraterrestrials. *The UFO Magazine, UFO Encyclopedia* by William J. Birnes states: "The work done by geologists who believe that the Sphinx suffered from water erosion and not wind erosion…throws a new light on the possibilities that those who built the Sphinx were of a civilization possibly lost to what we take to be history, if, in fact, they are even of this earth."

Brazil

Brazil is another country high on the list of having been visited by extraterrestrials in early history. The belief of star beings visiting Brazil comes from old Brazilian legends and statuettes of beings that appear to have had the capability of flight. The legends state that beings came from the sky and taught the people agriculture, astronomy and medicine, as well as other fields necessary for advancement. One account in particular stands out. It involves an extraterrestrial spaceman, by the name of Bep-Kororoti, who was worshipped by the Kayapo tribe (a group of people that lived near the Amazon basin). Bep-Kororoti was believed by the people to be a cosmic warrior of sorts. However, he was later venerated as an astronaut type of being that had traveled from the stars to Earth. Bep-Kororoti carried a dangerous and very powerful weapon (perhaps this was why he was first considered a warrior by the people). He operated a spaceship that was capable of great destruction. In the beginning, the natives were afraid of him, until he eventually removed his spacesuit and they could see that he looked very similar to them in appearance and they could tell that he was a benevolent being. He has been described as having light skin and being very attractive. He remained with the natives for years, even marrying and having a child with one of them. He eventually left on his spaceship to return home, taking his family with him. Today there are still tales and celebrations centered around this strange humanoid being that is said to have brought the people knowledge.

Greece

It appears that Greeks too had access to high tech machinery in the ancient past. In fact, one of the most important relics ever discovered was located in the Aegean Sea. In April 1900, sponge divers located an ancient ship 150 feet beneath the surface. They were astounded to find that the ship contained numerous artifacts. Among them was what is known today as the *Antikythera Mechanism*, a device made of bronze and used to compute and display data on astronomical events. It has been hailed as the oldest mechanical computer ever discovered. In the History Channel's, *Ancient Aliens* episode "Alien Tech in Ancient Greece," (Season 10), author and ancient astronaut theorist David Hatcher Childress states, "The American scientists who were studying the Antikythera device actually said that discovering the Antikythera device was like finding a jet plane in the tomb of King Tut. It was so amazing to them. They had never, ever conceived that the ancient Greeks at 200 BC would have had the knowledge of mechanical devices like this." It was found inside an antiquated, coral encrusted metal box dating back to the 2nd century BC. The question is, where did the ancient Greeks at 200 BC acquire a technical device? We can assume that those being hailed as powerful gods (believed now to be extraterrestrials) interacting with humans in those days, brought fascinating devices with them from their home world, including computers like the Antikythera Mechanism. Today the Antikythera Mechanism sits in the National Archaeological Museum in Athens, Greece.

Another area of Greece that reportedly had advanced technology is the island of Rhodes. Rhodes is the place where some researchers believe that the *Antikythera Mechanism* may have originated. This is because Rhodes too was highly advanced for that period, having unexplainable high-tech equipment. It appears that 2500 years ago, the people on Rhodos had computers and artificial intelligence (AI) at their disposal. In the 5th century BC, the Greek lyric and poet Pindar wrote that at one time in history, Rhodes was decorated with animated statues. In his writings, Pindar recounted that the statues appeared to come to life, meaning, they moved, just as we see in our own technology today in robots. One wonders if these animated statues were a form of artificial intelligence, or if they were controlled via a motion detector or from a remotely controlled device. Either way, the ancient Greeks having moving technology denotes machinery, technology and systems that were far too sophisticated and progressive for their time.

Peru

Caral-Supe is an ancient city in Peru that was first discovered in 1905. At the time, it appeared to archaeologists to be a place of little importance. It was Peruvian anthropologist and archeologist Ruth Shady Solas, the founder and director of the archaeological project at Caral, who after scrutinizing Caral-Supe more closely, realized that it was at one time, an enormous, high level city for its time. What was discovered at the site amazed people in the region, and ancient historians around the world. What they thought were simplistic ruins turned out to be an enormous multifaceted development, with 30 major population centers, complete with pyramids, an amphitheater, residential buildings and more. Archeologists were also stunned to find when dating artifacts that Caral-Supe predated the Incas by more than three thousand years, dating back to approximately 2600 BC. That would make it over 4,600 years, making it one of the oldest locations in regard to ancient civilizations to be found in the Americas. Some researchers maintain that Caral-Supe is yet another civilization that was so forward-thinking, even cutting-edge for its time, that one wonders if extraterrestrials were involved in helping them in their advancements.

Authors Note: It is thought that out of the ordinary cities from the ancient past show that extraterrestrials may have been eager for humans to advance (which we have done rapidly) in order to more quickly take our place in the galactic community. An idea that has been brought forward is that most civilizations had beings from the stars helping them to progress. This is found all over the world, not in just one or two areas. It's very interesting and speaks volumes as to who and what we may be dealing with when it comes to benevolent extraterrestrials in our past, present and potentially our future.

The massive mountain city of Sacsahuaman is another Peruvian marvel. The building of this city is viewed by some as an obvious example of extraterrestrial contact. Sacsahuaman was located just outside of the Inca capital in Cusco, and was said to have been founded and built by the Incas. Several scientists and archeologists have questioned how it came to be built considering that it required thousands of tons of weight in stones. The quarries that produced the colossal boulders were located twenty miles away. These heavy blocks of stone weighed 200 to 360 tons a piece. The largest is twelve feet thick and twenty-five feet tall. Not only are they extremely heavy, but each block is different; yet they all fit seamlessly together. They were transported over 20 miles up a mountainside before being placed precisely into position, eventually creating an enormous city. A similar feat would be challenging even for engineers today. As stated with the Egyptians, some speculate that levitation or even teleportation may have been used to transport the huge stones.

Author's Note: One thing that stands out here, as a researcher of extraterrestrial and UFO phenomena, is the possibility that the Incas had help with this project from extraterrestrials because it was to be a fortress city. In history, extraterrestrials sometimes appeared when it came to the defense of certain cultures. It could be that this was a motivation for assisting with the building of this fortified city. Perhaps the extraterrestrials were attempting to protect the people in the city from some unknown foe.

Mali

A fascinating tale of a direct extraterrestrial connection, and one that has become rather famous in the subject of extraterrestrial contact, is that of the Dogon tribe in Mali, West Africa. This is one of those rare cases where it is accepted as fact that a group of people were visited by beings from another world. While the story may seem beyond belief to some, there is too much evidence to discount it. There are those of the opinion that this information alone should have sparked worldwide conversation, and the furthering of research about Earth being visited by extraterrestrials.

In Mali, south of the river Niger bend, lives a tribe of people named the Dogon. The Dogon built their villages in the valley of Bandiagara (the Cliffs of Bandiagara is a huge geological escarpment rising above the surrounding flatlands in Mali). The Dogon had refused to convert to Islam and therefore, they settled themselves along the defensible cliffs. In case of danger, they could shelter in one of the many hidden caves in the rocks. Their houses are made of mud. Due to the dry and hot climate the mud is as hard as stone. Their main trade goods are onions. Where the Dogon originated is unknown. However, they are believed to be the descendants of the ancient Egyptians. The Dogon are well versed in astronomy. Their astronomical lore dates back thousands of years to 3200 BC. In fact, for thousands of the years, the Dogon kept an incredible secret connected to the cosmos.

It was around 1931 that the Dogon announced their secret to the world. It was there, in one of their villages, inside the "toguna" which means the "house of words," that four Dogon priests shared

Dogon statues of gods and ancestors.

70

their advanced astronomical knowledge with two visiting French anthropologists. Their names were Marcel Griaule and Germain Dieterlen. The information from the Dogon was a part of their animistic beliefs. They had recorded this knowledge on stone tablets that they kept hidden. The guests learned from the priests that the star that we know as Sirius (located 8.6 light years from Earth) has a companion star that is not visible to the naked eye. They went on to inform the scientists that this star has a 50-year elliptical orbit around Sirius, and that it is an extremely heavy one. They even went as far as to say that this companion star turns on its axis. Quite a big claim and a lot of information from a culture that had not been a part of the mainstream world. Not only that, but at that point and time, scientists had no clue that there was a companion to Sirius! That information was yet to be discovered. It raises the question as to how the Dogon, who had no access to telescopes or other astronomical devices, knew so much about an unseen star? A star not known to modern-day scientists. One that wasn't even photographed until 1970. Yet, the Dogon knew it was there, and they knew of its details. *How?* Today, we now know of this star as Sirius B.

How the Dogon received this information is one of the most intriguing aspects of this story, because according to the priests, the Dogon people were given this information by extraterrestrials called the Nommos. According to the priests, the Nommos came to Earth ages ago from the Sirius star system. Their planet is one that orbits a star in the Sirius system. They are amphibious beings with the ability to exist in water or on land. The Dogon told the men that the Nommo prefer being in water rather than land, due to their fish-like tails, which apparently worked better in water. They traveled to Earth in a spaceship that revolved when descending to land. The Nommo gave the Dogon people quite a bit of information about the universe. Galactic information given to the Dogons from extraterrestrials thousands of years ago include:

•the Sun is the central point in our solar system
•the planets orbit the sun
•the planet Saturn has several rings
•the planet Jupiter has four major moons
•the Milky Way galaxy is an expanding spiral
•there is a second star cycling around Sirius called Emme ya Tolo
•Sirius B has a super-density

71

The Dogon knew all this information before the invention of the telescope, and before the discovery of Sirius B by modern-day scientists. In fact, scientists suspected Sirius B's existence as early as 1844. It was seen through a telescope in 1862. According to the legend, there is a third star, Sirius C. It is around Sirius C that the home planet of the Nommos orbits. Interestingly, most scientists do not consider any part of the Sirius system as a candidate for life. Apparently, they are not listening to the Dogon.

Author's Note: One wonders if some of the Nommos are still on Earth, or perhaps they left and then later returned. There are a number of stories and sightings of humanoid amphibian beings that are thought to be extraterrestrials and are believed to be living in the deep waters of Earth's oceans. They are said to be approximately the size of humans (sometimes a few feet taller). Could these stories be related to the Nommos? Are there Nommos in Earth's oceans today?

South America

The Incas were a large, complex civilization that existed in South America. They referred to themselves as "sons of the sun." This phrase indicates a belief that their ancestry began in the cosmos. Their people were located in Bolivia, Peru, and Ecuador with their ancestry reaching as far south as northern Argentina, as well as some areas of Chile. There are researchers that suggest, and some accept it as fact (these days), that the Incas may have had direct contact with beings that came from the stars and taught them how to establish their civilization and how to maintain it.

India

In the Charama region, in the Kanker district of India, scientists discovered a 10,000-year-old series of rock paintings and etchings that portray extraterrestrials and what appears to be spacecraft. The images show a type of alien that are commonly referred to as the Grays. There they are shown with large heads and large dark eyes, with no other discernible features. They are also curiously shown holding what appears to be a type of weapon. Some images show them dressed in spacesuits. In the background small spacecraft can be seen. This discovery is just more evidence that extraterrestrials visited Earth in ancient times. There are old tales told by the people of these villages that have been handed down by their ancestors that tell of the "rohela people," known as the small sized ones that would come from the sky in spherical shaped aerial spacecraft and land. The people claimed that they would take away one, sometimes two people from the village, never to be seen again.

This information is particularly fascinating because it shows that there were extraterrestrial abductions going on prior to the 1940s, which is when many believe that they began occurring. It apparently is not a modern phenomenon.

Anomalous Artifacts

The Earth has many secrets, but it appears that the Earth is giving up some of its secrets to its mysterious past. In the last few centuries, there have been a great number of anomalous artifacts that have been discovered around the world. These artifacts challenge conventional historical chronology by their very existence. They are evidence that the ancient world was a very different place than we thought. Scientists have unearthed ancient cities that we did not know existed, relics made from advanced technology, skeletons that appear to be nonhuman, artifacts made from material not found on Earth, and more. We are left wondering where these objects originated, who made them, and what are they doing in our ancient past? *If only the Earth could speak.*

Scientists in the categories of archaeology, geology, paleontology, and others from around the globe have discovered thousands of anomalous artifacts (sometimes referred to as out-of-place artifacts) that were undoubtedly constructed by unknown intelligences. These items date back from anywhere between 200 and 500 million years old. Experts believe that they are proof that Earth has been visited by extraterrestrials for thousands of years. This evidence shows that our ancestors not only witnessed UFOs in the skies just as we are seeing today, but that they had a physical connection to them. The extraterrestrials clearly walked among humans, sharing their knowledge with us. Our ancestors left behind artifacts, writings and other items that let us know these otherworldly beings were here and interacted with us. However, the story does not begin and end with extraterrestrials visiting Earth. These beings established a connection and relationship with humanity that has lasted to this day.

Due to space constraints for this book, I cannot list every anomalous item that has been discovered. However, the following are some of the most interesting discoveries of objects from extraterrestrials that lived and worked among humanity in the past. Each article has a story. Each one brings us closer to solving the questions of our ancient ancestry and our relationship with the cosmos.

As we delve into this history, we should question whether this information was left for us to discover in a certain time frame (*now?*), a period when it would be time for humanity to understand and embrace the notion that we are not alone in the universe. They say there are no coincidences. Perhaps humanity awaking to its past would awaken us to the present, and what may lie ahead. As we contemplate the craft we see in our skies today, it would be prudent to consider that whoever was here before, may still be here now...*just as we are*.

The London Hammer Artifact

The London Hammer artifact is one of those items that is so unusual that we have no rational explanation to explain its existence. It is this type of discovery that has made some question our origins, and just what happened in our ancient past. The London Hammer is a relic made of iron and wood that is older than the beginning of human history. It was found in London, Texas in the United States in 1936 by a couple by the names of Max and Emma Hahn who were on a hike. Along their journey, the pair noticed a rock with wood jutting out from its core. Thinking that it looked particularly odd, the couple took the rock home and broke it open using a hammer and chisel. What they discovered inside of

The London Hammer Artifact.

the rock surprised them. There was an item that resembled an antiquated hammer. It was such an intriguing find that they decided to have archaeologists examine it. The archaeologists learned that the hammer was embedded in rock that was over 400 million years old! The hammerhead is six inches long with a one-inch diameter. Of note, and great importance, is the fact that the hammer's head consists of more than 96% iron, which is significantly purer than anything nature can produce without the assistance of technology. Mainstream history tells us that humans have only existed for approximately 200,000 years.

It should be noted too that the London Hammer has not rusted since it was discovered. The finding of this relic seriously causes us to pause, because it significantly questions our knowledge of human history and our timeline. So, just how did this relic get here? Are we looking at an artifact from a pre-historic civilization that had advanced technology? Some speculate that it was either brought here or created by an extraterrestrial colony, started by extraterrestrials that lived on Earth during pre-human history.

For those that do not know, it is believed by some that there were extraterrestrial groups residing on Earth before humans made an appearance. Additionally, some believe that these beings were nonhuman and that they dwelled here before leaving Earth due to a catastrophe, or even died off due to an inescapable disaster. Some even speculate that this civilization may have been Atlantis.

The Drill Bit Relic

On December 13, 1852, John Buchanan, Esq., presented a baffling object to a meeting of the Society of Antiquaries. A drill bit had been discovered encased inside a piece of coal that was approximately 22 inches thick. It was buried inside antiquated clay and under boulders in Scotland. There was no indication that the coal had been punctured during drilling, nor was there any clue as to how the drill bit came to be encapsulated in the coal, implying that it was there when the coal developed, hundreds of millions of years ago. The society deduced that the drill bit was of a modern level of advancement.

There are two theories when it comes to the drill bit relic. Either humans existed on Earth well before scientists believe, or there was an extraterrestrial colony on Earth during that period that have since either disappeared or blended in. Just like the London Hammer. Also, there is the story of Atlantis. Some believe that

The Drill Bit Relic.

Atlantis was a real place with state-of-the-art technology and as the legend states, it was eventually destroyed. Atlantis is thought by some to have been founded by extraterrestrials. Could the story of Atlantis be true? Or could there have been another civilization that even predated Atlantis? Were there people from other worlds operating on Earth before the appearance of humans? Researchers believe this may have been the case.

The Coso Relic

One of the most unusual reports in recent years tells of a discovery in the coastal mountain range in Southern California. On February 13, 1961, Wally Lane, Virginia Maxey and Mike Mikesell, who were the co-owners of the LM&V Rockhounds Gem and Gift Shop, hiked into the Coso Mountains to search for unique rocks. During their search, they discovered a geode. It looked interesting enough to take back with them, which they did, with the intention of breaking it open. They packed it along with their collection of items from the search and eventually headed back. Later, they split it in two. What happened next shocked them. Inside of the geode was a mysterious item that resembled a modern-day spark plug. Additionally, there was what looked like a tiny coil in its upper area that is not found on contemporary spark plugs. After an examination of the object, a geologist dated it as being somewhere around 500,000 years old. The x-ray results for the item were also fascinating. Most notably it was revealed that the item was not organically created. Even though some have tried to debunk it, stating that it is a spark plug that was created in the 1920s, we know that cannot be the case because it would have taken a millennium for the geode itself to be formed around it. In the end, there is no rational explanation for how this occurred.

We should ask ourselves, how did a piece of equipment come to be inside of a geological formation from 500,000 years ago? This means that it was made hundreds of thousands of years before industrialized civilization. *How is this possible?* The conclusion made by some researchers about this and other anomalous objects dating back to pre-history is that someone was obviously on the planet, engaged in some kind of work, and they were *not human*.

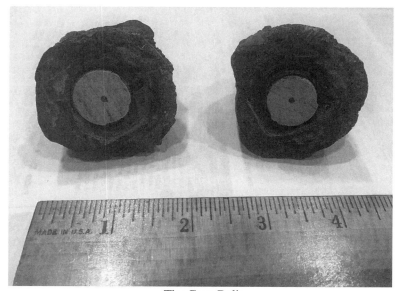

The Coso Relic.

Chapter Four
The Oceans, Earth's Final Frontier

"As humans we tend to believe that we have dominion over the Earth, but in the vast oceans beneath us, there could be all kinds of advanced civilizations even ones that have been here for much longer than we've been on this planet and they've come here from other solar systems and then came to our planet where they're now living underwater, and it seems incredible to us, but we may be seeing their ships, these USOs coming out of the water and there may be some highly advanced civilization that's in these vast oceans that we have yet to explore. Anything could be down there."
—David Hatcher Childress

There are UFOs coming and going in Earth's waters. They have been seen so often, with so many witnesses, that there is no longer a question as to whether or not they exist. *They exist!* As a result, this poses a great number of questions. Who is operating these craft? What is their goal? Why are they here? Why are they in Earth's oceans, seas and lakes? Those questions, dear readers, are what we should be asking. We hope they are benevolent, galactic friends. If so, then an introduction is past due. We must consider that if these beings have been here since the beginning, then the Earth may be just as much theirs it is ours. One can only wonder why they choose not to make themselves known to us. As I have stated before, it could be because we are a warring species. They may be worried about our reaction to them. Or, if they are extraterrestrials with bases and not a civilization, if they have come here recently for reasons unknown to us, then they may be under some sort of directive that we do not know or understand, much like the *Star Trek* prime directive. Perhaps it is a noninterference mandate. Or, they simply may not trust us, and wish to keep separate from humanity.

Additionally, there may be more than one humanoid, intelligent species in our oceans. It could very well be that just as on Earth's surface there are different types of people, also, in Earth's oceans, there may be different groups and civilizations. Some may be intraterrestrials as opposed to extraterrestrials. The intraterrestrials would be beings that developed in Earth's waters and have been here all along. Intraterrestrials could also be an extraterrestrial that came here ages ago and made this home. They may have existed in Earth's waters before the presence of humans on Earth. This author feels that beings that may have come here that long ago are no longer extraterrestrials as it has been too long, just as humanity, if brought here from the stars, is now considered to be terrestrial with extraterrestrial connections. Theories for this are complicated. Theories as to who these beings are go as follows:

•Extraterrestrials visiting Earth and hiding in Earth's waters for the purposes of exploration or mining.
•They are beings that were seeded on Earth, just as humanity may have been, that have been here all along.
•They may be connected to inner Earth.
•They may be amphibious extraterrestrials that came to Earth from a watery world and took up residence here.

Unidentified submersible objects (USOs) have been seen in Earth's large bodies of water for decades. A USO is essentially a UFO that enters and exits water. We could also say that a UFO becomes a USO once it stops flying, then submerges below water. They are in fact a part of Earth's extraterrestrial history. However, most people are not even aware of them. According to UFO investigators, they lurk beneath several of the unexplored bodies of water found on Earth. This is not surprising considering that we know more about the surface of the Moon than our oceans. That is an important statement considering that we have only explored less than one percent of the lunar surface. In fact, the Earth is covered 71 percent by water, yet we have only explored 5% of Earth's oceans. In fact, the deep-sea area of the oceans where it is perpetually dark, is 103 million square miles in radius. Given these facts, the oceans have become known as Earth's "final frontier" and are sometimes referred to as our "inner space." We do not know what is down there. That means that we are existing on Earth with beings that we know nothing about. While there are many questions when it comes to whether the Earth has an extraterrestrial connection, one of the most intriguing ideas is that there may be extraterrestrials living in our oceans and lakes. If there are, then we need to know who they are, why they are here, and how long they have been here.

As noted, USOs have been seen both entering and exiting Earth's waters. These large, unexplainable, fast-moving objects have also been detected on the radars of underwater military personnel in several countries. Not only have military personnel observed them entering and exiting the waters, but they have monitored them while traversing the waters as well. As of late, these USOs have been seen more frequently, and appear to be bolder in showing themselves. They clearly resemble spacecraft in the same shapes and forms as the UFOs seen in the skies. Because they descend, people often get a closer look at them than the ones observed in the skies. We can reason from these observations that without a doubt extraterrestrials are here, and for whatever reason, have positioned themselves in Earth's waters.

Considering the idea of there being extraterrestrials in our waters, this very much reminds me of my research on the possible existence of extraterrestrials on the Moon. As stated earlier, the Moon too is an area that man has explored on a very limited basis. There was, and still is much speculation about extraterrestrials residing on the Moon. Many wonder today about the strange anomalies seen there, including strange lights, clouds, UFOs and other mysterious phenomena. Afterall, according to Earth's scientists, nothing should be going on there. Nothing can live there. No one can survive there, yet there is quite a bit of evidence that states otherwise. The same is true of our oceans (and other large bodies of water).

I covered moon anomalies in my previous book, *The Moon's Galactic History: A Look at the Moon's Extraterrestrial Past and its Connection to Earth*. It amazes me that once again I find myself in a research position to look at yet another place in our Solar System (and right at home), that may be harboring life for a very long time without us having known it about. From the reports, there just may be beings living in the deepest part of the oceans. Tales of humanoid beings existing in Earth's oceans go back thousands of years. There are many tales of mermaids and spirits of the ocean, etc. Perhaps those tales had some merit. However, this author does not feel that those legends are connected to the USOs seen today.

They are, I believe, two very different phenomena. I do not feel that these USOs fall into the realms of myth and fantasy. In fact, from their descriptions, they are very different from anything we have imagined so far. From the descriptions by observers of these craft, these beings exhibit extraordinary abilities in the area of technology, appearing to be far more advanced than humans. About "underwater UFOs," *The UFO Magazine, UFO Encyclopedia* states, "UFOs are said to be not only capable of navigating through earth's atmosphere, but also of traveling great distances under our oceans. There are numerous reports of underwater UFO bases, such as off Puerto Rico (The Bermuda Triangle), and in the Eastern Pacific, and of encounters with these craft either traveling through, entering, or exiting oceans and lakes."

When the Soviet Union collapsed, Russia's Navy declassified the records of Cold War UFO sightings. The reports indicated that approximately 50 percent of the UFO incidents within the Soviet Union were associated with the oceans. Another 15 percent were related to lakes. The radar on Russian submarines, on many occasions, showed readings of USOs traversing the waters at tremendous speeds. Estimates revealed speeds in the area of 230 knots, or 400 kph. Travelling at such speeds is difficult to accomplish and shows that these USOs ultimately defy our laws of physics. One might ask, if USOs are so prevalent, would we not have had a direct encounter with them by now? We should remember that the majority of our oceans remain unexplored, unobserved, and unmapped. They could be residing in areas that no one has been to or seen before. Also, we still do not have the ability to go very deep into the oceans for long periods of time. Long story short, *anything* could be down there. One possibility is that there may be more than one extraterrestrial group existing in Earth's waters. Still, with that said, there are some reported encounters between USOs, humans and even humanoid beings in our oceans and lakes that have been reported from different parts of the world.

USO-UFOs

UFOs have been seen in countries all over the world. However, researchers have found that some of the most active UFO areas are located near bodies of water. *Why*? In fact, as mentioned above, UFOs have been witnessed submerging into large bodies of water as well as exiting (a UFO becomes a USO once it submerges).

Moreover, just as there have been reports of UFOs that appear over and sometimes pursue cars, there are those that sometimes pursue boats and ships. There are hundreds of cases on record of UFOs hovering directly over boats, and in some accounts, they are observed beneath them. These incidents have occurred for centuries and are still occurring *now*. It is only at this time in Earth's history that we are beginning to pay attention to what is going on with UFOs and our waters.

Just what would be the motive behind extraterrestrials visiting or living in Earth's waters? The large deep bodies of water on Earth, our oceans, seas and lakes may be the place to set up base because deep water is a perfect place to hide from humans. This is because it is still very difficult for us to descend and stay in very deep water. It would therefore be easy for them to hide there. We have no idea about their technology. However, what we do know is they have the amazing capability to travel the cosmos and also Earth's waters.

Sites for Extraterrestrial Bases Beneath Earth's Waters

Ufologist and Soviet Naval Officer Vladimir Azhazha has been quoted as stating, "I think about underwater bases and say: why not? Nothing should be discarded. Skepticism is the easiest way: believe nothing, do nothing. People rarely visit great depths. So it's very important to analyze what they encounter there." It is reasonable to assume that if there are USOs flying in and out of the waters, then there may be bases located within Earth's waters where these craft are stored, and where an underwater race of beings may be dwelling. The topic of USOs is a totally unexpected phenomenon. Yet it exists, and no one knows what to do about it. There have been USOs that have followed and sometimes taunted military submarines, just as the occasional UFOs have been known to do with airplanes. With all of our technological know-how, in an age when we are looking to go to Mars and entertaining the idea of colonizing other areas of the Solar System, we find that we have a bewildering situation that thus far, we have no resolution to.

We have spent so much time in past years studying the stars, looking for life in outer space and documenting UFO activity, that we have been missing very important clues that there is something going on right here in our waters. Notwithstanding, we now know that we are not alone in the cosmos, and it appears we are not alone in our deepest oceans. The following is a list of areas that may hold extraterrestrial bases.

Golfo Nuevo, Argentina

In Argentina's Golfo Nuevo (located 650 miles southwest of Buenos Aires) on February 1960 there was an incident involving a USO in the waters off the coast. The Argentine and U.S. navies worked jointly for two weeks, using a large number of underwater explosives to bring to the surface what appeared to be two USOs that were maneuvering beneath the waters of Golfo Nuevo, which is an area of approximately 20 to 40 miles. Since that time there have been several reports of UFO and USO phenomena in that area. Some believe that not only is Argentina a hotspot for UFO activity, but there may be an extraterrestrial base existing in its waters as well.

North Island, New Zealand

North Island in New Zealand is another area where UFOs are frequently seen entering the sea with the prospect of there being a base located under the waters. Reportedly, there was a surge of USO activity between the months of January and March 1995. The craft were witnessed at all hours of the day and night. On one occasion in particular that happened on March 9, 1995, witnesses reported seeing a large, illuminated, silver colored UFO that pulsated as it moved. It also had a mysterious red hue of something unidentified trailing behind it. The airport personnel in the control towers at the Rotorua and Hamilton International airports were privy to the sighting as well. Additionally, citizens telephoned area radio stations after witnessing the same UFO that day.

Puerto Rico, USA

In Puerto Rico there have been numerous reports of UFO and USO sightings. They are often seen near the northeastern coastline. Spacecraft have been witnessed entering and exiting the water there for several years. The sightings are so prevalent that the U.S. Navy has become involved and is said to be monitoring the UFO/USO activity in the waters along the coast.

Lake Titicaca, Peru

Perhaps the most startling information regarding a possible underwater extraterrestrial base come from Lake Titicaca which is located on the borders of Bolivia and Peru. The entire area is full

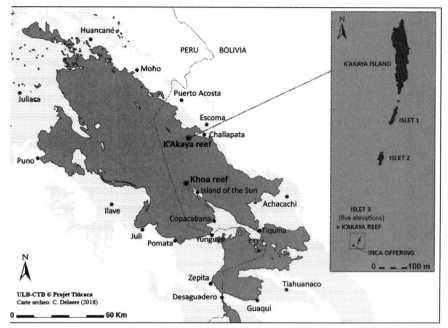

A map of Lake Titicaca.

of UFO and USO activity. There are those that believe that Lake Titicaca is home to an ancient race of beings that reside beneath the waters. Intriguingly, and what may be a major connection here, is that the ancient city of Tiahuanaco (one of the oldest cities on Earth) rests on the southeastern shore of Lake Titicaca. Within Tiahuanaco is the Sun Gate of Tiahuanaco, a mysterious antiquated relic with a doorway that holds astronomical symbols containing information that some believe was given to the ancients by extraterrestrials. What's even more interesting is that there have been several mysterious writings and statues found near the lake that appear to show ancient Mesopotamian underwater gods. The gods portrayed in the statues are believed by the locals to be images of gods that came from an ancient civilization that had once existed under the waters of Lake Titicaca.

Not very long ago, a group of people visiting the area filmed a large, circular submerged object moving slowly under the water. This sighting suggests that there is something in the lake, and that perhaps the legend of a civilization being in the deep waters of the area are true. Of course, the ancients would have referred to the beings as gods. Today, as we move forward with the research of Earth's galactic history, we now know that there is most likely an extraterrestrial connection here, with a possible extraterrestrial base or civilization in those waters. As in many of the other accounts given here, it appears that if true, then these beings have been there throughout Earth's history.

Lake Erie, Ohio, USA

Lake Erie is one of the five great lakes of North America. What most people are not aware of is that Lake Erie has a long history of UFO and USO activity. Reportedly, fast moving UFOs have been seen entering the waters of Lake Erie. In an incident that occurred in 1988, a UFO purportedly landed on the lake on a day when it was completely frozen. Shocked witnesses contacted the Coast Guard to report the incident. The craft was described as having red and blue lights and made an unusual noise. Witnesses also reported that there were strange "triangular shaped objects" being "jettisoned" from the UFO. Eventually, the UFO disappeared. Observers believed that it had descended into the depths of Lake Erie. What is interesting in this account is that this craft landed on an iced-over Lake Erie and proceeded to essentially somehow make its way through the ice. Perhaps these jettisoned triangular objects were made by a kind of tool designed to dig. This tells us that there is something beneath those waters that the visitors were attempting to get to. Was it a base perhaps?

Lake Baikal, Russia

Lake Baikal is a rift lake in Russia. Located in southern Siberia, it is nearly 30,000,000 years old and is the largest freshwater lake in the world. It makes up 22-23% of the Earth's freshwater surface water. It is also the deepest lake on Earth—reaching a depth of a little over a mile—and the clearest. An estimate as to how far you can see into the lake is approximately 130 feet. It is also one of the main UFO hotspots in Russia. States J.M. Plumbley, in an article titled "Part of your world: terror in the depths of Lake Baikal," dated October 5, 2017, "The surrounding villages have witnessed hovering lights in various colors and formations, as well as silent discs that have floated low in the sky for so long people threw rocks at them from sheer boredom." Of all the bodies of water discussed in this section, Lake Baikal presents the most evidence for having an extraterrestrial base beneath its waters. There, fast moving USOs have been observed, and in one account there was an incident involving extraterrestrials.

In 1977, scientists in a submersible at approximately 3,900 feet down with the lights turned off, were examining how far sunlight could reach into the lake. According to the account, two bright lights appeared, one from above and one to the rear of them. Shortly after, the lights disappeared. It seemed that someone was observing the submersible. Whoever it was remained silent, and showed no aggression.

However, this was not the case in a second incident that occurred in the lake where humanoid extraterrestrials were encountered. The incident is well documented. Unfortunately for the men that encountered them, several did not return to tell the story. Before relating that tale I will describe a prior humanoid encounter.

During Lake Baikal's long history of UFO sightings, several witnesses have spoken about seeing an enormous "mothership" over the water. Some also recounted seeing humanoid extraterrestrials exiting the craft and descending into the lake. Reportedly, they were wearing some type of "shiny suits." This account is especially interesting, as they did not seem to be hiding themselves from viewers as they went about their work. This scenario occurred before the next account.

According to former Soviet naval officer and famed ufologist Vladimir Azhazha, declassified "secret" files released by the Russian government state that in 1982 seven military divers, performing standard training exercises in the depths of Lake

A map of Lake Baikal.

Baikal, came across an enormous, oddly shaped, underwater vehicle that moved faster than anything they had ever seen. Days later, the divers saw a team of humanoid extraterrestrials (although they were said to be clearly nonhuman) beneath the waters at approximately 150 feet. Their outfits were also described as "shiny." Although there is no confirmation, one can imagine them to have been the same beings that were observed leaving the mothership earlier on. The extraterrestrials also wore oxygen masks, which have been described as small and are thought to have been made by advanced technology.

Unfortunately for them, the divers attempted to capture the extraterrestrials. As they tried to secure them, the extraterrestrials used what was described as an advanced sonar wave weapon. This device killed three of the divers. In the process, the other four men retreated. Reportedly, some of the survivors sustained injuries.

There have also been discussions about strange images taken of Lake Baikal by the International Space Station (ISS). NASA images show what looks like a base located beneath the waters there. In 2009, astronauts onboard the ISS photographed two mysterious circles in Lake Baikal's ice. This has led to debate over what they are, and what or who, may have created them. It is speculated that the circles were created either as a result of global warning or by some sort of underwater vehicles. Some researchers maintain that the images released by NASA may confirm that Lake Baikal is home to an extraterrestrial base. In an article for the *Time for Disclosure* website titled "NASA Pictures Reveal Underwater ET Base in Lake Baikal," dated September 8, 2021, ufologist Nancy Thames writes, "One of the saucer-like cracks was found near the southern end of the lake, while the other was close to the center of the lake. Both anomalies were symmetrical and perfectly round, pointing towards the idea of a spaceship or even a mothership that broke the extremely thick ice on its way out. Could this be one of the underwater 'vehicles' spotted by the Soviet divers in 1982?" One wonders.

The Mariana Trench, Western Pacific Ocean

The Mariana Trench (also known as the Marianas Trench) has been referred to as "the world's most enigmatic and chilling destination." It is a crescent-shaped trench located in the Western Pacific, near Guam. It is said to be the most mysterious part of our oceans. Positioned approximately 200 kilometers east of the Mariana Islands, it is the deepest oceanic trench on Earth, extending for more than 1,580 miles (2,540 km) with a mean width of 43 miles (69 km). Its depth is a minimum of nearly 36,000 feet. Simply put, it is the world's deepest place. In an article titled "Marina Trench: The deepest depths," by Becky Oskin, published in *Live Science*, May 16, 2022, it states, "The Mariana Trench is the deepest oceanic trench on Earth and home to the two lowest points on the planet." Extraterrestrials are believed by many to exist within the trench. If there, then they are truly a part of our galactic history, because more than just a base, an entire civilization is believed by some UFO researchers to exist there. Given the data on the trench, it is difficult to understand how anything could tolerate the environment there. Sunlight hasn't hit bottom of the trench in a billion years. Temperatures are just a few degrees above freezing, and there is crushing water pressure. Still, marine life does thrive there. For that reason, we can only imagine what an advanced species from another world is capable of developing in the fields of science and technology that would allow them to live there. If there are extraterrestrials in the Mariana Trench, it would be difficult to even locate them, let alone study their ways and habits. We would also need to find a way to communicate with them. Wherever the beings came from, it would be difficult for us to meet and interact with them unless they initiate it. Whoever these beings are, it does not appear that they have any interest in interacting with those on the surface, namely, us.

Point Dume, California, USA

Sometimes the least expected places turn out to be where one might see UFOs, USOs and in predicting that an extraterrestrial base may be located. One of these places is Malibu, California. For those not familiar with this popular part of Southern California, Malibu is a beach city located 30 miles west of downtown Los Angeles. It is a popular tourist area and is well known for its idyllic climate and Hollywood stars. It is also known as a UFO and USO hotspot. Several ufologists believe that in the depths of the ocean near Malibu, there may exist an extraterrestrial base. This idea is also fueled by reports of a massive, out-of-place construction located approximately 2,000 feet beneath the waters, measuring nearly three miles wide. The structure is known as Sycamore Knoll. Several UFO researchers believe it to be extraterrestrial related.

The mysterious Point Dume in the Pacific Ocean off Malibu, California.

The Shag Harbour, Nova Scotia, Canada

One of the most recognized USO events transpired in Shag Harbour, Nova Scotia. The "Shag Harbour incident" as it is known, occurred on October 4, 1967, in the small fishing town on the South Shore of Nova Scotia. On that day the residents of Shag Harbour experienced something they would never have imagined. In the sky, witnesses saw what appeared to be a spacecraft moving over the Atlantic Ocean. Four orange lights were observed on the craft. As they watched, the craft descended rapidly and appeared to crash into the water. Residents notified the Coast Guard. By the time the Coast Guard arrived, the craft had submerged beneath the waves. Reportedly, yellow foam could still be seen on the surface of the water where the craft was last been seen before it either sunk or purposely submerged itself.

Treating it as an emergency situation, and presuming it had crashed, a rescue operation was put in place that included both the Coast Guard and unofficial town residents that wanted to assist in the search for survivors. The area was thoroughly searched; however, nothing was found. There was no wreckage, debris, or even a record of planes that were scheduled to fly over the area, and no aircraft were missing. What happened that night was officially written off as a downed UFO. An interesting and telling comment was made in an article from the *Exemplore* website titled, "Unidentified Submerged Object: The Underwater UFO at Shag Harbour," August 9, 2022. It states, "The Shag Harbour incident, in fact, is one of the few times authorities have thrown up their hands and written off a sighting as a UFO." Whatever this was, it was heading somewhere. We can assume that the UFOs have a reason for submerging. Could there be an ancient civilization or a base in the deep waters of Shag Harbour?

Miami, Florida, USA

Perhaps the UFO experience of Filiberto Cardenas can shed some light on the above information and whether there really are bases or cities in Earth's waters. Cardenas' experience gives us a peek into just what may be going on in the mysterious depths of the oceans. On the evening of January 3, 1979, Cardenas and three family friends were traveling on Okeechobee Road, in Miami, Florida when his car engine suddenly stopped working. Cardenas and one of the friends exited the car to check under the hood, when he along with his companions heard a loud humming noise. Suddenly, a large spaceship appeared above the car. It had a bright blue-violet ray of light emanating from it. Without warning, the light enveloped Cardenas and he found himself unable to move. The ray of light then pulled Cardenas into the craft, in front of his three shocked friends. The craft flew away with Cardenas.

Two hours later, a disoriented Cardenas was located by a policeman 16 miles from where he had been taken. He then told a remarkable story. He stated that the ship had traveled a good distance until it eventually reached an oceanfront area on the coast. There they entered an *undersea tunnel*. He said that at that point, he could see the water whooshing by, through a window. He noted how easily the ship was able to traverse the water. He stated that he felt no resistance to the water as they traveled through it, indicating that their technology was highly advanced. He described the extraterrestrials as normal sized and human looking. He stated that they used telepathy to communicate with him in fluent Spanish.

The extraterrestrials warned him against wars and disasters that would threaten life on Earth. The extraterrestrials were dressed in dark, tight-fitting, once-piece jumpsuits, with a head covering. In the front of the jumpsuit, located in the right breast area, there was an insignia with what appeared to be either a snake or the letter S. Over the "S" was an X. Once they reached the end of the tunnel, they arrived at a huge underwater metropolis. He was later taken inside of a room and led to a seat made of stone. He was given a drink that he described as having a taste similar to that of honey. Shortly afterward, he was visited by several people. One individual was human. This person greeted Cardenas and made a point of telling him that he was welcome there. He told Cardenas that he was from Earth and lived amongst the extraterrestrials.

Afterward, Cardenas was escorted to a building, and was led into a small room where he was examined. Cardenas stated that during the examination there was no pain. When the examination was over, he was returned home. A few weeks passed, and Cardenas found himself being telepathically contacted by the extraterrestrials. He was instructed to return to the original area where he had first encountered them. Interestingly, Cardenas requested that his wife Iris join them. The extraterrestrials approved and Iris went along. During the meeting, the extraterrestrials expressed the importance of universal love in the well-being of Earth and humankind's progression.

It should be noted here that in the course of one of Cardenas's encounters with the extraterrestrials, hundreds of people at Miami International Airport reported seeing a large UFO along with two smaller spherical-shaped UFOs waiting nearby. Several of the witnesses were later questioned, and all reportedly confirmed seeing these craft in the same location during the period that Cardena's meeting with the extraterrestrials had transpired. If Cardena's story is true, and this author believes that it is, then this tells us that there is an underwater city in the Atlantic, and there may be more throughout the world.

A Water World

Some researchers theorize that if in fact there are beings existing in the depths of some of Earth's large bodies of water, that they may have come from outer space sometime in Earth's very distant past. It is suspected that they may have come from a watery planet. If we are to accept that there are others in the universe, the idea of a water world may not be so far-fetched as it may sound to us land-faring humans. There may be water worlds out there that could hold a variety of lifeforms. They may also be very much like Earth with both large areas of land and water. If these worlds have land as well, then it is possible that they have technologically advanced civilizations that are similar to our own, even though they are particularly proficient in the water. There are two very good examples of this hypothesis. In a 2013 article published by Space.com titled "What Might Alien Life Look Like on New 'Water World' Planets?" by Mike Wall, we learn of two recently located planets that may possibly be oceanic worlds. Scientists theorize that the oceans on these planets could hold a large variety of life. These planets are two distant exoplanets named Kepler-62e and Kepler-62f. They were revealed during a NASA press conference that was held on April 18, 2013.

These planets are among the most favorable candidates for life-sustaining planets discovered outside of our Solar System. From examining computer simulations, scientist believe that these planets are enveloped by continuous oceans. Interestingly, they are estimated to be 1.6 and 1.4 times larger than Earth. They also orbit in their own star's habitable zone (the area around a star where a planet could experience temperatures similar to those found on Earth, allowing for the possible existence of liquid water and of life). Most mainstream scientists believe that life on Earth began in the oceans. Therefore, scientists theorize that the same can be said for other worlds that have large bodies of water. Could the beings located in Earth's oceans be from a world similar to Kepler-62e and Kepler-62f?

There are cases of extraterrestrials that visited Earth that are believed to be water-faring beings. The extraterrestrial group the "Nommos" come to mind. These are the amphibious extraterrestrial beings that visited the Dogon tribe thousands of years ago and gave them information about the galaxy. The Nommo said they came from a world made up mostly of water. When visiting Earth, they would go in and out of the water. In fact, they stated that they preferred water to land. We should ask ourselves *where the Nommo are now. Did they leave Earth, or did they stay after meeting with the Dogon?* There have been beings sighted in the oceans that resemble them. Is it possible that some of them remained on Earth and built cities under the oceans?

One Strange Tale

There was a strange tale told on a social news website where real encounters of the mysterious and unusual are shared. In one account a person told of their experience that involved beings existing in the ocean depths. The story was honest, genuine, and gripping. (*Author's Note:* The person remains anonymous and there is no corroborating this story. However, it is too fascinating a tale to not incorporate here). I am including it here as something to think about because it so closely relates to this chapter. If true, it gives us some idea of what may be awaiting us as we travel to the water depths of this world one day.

Just imagine that you are in a deep-diving submersible. You sit down on the ocean floor at a depth of approximately 12,000 feet. You are surrounded by darkness. What do you think you will see once the external lights are activated? Perhaps you would expect to see marine life that no human has seen before. Or you may find something even more astonishing. What if you found humanoids outside of your submersible, and they were looking back at you? According to one strange tale, this could happen. This is because, if there is even the remotest chance that this story is true, then there are humanoid beings existing in Earth's oceans. According to the account, during a marine life associated mission in the early 2000s, this person along with a team, were assigned to investigate several beached whales (in an undisclosed area of the world), when they made a shocking discovery. To their surprise, they found that the flesh of the whales had been cut into, and pieces of their flesh had been extracted. Simply put, rolls of meat had been removed from the bodies of these whales. *But by what?*

According to the report, the whales washed up on the beach with the incisions already in them. The scientists noticed that the areas that were cut had also been singed around the edges. They deduced that the item used to singe the edges was a type of laser instrument. Baffled and startled at this odd finding, the scientists ordered a hydrographic survey (a civil engineering service that collects information about a specific area of water) be performed in the region. Shockingly, the hydrographic survey and other research performed in the area showed undisputable evidence of an advanced species of humanoids living on the ocean bottom.

Scientists were able to observe them using a high-tech submersible that came with exclusive oceanic surveillance technology. This allowed them to see into the depths of the ocean, and the team learned quite a bit. These beings were extremely advanced technologically, and were equipped with stunning physical abilities when it came to the water. They moved at lightning speed, said to reach over 70 knots. The team observed the beings communicating and, according to the story, they would make noises that were similar to some aquatic animals. Even more interestingly, if not alarmingly, the beings had the capability of producing a precision sonar blast. They used the sonar blast on the submersible and did some damage. Whether they were afraid of the submersible, or simply did not want to be observed is unknown. However, if this story is true, then it appears these beings, cannot be easily approached.

Their description is equally intriguing. First and foremost, they are humanoid. They do not resemble in any way aquatic life. They do not have fins or gills as often portrayed in science fiction. They are tall and extremely slender, with a glow of light that radiates around their bodies. Their bodies are enveloped in a substance akin to elemental mercury, which appears to be in motion. Their bodily movements are very fast and sharp, and they are identical in appearance. They have been described as having entirely white eyes, no hair, and no discernible ears were seen. Their mouths are wide, but without lips. Male and female could not be distinguished. What's even more perplexing is the way they moved in the water. They did not appear to swim, and they did not move the way a human would in water, nor a fish. They have what appears to be superior capabilities when it comes to water, unlike any known creature.

Any imagining of a mermaid type being here is incorrect. They were nothing of that ilk, it appears from this account. They moved swiftly, and seemingly without switching positions. What is bewildering is that these beings do not appear to be affected by the depths of the ocean. When it came to the submersible, they were curious and appeared to know that they were under surveillance. Could this have been the reason that they fired a sonar blast at the hull of the submersible?

The account gets even more mysterious with the introduction of habitats and vehicles. The vehicles were located via sonar. Some are said to be extremely large, and ridiculously fast. The account states, "They would move faster than anything should be capable of moving underwater." Habitats were also located. They are said to be hexagonal and connected. Of course, no one knows from what material they are made. The article also stated that habitats have been located in other ocean areas and are believed to be those of these same beings.

In this author's opinion, these humanoid underwater beings may exist in habitats that are not necessarily water filled. I should note here too, that the mercury fluid substance and white eyes could just be a type of suit designed to help them move through water. If this story is real, and the beings really do exist, they may be just as capable on solid ground as they are in the oceans. They may also be responsible for some of the USOs we read about earlier. They clearly have technology and abilities that we simply do not understand. They may have chosen our oceans because of the privacy. Also, we have no idea how long they have been here. *Or why they came.* Also, one more thought to consider: there just may be different types of humanoid beings (extraterrestrial or intraterrestrial) living in Earth's oceans.

What better place, if they have the technology, for extraterrestrials to be on Earth without detection, considering we do not know what is in our oceans. There have been too many sightings of USOs going into the ocean, and even more of lights and other unnatural phenomena seen by people moving through the oceans, to disregard the idea that someone from elsewhere may have come to Earth in the distant past and be dwelling there. Let's remember that we have only explored 5% of the oceans. In fact, the deep-sea area of the oceans, that is perpetually dark, is 103 million square miles in area. Being that the oceans are the world's "final frontier" and have even been referred to as our "inner space," according to some scientists, we do not want to end up being surprised that there is an advanced humanoid civilization from outer space hiding in the oceans. That could prove disastrous as our own people may not welcome them. Given the vastness and depth of Earth's waters, they could have entire cities that we know nothing of. However, as we progress in our deep-sea oceanic technology, we may soon learn more about potential extraterrestrial oceanic visitors and neighbors.

The account also gave this bizarre information. It stated that there are several areas around the globe where these beings exist. The Mariana Trench is one of the main places that they are located. The account described them as being highly evolved and seemingly invincible since they can exist in deep, highly pressurized waters. They are believed to have evolved far beyond humans and have advanced technology including craft and some sort of housing. There appears to be a good number of them as well, as indicated by their facilities off the coast, near Cyprus Island.

This is a fascinating story if true. If it is fiction, then given the limited amount of information on USOs, it is at least interesting to consider. One thing we do know for certain is there are UFOs entering and exiting Earth's waters all over the world. That has been documented, and we wonder, *who are they?*

Christopher Columbus on the Atlantic Ocean

I would like to end this chapter with an extraordinary event. It is no surprise that one of the people that observed USOs was Christopher Columbus. He saw UFOs submerge during his first voyage. Columbus kept journals of his travels and, fortunately for us, we have his writings today and can see for ourselves what he reported. On October 11, 1492, at 10:00 pm, Columbus witnessed something amazing. As he and his fleet sailed across the deepest waters in the Atlantic Ocean, they were astounded to see intermittent lights moving beneath the waters. He later witnessed an immense spherical shaped object leaving the ocean! Later he observed a large intermittent light that moved from the ocean into the sky. He wrote that the light was brighter than any light he had ever seen. His crew, which consisted of 120 people spread out across a three-ship Spanish fleet, were astonished. Due to a lack of knowledge, he likened what he saw to a candle moving upward and then lowering in the night. What's even more interesting is this was not a one-time occurrence. Over the next two months, Columbus wrote of other strange events while on the waters, including strange sightings and odd events while observing the cosmos. On September 17 and September 20, he wrote about how there were mysterious lights in the sky that moved. Columbus wrote, "The star moves from its place, but the needles remain stationary."

What better place to have clear UFO sightings than on the ocean waters? It really is quite calm out there. Also, there is not much to do on a ship at night. Sailors most likely spent a good amount of time on deck stargazing and talking in the blackness of the night, with only the Moon and stars for light. Any strange lights in the sky or beneath the waters would be easily have been seen.

It is interesting to realize that extraterrestrials were monitoring Columbus and his crew aboard the fleet of ships. It is possible that the extraterrestrials knew that the men aboard those ships had no idea what they were looking at. The idea of spacecraft was far from their minds, so therefore the men must have been quite amazed. I believed that the extraterrestrials understood at that time that humanity was a young species that was still attempting to find their footing in the world and the universe in general. I believe this was a reconnaissance mission on the part of the extraterrestrials more than anything else. They may have a base in the waters there, and may be monitoring humanity, Earth, and our progress. Or they may just exist there for reasons we can only image. *However, learning from this experience of Columbus, we know they have been around for a while…*

Chapter Five
The Hollow Inner Earth

"Now that they are admitting there is an ocean beneath the surface of the earth, will they eventually admit to the inner Earth civilizations… Will they admit that there's a Sun in the Earth's core and an atmosphere for those that dwell within? That would mean they'd have to admit that much of the science about our planet given to us for the past few hundred years was fabricated."
—Order of Melchizedek

I would never have imagined that the topic of inner Earth would have a role in our galactic history. However, due to the numerous legends of a hollow Earth, inner Earth, and the idea of possible extraterrestrials living there, it most certainly has become a part of who we are and helps to round out this information of Earth's connection to the stars. It appears that this galactic history has several unexpected twists and turns.

Is the Earth hollow? Is there a civilization inside Earth? The hollow Earth hypothesis proposes that Earth is not a solid sphere but contains vast cavities underneath the surface. Inside of these cavities, that are believed to run deep inside the Earth, is thought to be another world, an inner Earth civilization. The thought of a civilization existing inside of Earth may have seemed absurd to most people on the planet in the past. However, with what we are experiencing today by way of extraterrestrial contact and disclosure, people's minds are more open to this possibility. We have learned, perhaps the hard way, that the world, the galaxy, and the universe is not what we thought.

There have been reports through the centuries from people claiming to have visited inner Earth. There are myths and tales about a civilization existing there. This is extremely interesting to me as I have explored the idea of the Moon being inhabited, and the oceans, and now it is time to turn my attention to inner Earth. For all those who do not believe this could be real: you will be disappointed. The problem we have in all these scenarios is that humanity has been asleep (so to speak). Humanity has been so immersed in the different ages and cultures and progressions over the years since we arrived on Earth (however that may have happened), we missed things. As we were "sleeping," other areas around us were growing, changing, thriving, and progressing right under our noses. We never really paid attention to what was happening around us, until now. The world is waking up and people are realizing what they have been missing. What is going on inside of the Earth, what lies beneath our feet, is not something we stopped to consider until now. In the time of learning of our galactic history and about extraterrestrials, it is time to turn our attention below.

Interestingly, this idea of a hollow celestial body is something that is beginning to become a recurring theme in the galaxy, as our Moon and Mars' moon Phobos are thought by some researchers to be hollow as well. Is this something that can be found in planetary bodies throughout the galaxy, or even the universe? Some researchers maintain that living inside of a planetary body is better than staying on the surface because people and the environment are protected from natural disasters (most especially one that could potentially wipe out life). We know that Earth suffers from calamities that occur all over the world, all the time, every year. In fact, due to these threats, some researchers have suggested that the way we are living on Earth, that is being on the surface, *is inside out*. Some feel that we are also easy targets for an advanced malevolent group of beings that may be intent on harming the planet and those on it. These are truly interesting thoughts that we are just beginning to understand may have merit.

The question is, are there people that figured all of this out ages ago and moved inside of the Earth? If they are there, who are they? Some believe that they are beings that came from elsewhere in the galaxy and created a world there. It may have been for the very same reasons as stated above. It may have been the most logical choice, especially if they had the technology to do so. Another theory is that this inner world is inhabited by intraterrestrials. These are humans that have been there since the beginning. They have remained safe and away from the chaos on the surface. The disasters that humankind has suffered on a worldwide scale did not affect them. It is thought that they remained below, continuing to progress, and are now superior in all matters to we on the surface. One last thought is that these, too, may be people that were seeded by an advanced race in the galaxy. These people ended up in this world below, while others developed on the surface. Recently, scientists have found a great deal of evidence showing that the Earth is hollow. The question is, if there is a civilization inside of the Earth, then to which of the above groups do they belong?

Hypotheses as to Who May be Dwelling Inside Inner Earth

•Humans that sought refuge inside of Earth eons ago. They may have been escaping a disaster on the surface. These people I would refer to as intraterrestrials. They are not really a part of our society, and for the most part are "alien" in their ways to those on the surface.

•Humanoid extraterrestrials who originally existed on Earth from a prehistoric civilization that for whatever reason moved inside the Earth. They may have moved inside for the same reason as given in the first hypothesis. There is a lot of speculation these days among scientists about a pre-civilization that existed before humans arrived on Earth. This discussion arrises because of the out-of-place artifacts that have been discovered, as well as ancient cities, that show the work of a highly advanced, highly skilled, highly knowledgeable group of beings. No one knows as of yet who they were or where they came from, although it is theorized that they were extraterrestrials that came to Earth. If this is the case then they would be far more advanced than humanity and may have achieved success in creating a world inside the Earth.

•Humans that were here in the beginning, but developed beneath the surface of Earth. They progressed alongside those living on the surface. However, they did not suffer setbacks as humanity did due to world catastrophes on the surface. Humanity is believed to have had to start from scratch building a worldwide civilization, and relearning the areas of science and technology, perhaps several times. Those inside the Earth are believed to have continued progressing with no gaps. They may even have aerial craft. Their craft may be some of what we see in the skies today.

•Extraterrestrials that came from outer space and took up residence inside the Earth. These beings may have come here fleeing their own world for any number of reasons, such as a calamity or an oppressive political climate. The idea of extraterrestrials living inside of planetary objects is being scrutinized more closely today by researchers, so it is not as far-fetched as it may sound. An extraterrestrial race with technology more advanced than ours may have come here and established a city inside of Earth. They may have done so because this was the way on their original home world, or they may have been avoiding humanity. They may have probed Earth and learned that it was inhabited. They would not have destroyed or interrupted life on the surface, but they certainly may have considered a civilization on the inside if they had the technology to establish it.

The Hollow Inner World

Once scientists understood that we may indeed be living on a hollow Earth, they set about learning about the inner Earth's topography. Some of this is being done using seismometers and the studying of seismic waves. With the use of this technology, scientists can penetrate, reflect, or refract even homogeneous rocks when they encounter boundary zones or abnormalities. As a result, they now have data on the topography of inner Earth. They learned that the inner world has a topography that is similar to that of Earth's surface, which is rough and rugged. Researchers have discovered massive mountain ranges (some even larger than those on Earth's surface), immense valleys and huge plains. These areas are located 660 kilometers (approximately 410 miles) beneath the Earth's surface. Scientists refer to this area as "the 660-kilometer border." There is even talk of a source of energy (some refer to this as a sun). One of the most surprising pieces of information to absorb when it comes to learning about the inner world is that there is a massive amount of water there. According to reports, there is three times the amount of water located inside the Earth than the entire amount found on the surface. This includes the Atlantic, Pacific, Indian, Arctic and Southern oceans as well as all the large seas and other large bodies of water. It is truly shocking to think about, and what is worse, is that most people are not aware of it.

We can only speculate when it comes to this power source that some refer to as a "sun." There are theories of course, as inner earth proponents believe that some sort of power source is located there. If indeed there is an advanced race of beings either intraterrestrial or extraterrestrial, they may have found a way to produce life-sustaining energy. On *The Conspiracy Show,* in an episode titled "The Earth May Be Hollow! A Journey Inside!" (S2E11), hosted by Richard Syrett, inner Earth researcher Brooks Agnew commented on the topic stating, "Inside the planet we probably don't have a fusion source of light like we have here. It's probably a very hot iron core, like one solid iron crystal and if that's so and it's anywhere around 5000 degrees, it's probably glowing white hot and if it's glowing white hot it's a source of light." On the same show, Rodney Cluff, author of *World Top Secret: Our Earth is Hollow!,* had this to say on the matter: "The inner sun they estimate to be about 600 miles in diameter. It generates electromagnetic energy, and it comes out in the form of light and heat that gives life, and life to us, and the people inside the Earth." Admiral Richard Byrd, who claims to have visited inner Earth, reported that there's a levitated sun that's made of refractory crystals that are energized by the solar Sun.

Son Doong Cave – An Example of Inner Earth? A Connection to Inner Earth?

Our Earth is believed to have a vast network of underground, honeycomb-like tunnels that connect many parts of the world. They are believed to go on for hundreds of thousands of miles. These tunnels are thought to lead into huge caverns and caves throughout the planet. Some are thought to extend deep down into the inner Earth, where the inner Earth civilization can eventually be located.

There are some areas in the world today that researchers believe may be an example of what to expect should we ever visit the inner Earth. Scientists are locating tunnels, caves and what appear to be hidden entrances leading into the Earth that humanity never knew existed. Not only that, but some of these openings lead to what appears to be "worlds" unto themselves, some with their very own ecosystems. Strange creatures never seen before are sometimes found in these deep, dark locations. Many believe that if these caves and tunnels are explored in depth, then they will lead to the mysterious, legendary inner Earth civilization.

One example of a place that was recently discovered and that appears to be a world of its own, and that may be viewed as a smaller version of what we may find deeper inside the Earth, is the Son Doong Cave. The Son Doong Cave is located in Quang Binh Province, Vietnam. It is the largest cave passage in the world. In 1991 logger Ho Khanh discovered a mysterious entrance that led to a concealed cave in the mountains whose entrance was covered with dense jungle foliage. Khanh could see from a distance that the terrain that would take him to the consisted of steep cliffs that he simply couldn't traverse, and so he turned back. It was almost 20 years before the cave would be explored, which was accomplished by the British Cave Research Association. It was only then that the true nature of what had been hidden for so long was discovered. What they found was shocking. This hidden cave is a world of its own, located inside the Earth. Data on the cave follows:

- •The cave is 40 stories high
- •It is nearly 3 million years old
- •It has a thriving jungle
- •It has its own localized weather system
- •It has its own ecosystem
- •It has a rainforest named the Garden of Edam (not Eden)
- •It has a large river
- •It extends through the Earth for nearly 6 miles
- •It runs extremely deep inside the Earth
- •Trees and vegetation grow abundantly
- •It holds the largest stalagmite ever found
- •It has an abundance of rare limestone pearls

As you can imagine, it is also known for its great beauty. It is unlike anything anyone has ever seen before. No one would have believed that such a place existed. It was there all along. Some believe that it is a preview of what is to come, when we journey even deeper inside the Earth. There is one caveat though. There have been what are referred to as "strange beings" seen in the area, and they are believed to dwell within the cave. Some believe these beings are extraterrestrial in origin, others maintain that they may come from deeper within the Earth. They have been described as "reptilian-type humanoid beings." People in the area believe they live deep within the cavern. On the popular History Channel series *Ancient Aliens*, in an episode titled: "Terrifying Humanoids Emerge from Subterranean Realm," author and investigative mythologist William Henry talks about these creatures stating, "What's fascinating about this is that these reptilian-type humanoid beings are similar to the seraphim, or the winged serpents in Kabbalistic tradition. The seraphim are said to have gone and lived in the inner Earth, according to Kabbalistic teaching."

Today's beliefs about beings referred to as "Reptilians" are that they are a race of malevolent beings from another world, and *some* are here. However, the Reptilians are not the only extraterrestrials residing within the caverns of Earth. The inner Earth is vast. All may not be residing together, just as on the surface, there are different areas with different types of people and animals.

One would not have suspected that the inner Earth scenario would be a part of our galactic history. However, it is so. In his presentation *Inner Earth Worlds* (17 July 98) in Detroit, the esteemed researcher, metaphysician and historian Dr. Delbert Blair gave detailed information on his research into inner Earth stating, "The world within is said to be an area of Earth that they don't talk about. And that there is more livable space inside our planet than on the surface. The problem that comes about is that there are creatures or things living down there already and have been for centuries. They say that there are cities down there. Some of the cities are no longer inhabitable, some are actually inhabited. ...You can go from any continent on our Earth and down somewhere, you start running into one of these tunnels, one of these cities, one of these caves." Blair compared the size of one of these tunnels to the U.S. city of Detroit, stating that some of the tunnels are so large that the city of Detroit can fit into one four times. Those are the kinds of areas we are looking at when it comes to what is inside of our Earth. In addition, he mentioned rivers flowing, an atmosphere, a standard temperature of around 60 degrees, openings on Earth (up to 305 that are known), creatures that are not found on the surface, and the possibility that there are more layers to the Earth than we have been told, meaning, anything could be down there! There could be extraterrestrials there and/or intraterrestrials.

Thought has it, too, that some of what we refer to as cryptids may be becoming from some of these tunnels and caverns inside of the Earth. If there is another world down there, then the creatures, and animal life there might be different from what is on the surface. Sightings of cryptids go back thousands of years. They used to be a bit more elusive than today. Today, with the internet and phones everywhere, there are strange creatures being seen more often. They are coming from somewhere. There is a theory that they may have been placed on Earth by UFOs. Are these some of the unexplainable beings seen on the surface? Are they taking refuge inside some of these caverns? Perhaps the inner Earth caverns have just as many interesting animals as we do on the surface.

Blowing Cave

A remarkable story that American author Jerome Clark wrote about in his book titled *Extraordinary Encounters* is connected to the inner Earth topic. It involves "Blowing Cave," which is located in Cushman, Arkansas. Although this cave is visited by tourists today, it has an incredible backstory to it. A man by the name of George D. Wight and some friends allegedly discovered an underworld civilization when exploring Blowing Cave. Wight and his friends had been inspired to visit the cave by a series of stories published by *Amazing Stories Magazine* that were authored by Richard Sharpe Shaver. Shaver claimed to have discovered the inner Earth civilization, and later wrote stories inspired by his original adventure in inner Earth. The name of the series was *The Shaver Mystery*. Shaver recounted in his stories how he had visited inner Earth and located an advanced civilization. He claimed that two advanced races named "Tero" and "Dero" (one was a benevolent race the other malevolent) lived inside the inner Earth.

George Wight, who was from Michigan, studied ufology. Wight was a fan of Shaver's work and was familiar with his claim of having discovered an underworld civilization. According to Clark's account, Wight was at first skeptical of the claims made by Shaver of having discovered an underground city. However, he also held a great interest in spelunking. He would sometimes explore caves with a friend of his by the name of "David L." and a few others. Another friend mentioned in Clark's book was a man by the name of Charles A. Marcoux who was a columnist for a UFO newsletter (as was Wight). According to the story, Marcoux was a firm believer in Shaver's claims of discovering an underground city. Marcoux even went as far as giving lectures on the subject.

In 1966, Wight and 11 other people traveled to Arkansas to explore Blowing Cave. This expedition was to last a week. According to Jerome Clark Marcoux was later given a diary written by Wight about the group's exploration of Blowing Cave. Clark says that Marcoux stated:

> The manuscript related that while exploring Blowing Cave, the group spotted a light at the end of a tunnel. As the spelunkers approached it, Wight noticed a narrow crevice, just big enough for him to squeeze inside it. There he found clearly artificial steps. He called his friends, and they climbed through the opening. On the other side the opening expanded, and they were able to walk upright. "Suddenly," Wight wrote, "we came into a large tunnel/corridor, about twenty feet wide and just as high. All the

walls and the floor were smooth, and the ceiling had a curved dome shape. We knew that this was not a freak of nature, but man made. We had accidentally stumbled into the secret cavern world."

According to the diary, as they moved further inside of the cavern, they met people that appeared human, except for having a bluish hue to their skin. They were informed that they had been allowed to locate and enter the passageway because their intentions were noble. This had been proven to them through a special device they had for monitoring people's mindset. The team was told the passageway continued for hundreds of miles deep inside the Earth, and led to cities that were inhabited by people and beings which included, to quote Jerome Clark, "serpent-like creatures" and "Sasquatch like hairy bipeds." One can only wonder when reading this account if these "serpent-like creatures" were the Reptilians as mentioned in the Son Doong Cave account. What is also interesting here is the mention of the "Sasquatch like hairy bipeds." It has been speculated that sasquatch beings, also known as bigfoot, may be coming from inside the Earth.

The group was taken to a type of elevator that took them deep underground to where the cities were located, which they were told was hundreds of miles down. They were amazed when the doors opened to what appeared to be a "city of glass." They were told that the people escorting them were the progenys of people who ages ago had gone underground to escape the Great Flood. When their ancestors had fled the flood, they discovered a civilization that was already there existing inside of inner Earth. They called them Teros. The Teros were living inside of inner Earth when the people from the days of the Great Flood were just getting going on Earth.

After the trip, Wight decided not to return home. He preferred to remain in the underground city. The other members of the team returned and attempted to convince the world of what they had seen, but to no avail, as people did not believe their claims. The account goes on to state that Wight resurfaced in 1967. He had wanted to give a written account of his experience to Charles Marcoux. He located David L., who for reasons unknown had abandoned the ufology area of study. One wonders if this could have been due to ridicule over the team trying to tell their story when they returned, and the backlash that surely followed. Wight requested that David

L. give the journal to Charles Marcoux. According to this story, Wight wanted Marcoux to know that he believed him about there being an underworld civilization. Afterward, Wight returned to inner Earth. He was never seen or heard from again.

The diary was not delivered to Charles Marcoux until 1980, when David L., who apparently had lost track of him, managed to locate him. Wight had written the following words to Marcoux: "Yes, Charles, all that you told us is true... I owe you a debt of gratitude, because the Teros healed my crippled leg, instantly. I am grateful for more than just that, and I have left these notes and somewhere a map so that you, too, can...visit with these people... Maybe we will meet here someday."

There have been visitors to Blowing Cave since that time. So far (as far as we know) no one else has encountered inner Earth people in this cavern. Given how many things are hidden in this world, and how difficult it is to get all information regarding mysterious phenomena this is not surprising notwithstanding the fact that if these people exist, they may not want to be found. However, if this story is true, there are few items of note:

•The glass city seen by the group is interesting because Admiral Richard Byrd who also claims to have visited inner Earth, described the city he saw as a "crystal city." Is this a coincidence? Although these two entrances to inner Earth are in different areas of the world, one wonders if these cities were built by the same group of beings.

•The reference to "Noah" is extremely noteworthy. We do not know if these beings used the name "Noah" or if the reference came from Wight himself when the beings told him that they were the descendants of those that had escaped the Great Flood and went underground. However, there is a theory that some who fled the Great Flood went underground. We do not know if Wight had any religious associations. It is also believed that the Atlantans and non-Atlanteans alike went underground to escape that destruction. Could the tales be true and all that attempted to escape the disasters went inside the Earth and found beings already living and thriving there?

Interestingly, Noah himself was different from the rest of the populace of his day and is believed to possibly have been connected to beings from outer space, and perhaps even fathered by an extraterrestrial being from the royal Anunnaki line. According to one legend, he was the son of Enki who was a powerful leader, and himself the son of the ruler of Nibiru. *The Encyclopedia of Angels: An A to Z Guide*, tells us, "According to the book of Enoch, as a baby, Noah was surrounded by a brilliant light that glowed in the darkness and would light up an entire room. His father, Lamech, believed that the baby was fathered by the angels and was not his own child." There was something very different about Noah and given what we are learning about the gods and the cosmos, and how we are related to extraterrestrials, one wonders if this extraterrestrial linage is connected with the information shared in this story of Wight and his companions. Could it be that Noah's descendants went inside the Earth and were helped with surviving by an extraterrestrial group, namely the Anunnaki?

•Reference was made to other creatures being inside inner Earth, creatures that were not human and were not a part of the main populace. This is the same situation we have on the surface in the case of humans vs animals. As I pointed out above, we are seeing an increase of strange creatures around the world. I have personally wondered if they are coming from UFOs bringing them here and dropping them off, or if they are coming from beneath the Earth. In Wight's account, a sasquatch type of being was named, and what were described as serpent-like creatures. Again, these references have been made elsewhere in the world and there are said to be several openings to inner Earth on the surface. Here, the account says that Sasquatch-like hairy bipeds exists down there. *Coincidence*? There is also the reference to the serpent-like beings, which of course reminds us that there are a notorious group of extraterrestrials known as the Reptilians (also known as the Dracos), and that many have been seen across Earth, often in and near caves.

If the story of Wight and his team locating inner Earth is true, then it is fascinating. If not, whoever made it up connected a lot of dots in the research being revealed around the world today, that I might add was not available in 1967 when this exploration of Blowing Cave took place.

I will end this mysterious and wondrous tale by saying, I wish that George Wight was available for an interview on this experience. However, according to Jerome Clark's account:

...all evidence of his ever existing began to

mysteriously disappear from the surface. Birth certificates, school records, computer records, bank records, etc., all seemed to vanish, apparently the work of someone in a very influential position.

Whatever is going on inside the Earth, especially with the repeated accounts of advanced technology being discovered that appears to have come from elsewhere…I believe that it started with extraterrestrials coming here in the beginning of human history, and that what is happening on Earth today is coming from those beginnings. Everything happening on the surface, inside the Earth, in the oceans is all connected to our galactic heritage. Perhaps everything is coming to a head in this time of disclosure. We are learning about our galactic history and extraterrestrial connection both above and below. We appear to have neighbors, friends, and cousins in all places. It would be easy to dismiss Shaver's claims except for the fact that there are other testimonies to an inner Earth civilization. This author believes in not dismissing people's stories, and that all potential evidence should be examined.

Agartha—Shamballah

According to legend, Agartha is a magnificent, utopian kingdom that is located inside the Earth. There are several tales that talk about this underground paradise. One involves Buddhist teachings. The Buddhists believe that Agartha is located deep within the center of Earth. The Buddhists believe that there are millions of people residing there. They also believe that Agartha is made up of several cities. Agartha is thought to be a sophisticated metropolis that has grown in technology that far exceeds our own. The people of Agartha are said not to want to have anything to do with the surface governments and humans, and seek to avoid them. The capital, according to Buddhist beliefs, is called Shamballah (also Shambhala). Shamballah is where the "Sovereign Leader" resides. Buddhists also believe that the Dalai Lama is the representative to the Sovereign Leader of Agartha. The messages of this Sovereign Leader are said to have been communicated to the Dalai Lama for thousands of years. It is believed that these inner Earth dwellers have helped humanity after times of disaster. Interestingly, this was relayed to Admiral Richard Byrd when he visited inner Earth (see below).

The Russian explorer Nicolas Roerich published that a Tibetan priest had disclosed to him that the capital of Tibet was linked by a passageway located inside the Earth to Agartha. The entrance to this pathway is said to be guarded by Buddhist priests that are sworn to secrecy. They are tasked with keeping outsiders from entering. Those fortunate enough to be allowed entry journey deep into the Earth, where they will locate this kingdom, which according to accounts is a marvel to behold. If Agartha is real, then where did these people come from? Some believe that they came from the stars and set up their home here inside of inner Earth. Others believe them to be people that progressed on the Earth's surface and were forced inside of the Earth due to warring on the surface or a natural disaster. Whoever they are, if the stories are true, then these people have extremely advanced technology and great wisdom. As I have explained earlier, it is not unheard of for others in the universe to set up their homes inside of a planetary body. In Earth's case it is said that there is more room for living on the inside of Earth than the outside. So then, *is Agartha real?* The closest proof that we have that Agartha exists comes by way of a man who claims to have visited there. I should note, he was not looking for inner Earth when this incident took place. This person was a highly respected, decorated, trusted military officer, who came upon Agartha in the weirdest way: while he was flying an airplane. What happened during that flight has become legend. His name is Admiral Richard Byrd.

Byrd was an explorer of both poles, more famous for his work in Antarctica. The following story seems quite far-fetched, and comes from a diary that Byrd supposedly kept that wasn't published until well after his death. As I have stated, I am a proponent of presenting more information rather than less, so I include it here.

The story goes that on February 19, 1947, Admiral Richard E. Byrd left his base camp and flew northward to the area of the North Pole, for a secret mission. As he flew over the icy land of the Arctic, he soon found himself in an area that he didn't recognize. He was startled to see not ice, but a land with tress, vegetation and what appeared to be a woolly mammoth. What he witnessed confused him. He was having a difficult time understanding where he was, and why he was seeing what he did, when he encountered a disc-shaped flying craft near his plane. He was contacted by the individuals that were flying the other craft and was escorted into an opening that led to the inner Earth civilization. There, the admiral saw a magnificent, shining crystal city and interacted with members of a civilization living inside inner Earth. According to Byrd, These beings are far more advanced than us surface dwellers. He was given a somber message and warning for those dwelling on the surface from the Master, who knew about humanity's troubles. Byrd supposedly wrote down the events of his experience. The following is an expert from this supposed diary, that consists of the warning to humanity from "The Master."

Excerpt from *Admiral Richard Byrd's Diary*:

"I bid you welcome to our domain, Admiral." I see a man with delicate features and with the etching of years upon his face. He is seated at a long table. He motions me to sit down in one of the chairs.

After I am seated, he places his fingertips together and smiles. He speaks softly again, and conveys the following. "We have let you enter here because you are of noble character and well-known on the Surface World, Admiral."

"Surface World," I half-gasp under my breath! "Yes," the Master replies with a smile, "you are in the domain of the Arianni, the Inner World of the Earth. We shall not long delay your mission, and you will be safely escorted back to the surface and for a distance beyond. But now, Admiral, I shall tell you why you have been summoned here.

Our interest rightly begins just after your race exploded the first atomic bombs over Hiroshima and Nagasaki, Japan. It was at that alarming time we sent our flying machines, the 'Flugelrads,' to your surface world to investigate what your race had done.

"That is, of course, past history now, my dear Admiral, but I must continue on. You see, we have never interfered before in your race's wars, and barbarity, but now we must, for you have learned to tamper with a certain power that is not for man, namely, that of atomic energy.

Our emissaries have already delivered messages to the powers of your world, and yet they do not heed. Now you have been chosen to be witness here that our world does exist. You see, our culture and science are many thousands of years beyond your race, Admiral." I interrupted, "But what does this have to do with me, Sir?"

The master's eyes seemed to penetrate deeply into my

mind, and after studying me for a few moments he replied, "Your race has now reached the point of no return, for there are those among you who would destroy your very world rather than relinquish their power as they know it..."

I nodded, and the Master continued. "In 1945 and afterward, we tried to contact your race, but our efforts were met with hostility. Our Flugelrads were fired upon, yes, even pursued with malice and animosity by your fighter planes.

So, now, I say to you, my son, there is a great storm gathering in your world, a black fury that will not spend itself for many years. There will be no answer in your armies, there will be no safety in your science. It may rage on until every flower of your culture is trampled and all human things are leveled in vast chaos.

"Your recent war was only a prelude of what is yet to come for your race. We here see it more clearly with each hour...do you say I am mistaken?"

"No," I answered, "it happened once before, the Dark Ages came and they lasted for more than five hundred years." "Yes, my son," replied the Master, "the Dark Ages that will come now for your race will cover the Earth like a pall, but I believe that some of your race will live through the storm, beyond that, I cannot say.

"We see at a great distance a new world stirring from the ruins of your race, seeking its lost and legendary treasures, and they will be here, my son, safe in our keeping. When that time arrives, we shall come forward again to help revive your culture and your race.

"Perhaps, by then, you will have learned the futility of war and its strife...and after that time, certain of your culture and science will be returned for your race to begin anew. You, my son, are to return to the Surface World with this message..."

With those closing words, our meeting seemed at an end. I stood for a moment as in a dream...but, yet, I knew this was reality, and for some strange reason I bowed slightly, either out of respect or humility, I do not know which.

Byrd's supposed experience is now legendary. After the visit to inner Earth, Byrd supposedly wrote in his journal all that he had seen and had been told. If this rather far-fetched story is true, as far as we know, the inner Earth civilization has remained hidden and silent as they continue to watch the events on Earth's surface. We can only speculate if one day they will emerge to assist or educate those above, before their dreaded prediction of Earth's future comes true. According to the conversation between Admiral Byrd and the Master, the people of inner Earth would avail themselves to assist possible survivors on the Earth's surface after a worldwide calamity that they believe would be caused by humans on the surface. We can only hope that our future does not go as the Master has said.

According to Byrd's supposed writings, the inner people were sophisticated, spiritual, and more technologically advanced than we are. They had survived the five Earth-wide cataclysms, with no break in their history or technology, unlike Earth's surface inhabitants.

It is said that Byrd returned to Washington, DC on March 11, 1947. During that period, he was questioned by high-ranking security forces. He was also examined by medical personnel and cleared. He was then ordered to remain quiet about his experience and was watched closely by high-ranking military officials. Being loyal to his oath as a military officer, he obeyed orders. He did not talk about his experience, and the people he encountered. However, Byrd supposedly kept the diary of his travels that was eventually made available to the public by a small press to read many years later.

Chapter Six
We Are Not Alone:
Signs, Signals, Messages,
& Clues

"Beware the bearers of false gifts and their broken
promises. Much pain, but still time. There is good out there,
we oppose deception."
— The Crabwood Crop Circle, August 16, 2002

Are there extraterrestrials out in space that are trying to communicate with Earth? Have they been sending us signs, signals, messages, and clues to let us know that we are not alone in the universe? In Earth's galactic history, we have a long line of such clues telling us that we are not alone. As we have grown and matured as a species, we can now recognize messages from otherworldly intelligences. We are not alone. We never have been, and the evidence is everywhere. The reality is that from the time humankind appeared on Earth, extraterrestrials have been visiting. This knowledge and the understanding of this fact is news for most people in today's world. We have been naively oblivious to the signs being shown us that we are not alone in the universe. The signs, signals, messages, and clues have always been there. The fact that humanity did not notice them speaks volumes about the mentality of the people of Earth, and the situation the world is in. Humanity for the most part has been too busy and too self-absorbed to entertain the idea that there are others in the universe. Even today with all this information coming out, people are still in denial, and going about their lives as if this is not happening.

In the early days any messages received were interpreted as being from "the gods," and "God." For many years it appears that the extraterrestrials knew that we were not ready to be cognizant of such signs. We were not yet ready to understand who we are. When they visited Earth, humans looked to them as gods and saviors. We depended on them. Perhaps this is the reason they "left." Maybe

115

this was the only way to help us to grow as a species and as an independent planetary civilization. However, those from space that visited us in the past, and are still out there and watching us today, have left us clues to their existence and who we are, hoping that one day we will wake up. For the most part they subtly give us hints and clues. Here lately, they seem to have stepped up the process for reasons we do not yet understand. There even appears to be an urgency in our becoming aware of them of late. There are more signs in the skies by way of UFOs and sightings. There are many people accepting the fact that we are not alone. Many others believe that all this talk about extraterrestrials and UFOs is nonsense; that is until they see one. Believe me when I say, more and more people are seeing them and having encounters. Therefore, can we really afford to not pay attention to any messages they may be attempting to relay? These signs, signals, messages, and clues have come to us in many ways. Some were obvious, some were more understated. Some were with direct contact.

There are many reasons that extraterrestrials may be leaving signs, signals, messages, and clues instead of simply "beaming down," as they do in *Star Trek*, and confronting us. We should first understand that there are many different forms of life all around us. There are beings right here on Earth that people are not aware of. People have caught glimpses of them here and there, but there is no interaction on a large scale or regular basis. Those of you that have had experiences with strange beings that you cannot explain will know what I am talking about. It is too much for me to get into in this limited space. Perhaps that will be another book. However, the same applies to outer space. There is unlimited potential for extraterrestrial life that goes far behind anything we think we know, or anything we have ever imagined. There are beings in different forms, and at different levels of technology, living in different worlds.

All extraterrestrials are not equal in their science and technologies just as we are not on Earth from country to country. Some may be able to visit Earth directly due to their natural form and technical capabilities, while others are more limited. Therefore, we may find ourselves being contacted in a variety of ways. We just need to understand this and look for what has been left for us as far as physical signs, signals, messages and clues and other possible methods of communication, including telepathy.

This chapter reveals *some* of the signs, signals, messages, and clues that we are not alone from beings out there that, it appears, are trying to make contact for various reasons, just as humanity is attempting today by sending signals into space. For those that have never been exposed to this information, I promise you, it will be eye-opening!

Some of the means by which extraterrestrials are trying to tell us that we are not alone include:

• Technology
• Channelers
• Telepathy
• Crop Circles
• UFOs
• Appearances of extraterrestrials
• Light formations in the skies
• Strange Sounds in the sky
• The internet
• Entertainment
• Social Media

For the most part, they will not just show up at someone's door (so to speak) although, according to reports, direct contact has been known to happen. You will find some examples of these communications further into this chapter. We can imagine that in the many years that humans have been on Earth, there have been occasions when our cosmic brothers and sisters, outside of the original creators and planet seeders, may have attempted to communicate with us. Their reasons for attempting communication are something that we can only imagine. Their reasons may be similar to ours as we send out signals into space searching for intelligent life. If we were to contemplate the subject, according to the research, they could theoretically be contacting us for any of the following reasons:

1) like humanity, they too are searching for intelligent life in space
2) they want to let humanity know that we are not alone in the universe
3) they are responding to our signals that we sent into outer space
4) they wish to help us advance
5) they are in trouble and need assistance
6) they are warning us of some danger
7) they are looking for allies in the galactic community

117

8) they are seeking to barter and trade
9) they are involved in reconnaissance missions for a nefarious purpose
10) they seeking to prepare us for a spacefaring future
11) they are concerned about our use of nuclear weapons

In their signs, symbols, messages, and clues, just what are the extraterrestrials trying to tell us?

Messages from the Past in the Forms of Monuments and Artifacts

Could there be signs, signals, messages, and clues from extraterrestrials that visited Earth in the past that were left here to let us know that we are not alone in the universe? Would they have had the wherewithal to consider future humanity in this process? Perhaps extraterrestrials left certain objects for us to find, with that goal in mind. This could be the case with some of the monuments, relics and other objects discovered on Earth. There may even be items left behind that we do not recognize as signs. Could they have left them with the hope that these items would trigger something in us to help us to understand our origins? Or perhaps they were hoping that we would wake up to who we truly are...beings with a connection to the stars.

How would we know if extraterrestrials were attempting to communicate with us? Imagine that there is a world where you want to relay a message and make your presence known. You don't understand the language, but you need to convey an important, perhaps even lifesaving, communication. What would you do?

Extraterrestrials have been attempting to communicate with us since ancient times. In our ancient past they appeared to use physical objects and structures. Today, as humankind has advanced in technology and has become more sophisticated, they are using other methods to signal us. It also appears that there is more than one group that is contacting us, and these groups themselves are at various levels of advancement. Therefore, today we are receiving what appears to be a mix of messages in the forms of signs, signals, symbols, and other communications. We have already looked at the vast amount of information found connected to extraterrestrials in Chapter Three, *Our Ancient Past*. Now, however, we explore something quite different, and for many something even more amazing: how they have communicated messages through the ages. Below are just a few of the signs, signals, messages and clues that have come from beings we have yet to meet; but yet, are interested in *us*.

Signs and Clues

Since the beginning, humanity has been receiving signs that we are connected to the stars from what appear to be well meaning, benevolent extraterrestrials. Today we have ample evidence that suggests that we have been visited by these beings for millennia. The evidence comes by way of artifacts, ancient writings, petroglyphs, and other items that let us know that we are not alone in the universe, and we never were. Much of this information tells us that Earth has a direct connection to the cosmos. It appears too that the others may have been waiting for us to put the pieces to this cosmic puzzle together without their interference. I suspect that they are waiting for the day when humanity will come to accept the reality that they are here. Perhaps communications are more than just attempts to let us know that we are not alone, but may well be something even greater. One wonders too if there may be some urgency in the matter. As a new species in our galaxy, it has taken us some time to reach a point of maturity where we recognize that we are quite possibly a part of something greater than ourselves; the fact that we are more than likely a part of a galactic community. They may have been waiting for us to understand that we come from the stars. One wonders, too, if they are attempting to prepare us for first contact with the goal of us officially taking our place in a galaxy that is teeming with life. Will we be introduced to other worlds? Will others be alerted that we are here? Will we enter something akin to a galactic federation of planets? Perhaps, this is the reason they are trying to reach us, albeit subtly. They have apparently been leaving us clues as to their existence from the beginning. Also, they may have recognized that as a young race that was rapidly advancing, we needed to be made ready for the realities of the galaxy.

If advanced extraterrestrials were looking for a way to send us messages, they literally have space as their white board (so to speak). We can speculate that if there are peopled worlds out there, then they are at a variety of levels in their evolution. If we follow the Kardashev scale, we know that there can be worlds where the inhabitants are so far advanced that anything they do would appear like magic to us. Others may only be a hundred years ahead and are dealing with technology that is less superior.

There are mysterious objects on Earth that we cannot explain. Some have been studied for years and we still do not understand how they came to be here, nor their meaning. In our modern world, we are not encouraged to think out of the box and question. We often take what we are told at face value no matter how illogical it sounds, as long as it is an easy fit or simple answer. Many, however, want to know more and do question. Here you will find examples of things that are well known, but their purpose continues to elude us. These items have been theoretically linked to extraterrestrials.

Stonehenge

Stonehenge is a prehistoric monument on Salisbury Plain in Wiltshire, England dating back to 4000 BC. The boulders that make up Stonehenge weigh nearly four tons apiece and consist of a variety of rock types. Each monolith measures approximately 6.6 feet tall, is between 3.3 to 4.5 feet wide and approximately 2.6 feet thick. There are now only 43 of them left. When created, Stonehenge was aligned with the setting Sun during the summer solstice. As with several other monuments that are located around the world, there is no definitive answer as to how Stonehenge was created, nor what it was used for. Some believe that humans created Stonehenge, yet others maintain that there could have been no way for those living at that time to transport these huge stones, at their weight, from 150 miles away. It has been theorized that advanced extraterrestrials moved these gigantic boulders using teleportation, via the use of dematerialization at the point of origin and then materialization at their destination. This theory does appear like something right out of *Star Trek,* but believe it or not, if such technology exists out there in the universe, then it might be the only thing that would work in this type of construction. Many believe that this structure was erected as a burial ground, while others assert that extraterrestrials created it as a sign that we are not alone in the universe. They believe that these stones were a sort of clue for us and that they may even hold an unknown message that we have yet to understand.

Curiously, it is also speculated that the stones may have been a way of someone from space marking their territory long ago. It is said that visitors from the stars may have used the stones as a marker to claim Earth and all indigenous life on it as theirs. It is also believed that extraterrestrials may have in the ancient past created monumental remembrances of themselves that humans were not capable of building. These may have been created for us to understand that we are not alone in the universe, that extraterrestrials are here, and that they are more advanced than we are. These may have been ancient signs for us that people from other worlds came to Earth and spent time here. They may have understood that at some point we would see these monuments and put together that these were created by means unavailable to the ancient world, and that we would know they were out there. It doesn't take much to understand this. The scientists, however, will not admit to it. I don't know if the extraterrestrials understood just how stubborn human beings would be.

Pyramids

Thus far, pyramids have been located on Earth, Mars, the Moon, and Venus, with the most well-known being the great pyramids of Egypt. Today, several ufologists maintain that there may be a connection between the pyramids of Egypt and the others located in our Solar System. For centuries the pyramids of Egypt, and others around the world, were believed to be tombs for various kings and monarchs, and in some cases were thought to be gathering places for ritual ceremonies. Although this may be true in some cases, it is no longer considered to be the primary reason these structures were built, especially since others have been discovered elsewhere in the Solar System. There are those that believe the pyramids had many functions.

There are two lines of thought regarding the pyramids. One is that they were from previous civilizations that no longer exist, and the other is the idea is that they were placed there for humans to locate and start putting the "cosmic pieces to the puzzle" together about our past connections to other worlds, with the idea that we are all one cosmic community. It appears too that they are the product of one group that may be attempting to reach us, to make us aware of their presence through the use of what may be (at least to them) a universal symbol. They may also be seeking to convey the idea that they are connected to these planets, and that Earth may have an ancient connection to the planets that such monuments are located on. One can speculate that some of the planets in our Solar System, somewhere in the distant past, had intelligent life on them before it died out. For all we know, they may have been human or humanoid. We have no idea what happened in our cosmos' prehistory.

There has been talk for years of Mars and Venus once being inhabited. There is still talk today that someone is on the Moon (and there appears to be a cover-up involving that information). There is the idea too that the asteroid belt was a planet that was destroyed in a cosmic war. For all we know, it could be our ancestors that left those planets and came to Earth. Our cosmic ancestors may have placed objects here that we now see as mysterious artifacts to give us a message. There are said to be humanoids predominantly across the galaxy. Are these pyramids clues that this same group was with us in ancient times? This situation with mysterious artifacts on Earth is very similar to the story of *2001: A Space Odyssey* (a novel by Arthur C. Clarke later made into a movie by Stanley Kubrick). The story involves the locating of an ancient relic left on the Moon by advanced extraterrestrials millions of years before, that was found by astronauts that recognized it as a sign that advanced extraterrestrials exist.

What is also interesting about this particular sign is that researchers suggest that the pyramidal form predates the pyramids of Egypt. They have pondered whether otherworldly beings invented the design of the pyramid structure for us, or if they were sticking to a previously existing prototype. One wonders if it is a symbol that they are leaving throughout the Solar System and perhaps other parts of the galaxy as well. It would be interesting if one day we were able to know the dates of the origin of the purported monoliths located on Mars, Venus and the Moon. This would help us to better understand these potential signs.

It is speculated too that these advanced beings used the pyramid design to send a message to future generations that there exist other worlds with civilizations out there whose advanced science and technology exceeds anything that we are capable of. These sophisticated, complex, forward-thinking beings that came from another world surely knew that the pyramids would be examined, leading us to the conclusion that other galactic societies exist, visited earth, and are waiting for us to one day make contact.

Today, as we look back on human history, we can see this may have been a sign that they were (and still are) attempting to communicate with us. Undeniably, these extraterrestrials have left an unforgettable impression on humanity, as we continue to question the origins of the pyramids. In modern times we continue to question where they came from, who put them there, how they accomplished the building of them, and why they were placed here in the first place. With the possible discoveries of this same type of structure on other planetary bodies, it of course propels our thinking forward and encourages us as a worldwide society to reach for the stars, which may be what they wanted all along. *Should we say thank you?!*

The Nazca Lines

Continuing, we look at a series of large, oversized geoglyphs that were made on the floor of the Nazca Desert in southern Peru. Created in predominantly straight lines, officially, they are said to have been made by people who made depressions in the desert floor by extracting rust-colored stones while leaving the tan color of the soil located underneath the stones visible. That is the theory. It sounds well and fine until we learn the size of these glyphs and understand that they could not have been viewed except with aerial technology. The lines are thousands of years old, but the world did not know about them until we began to fly. According to the mainstream however, back then, there was no such thing as aircraft.

These images portray geometric shapes, and various plants and animals. They are estimated to be 2,000 year old. The images include fish, hummingbirds, lizards, llamas, monkeys, sharks, spiders, orcas and more. Some of them are very complicated

A photo of a portion of the Nazca Lines and the hummingbird glyph.

123

designs, while others are more simplistic forms. Some of the images are a whopping six hundred feet across. There are literally hundreds of these glyphs, and yet no one knows who created them or what they were used for. They are in fact one of the world's greatest mysteries—and that may have been the point of these rather odd, out-of-place designs.

So what were they used for and who created them? Surely, the people of that period outside of Peru did not know about them. They could not see them. Obviously, the people that created them understood their meaning. Or could they have been as the crop circles today, created by an unseen force that for whatever reason placed these images on the ground? To say that the people created them is a stretch given the size of them, and it would have been incredibly difficult to achieve that artistry on the ground in such perfect lines (similar to the crop circles). Even though the people of Peru over the centuries were aware of the lines, they themselves were unable to see the magnitude of the images as well as the scale of the lines. They would not have known that they were essentially enormous images in various forms.

The lines were discovered in 1939 by Paul Kosok, an American, irrigation scientist. Kosok noticed the lines as he was flying over the territory. He initially assumed they were some sort of antiquated irrigation system. Eventually, Kosok examined the images from both the ground and air. In his findings he deduced that the images had an astronomical connection.

After many years of discussion surrounding the Naza lines, some of the ancient astronaut proponents today believe that these enigmatic pictographs are evidence of extraterrestrial visitation to Earth in the distant past. This may be the most plausible theory. If they are correct, then what was their purpose? Some ufologists have suggested that they were runways for extraterrestrial spacecraft since they can only be seen from the sky. While that is a popular theory, it is also possible that these lines were a sign to future humanity that we had visitors that wanted to leave their mark. The designs are such that one wonders if all the images and depictions made were even familiar to the Peruvians. Some of the lines are said to point to certain celestial bodies such as the Sun and Moon, giving them an astronomical connection. Even though the lines have been examined for over 80 years, there are still no concrete answers as to what their purpose was. This is just another demonstration to humanity that there are other forces operating outside of Earth, and a sign that we as a species should continue our journey for answers to our extraterrestrial history.

Signs in the Solar System
The Sun

Several astronomers and researchers have stated that they have seen strange objects near the Sun. In one account there is a UFO that appears to be either "extracting energy" or "refueling from the Sun." There is also the idea that there are extraterrestrials living inside of the Sun, as UFOs are believed by some to come from inside the Sun, and some believe that they may in fact be visiting Earth. *Can this be true?* It seems incredible! However, it is smart to investigate all possibilities when it comes to Earth's galactic history.

The question of whether there are extraterrestrials visiting the Sun or even existing there is not new. It has been around for centuries. In his book titled *The Extraterrestrial Encyclopedia,* author David Darling, Ph.D. writes:

> Before the nature of the Sun was properly understood, there was no shortage of speculation that it might be inhabited. Lucian played with the idea, almost two thousand years ago, in his *True History*, while in the early seventeenth century Campanella built an entire utopian narrative around it in his *The City of the Sun*. More remarkably, as late as 1795, the distinguished astronomer William Herschel maintained that the Sun was essentially a large planet with a solid surface, surrounded by two layers of clouds. An opaque lower layer shielded the solar inhabitants from the heat and light of the glowing upper layer which he thought was similar in nature to Earth's aurora though on a grander scale.

The prominent German-British astronomer William Herschel believed that life existed on all the cosmic bodies in the solar system including the Sun. To his credit, Herschel was the creator of sidereal astronomy for the systematic observation of the heavens, and he also discovered the planet Uranus on March 13, 1781. In addition, Herschel created a theory of stellar evolution. He became the first president of the Royal Astronomical Society in 1820. Given his reputation, many took his ideas seriously. With everything that we are learning today, one wonders if Herschel was on to something when it comes to the Sun. Although today, in the mainstream, his theories would be dismissed entirely. In the *Royal Society's Philosophical Transactions* in 1795, he considered the idea that extraterrestrials may exist on (or inside) the Sun, writing, "The Sun ... appears to be nothing else than a very eminent, large, and lucid planet ... Its similarity to the other globes of the solar system ... leads us to suppose that it is most probably ... inhabited ... by beings whose organs are adapted to the peculiar circumstances of that vast globe." Very interesting! Herschel spent much of his life looking for intelligent life in the universe. I imagine that he would be especially excited about what is unfolding on Earth today.

Even more fascinatingly, Darling continues in his book stating:

> More recently, with the realization that alien life might run along completely different lines to the terrestrial variety, scientists and science writers have revisited the possibility of organisms living inside or on the surface of stars. Speculations about plasma-based life inhabiting the interior of the Sun or other stars have been made by A. D. Maude and later elaborated by Feinberg and Shapiro.

An article titled "NASA Video Shows Giant UFO Hiding Near Sun, Hit By Solar Explosion" (International Business Times, July 17, 2019) by Inigo Monzon states, "A new planet-sized UFO was spotted by NASA's observatory hovering near the Sun. In the video provided by the space agency, the UFO remained motionless even after getting hit by a massive solar explosion." No one knows of course what the object is, although there is speculation that it is a massive extraterrestrial ship. If this is the case and that is a spacecraft, then this would require unimaginable technology created by a race of beings that are millennia ahead of us, and just may fall under the type 3 category of the Kardashev scale. The video of the UFO is from the space agency's Solar and Heliospheric Observatory (SOHO). Regarding SOHO, NASA's website states, "Launched in December 1995, the joint NASA-ESA Solar & Heliospheric Observatory mission—SOHO—was designed to study the Sun inside out, from its internal structure, to the extensive outer atmosphere, to the solar wind that it blows across the solar system. Over more than two decades in space, SOHO has made many new discoveries, adding to scientists' understanding of our closest star." It is doubtful that anyone expected to find UFOs! The video taken by SOHO, shows a gigantic UFO in the lower vicinity of the Sun. The UFO is estimated to be five times larger than the Earth, and was seen exiting the Sun. This account leads to a great deal of questions of course such as, "Where did it come from?" and "Who created it?" Additionally, on his popular website, UFO Sightings Daily, UFO hunter Scott Waring shows remarkable imagery taken from SOHO of UFOs shaped like cubes (August 4, 2011) that are located near the Sun.

If that account isn't strange enough, there are researchers that suspect the Sun may be hollow and may be home to extraterrestrial worlds existing on the inside. They are theorized to be able to enter and depart the Sun via an advanced, high tech doorway located on the surface. In a second account from March 11, 2012, there is a UFO with what appears to be a tube-shaped object extracting energy from the Sun, in a refueling type fashion. In the above referenced article Inigo Monzon states:

> Based on this concept, it is possible to think that the escaping solar flares from the Sun could be caused by the opening of the star's door. This is probably the reason why UFO sightings near the Sun are almost always followed by solar explosions. It could also explain why the objects are not affected by the solar flares even though they are known to have devastating effects.

In another example of UFOs near the Sun, there is a story of a strange sphere that was filmed sitting near the Sun during NASA's Solar Dynamics Observatory mission (SDO), which launched on February 11, 2010. NASA talks about the incredible goal of this mission on its website stating, "Since it launched on February 11, 2010, NASA's Solar Dynamics Observatory—SDO—has been our unblinking eye on the Sun. SDO studies how solar activity is created and drives space weather. The spacecraft's measurements of the Sun's interior, atmosphere, magnetic field, and energy output all work to help us understand the star we live with." According to sources, images from the SDO reveal a strange spherical object in the orbit of the Sun. In a video from the popular YouTube channel TheSimplySpace, where strange and unusual goings on in space are documented, the object can be seen very clearly. In the video titled "First Real Mysterious Photos from Space That Cannot Be

Explained!" under the heading "the strange sphere," the narrator states: "This mysterious sphere was stationary for several days before moving away from the Sun again. Based on the images one can assume that the object would suck energy from the Sun."

You may be asking how what is going on with the Sun connects with Earth's galactic, extraterrestrial history? It does because some researchers believe that the ships on and around the Sun may be visiting Earth. If any of the fantastical events that we have read about here are true, then it is possible that Earth has a connection with the sun.

Venus

Venus, one of the brightest orbs in the night sky, is known for its beauty, and for being a symbol of love and romance. The Romans named it after the goddess of love in their mythology. However, the planet Venus is quite different from what we imagine. With a mass and size that is very close to that of Earth, its atmosphere is the densest of all the four rocky planets in the Solar System. In fact, it is approximately 90 times the pressure of Earth's atmosphere. Bleak, desolate, dry, and oppressive, Venus' temperatures are sweltering. In a word, Venus is hellish. The question is, "Was Venus always like this?" The answer is a resounding *no*. Scientists have proven that Venus' environment at one time was comparable to that of Earth. As a result, scientists believe that Venus was once a beautiful, welcoming, livable planet, complete with a breathable atmosphere and oceans.

Pictures from space taken by NASA's *Magellan* spacecraft (originally named the *Venus Radar Mapper)* showed astonishing images. There were pictures that showed channels that resembled parts of rivers that have since dried up. However, there are researchers that maintain that these were not water channels, but thoroughfares created by a civilization that once existed on Venus. Images of Venus also show silhouettes of pyramids, as well as a construction that resembles the Egyptian Sphinx. This information and more has convinced researchers of the possibility that Venus at some point held an intelligent civilization. *The UFO Magazine: UFO Magazine Encyclopedia*, states this: "NASA has discovered an array of pyramids and a Sphinxlike structure, not unlike the structures that are thought to exist on Mars." The same can be said of the Moon. There appears to be a connection between Venus, Earth, Mars and the Moon. Somehow, somewhere in our ancient past, it appears that we were all linked together. If this is true, then we can include Venus in the Earth's galactic history in ways we never imagined. Moving forward, we just may find that there is ancient connection, perhaps one involving an ancient war that is tied to the Earth, Moon and Mars, and perhaps extraterrestrials that have a connection to all of these planetary bodies and others in the solar system. *Stay tuned!*

The Moon

In *The Moon's Galactic History: A Look at the Moon's Extraterrestrial Past and Its Connection to Earth*, I covered quite a bit of information on how the Moon may be inhabited. When it comes to the inhabitants, one wonders if they have attempted to contact humankind, given that we are their closest neighbors. If there really are lunar inhabitants, and they are aware of us, would they try and reach us? What would their methods of communication with Earth be? What would be the signs and clues that they are there? There is a chance of course that if lunar inhabitants have attempted to communicate with Earth, that is information that the public is not be privy to. Still, there may be beings there that are attempting to let us know they are there.

There have been strange events on the Moon that can be interpreted as an attempt to communicate with Earth accounts of what could be interpreted as signals coming from the Moon. Could these beings be looking for ways to communicate with us from the Moon? In fact, since the creation of the telescope, astronomers have witnessed strange events on the Moon such as unexplainable moving lights and objects moving across the lunar surface. Something in the form of mist and fog has been seen bellowing up from the surface. There are lights positioned along the rims of craters. All of these and more could be signs to let us know they are there.

Did Extraterrestrials Attempt to Send Signals During the Apollo Moon Missions?

The Moon is known to have an array of strange phenomena surrounding it, from strange lights to rumors of UFOs seen near the Moon and other mysterious events. Most people do not know that during the Apollo missions, there were instances when extraterrestrials appeared to be attempting to communicate with the astronauts. One such person was Alfred (Al) Worden. Worden was a former NASA astronaut, teacher, pilot and the first interplanetary spacewalker. He is the author of *Falling to Earth: An Apollo 15 Astronaut's Journey to the Moon*. Worden served as the Command Module pilot for the *Apollo 15* mission to the moon, where he performed scientific experiments, made visual observations, took photographs, and mapped the lunar surface. In later years, Worden espoused beliefs in UFOs and extraterrestrials.

In a documentary made to commemorate the twentieth anniversary of the astronaut's first landing on the Moon, Worden expressed his beliefs that extraterrestrials had visited Earth in the distant past. Worden stated in an interview that the vision of the biblical prophet Ezekiel was that of an extraterrestrial spacecraft. In fact, he likened it to NASA's Lunar Module. During the *Apollo 15* mission, Worden heard a message in an unknown language while in space. According to the account, Worden heard a mysterious transmission come over the radio in what is thought to have been an alien language. He first heard breathing, then a whistling sound, and then someone speaking. The words were repeated continually. The odd transmission was recorded, and Worden sent it to NASA. The words were, "Mara Rabbi Allardi Dini Endavour Esa Couns Alim." Linguists were unable to translate it at the time. The transmission was leaked and broadcast on French public television. This is said to have occurred once before it was censored.

The well-known French historian and author Robbert Charroux, who was known for his writings on the ancient astronaut subject, allegedly published the transmissions which had been suppressed in the U.S. Researcher Steve Omar/En Mar, in his article titled "The Moon is a Foreign Nation," writes, "On public FRANCE INTER TV on August 3rd, 1962, at 8:00 A.M., and also in the weekly magazine *Le Meilleur*, was another leak that was covered up fast." Alain Ayache reported:

> Why has no one Spoken of the mysterious message heard on the Moon—20 untranslatable words? Perhaps it proves that other men exist, something that N.A.S.A wished to hide...words which really sow the Seeds of panic. Everything was going well that day on our Moon, then at 11:15 an extraordinary fading occurred and contact with Houston was lost. Worden, who oversaw telecommunications, had his attention drawn by a breathing sound and a long whistle. A sentence was constantly

repeated on one note, varying from a small to a shrill tone, and from lightly stressed sounds to raucous exclamations. Luckily the transmission was recorded on Lem's tape recorder, and Worden transmitted it to N.A.S.A. Here are the 8 separate words .... "MARA RABBI ALLARDI DINI ENDAVOUR ESA COUNS ALIM."

Another mysterious account of an alien language being spoken and heard involves astronaut Gordon Cooper Jr.. Cooper served onboard the *Mercury 9* and *Gemini 5* space operations. NASA's Project Mercury and Project Gemini engaged in missions that were undertaken in preparation to someday put astronauts on the Moon. Cooper began his career as an aerospace engineer, a test pilot, and an Air Force pilot. He was one of the seven original astronauts assigned to Project Mercury. During his professional career, Cooper had mysterious experiences as a civilian and when serving aboard each of the NASA missions.

According to reports, on May 16, 1963, while in orbit over Hawaii aboard *Mercury 9* (the last of the Project Mercury missions), Cooper heard a mysterious voice speaking in an indecipherable language over the radio. This was said to have been on a special radio frequency. The transmission was later examined by analysts, and it was determined that no known earthly language matched what was on the tape! On that same mission, Gordon reported seeing a large green UFO approaching his craft as he crossed over Australia. It was also picked up by tracking stations before it suddenly vanished. We can only speculate whether the strange language that Cooper heard was the same that was heard by Al Worden. I wonder too if the language came from the craft that Cooper witnessed. There was never any official word on what the UFO was. Some ufologists maintain that the space program is being watched by extraterrestrials, and that they are especially interested in humanity's progression into space. It is thought that what Cooper picked up on the radio, as well as the UFO, may have had a connection to that hypothesis.

In yet another incident, the *Apollo 10* astronauts heard strange, unidentifiable sounds when orbiting the Moon. They referred to these noises as "space music." There are transmissions of the men commenting on what they were hearing.

LMP: That music even sounds outer–spacey, doesn't it?

You hear that? That whistling sound?

CDR:Yes.

LMP: Whooooooo.

CMP: Did you hear that whistling sound, too?

LMP: Yes, Sounds like—you know, outer space type music.

CMP: I wonder what it is.

CDR: What the hell was that gurgling noise?

LMP: I don't know. But I'll tell you, that eerie music is what's bothering me.

CMP: God damn, I heard it, too.

LMP: You know that was funny. That's Just like something from outer space, really. Who's going to believe it?

CMP: Nobody. Shall we tell them about it?

LMP: I don't know. We ought to think about it some.

Nearly four decades after the *Apollo 10* mission, recordings were found that confirmed that the astronauts had been baffled over mysterious sounds as *Apollo 10* traveled to the far side of the Moon. After the astronauts returned from their trip, the tapes from onboard the spacecraft had been transcribed and filed away inside of the NASA archives. They were located by accident in 2008. Experts attempted to explain the odd noises away as radio interference. It has been argued that the Apollo astronauts, who are among the smartest and best trained men to send up on these missions, would have known radio interference when hearing it. Clearly then, this was something else, something far more mysterious. Could it be that extraterrestrials on the Moon were attempting to contact the astronauts through these enigmatic sounds? Could it be that extraterrestrials were aware that the astronauts were circling the Moon and were attempting to let them know they were there? Today, we have several accounts of UFOs being seen near the Moon, and in some cases following the Apollo missions. It is therefore no surprise that they may have used some sort of "signal" to inform the astronauts that they were not alone.

More Speculated Signs, Signals, Messages and Clues from the Moon

The Moon is important when it comes to the topic of Earth's extraterrestrial history because there are so many variables as to who may be there and why. The Moon has a lot of interesting phenomena going on, and it just may be that some of it is aimed at humanity. In my last book, *The Moon's Galactic History, A Look at the Moon's Extraterrestrial Past and Its Connection to Earth*, I included a number of items and events that just could be signs and messages aimed toward Earth. Whoever is there may be advanced enough to monitor Earth, but have no clue as to how to communicate with us. In one scenario in my book, I talked about lights blinking intermittently from the surface of the Moon. One wonders if these lights were designed for us to see. If so, could they have been a distress signal or warning sign? A passage from the book states:

> Mysterious flashing lights have been observed on the lunar surface. Reports of these intermittent lights date back to the 1800s. On July 4, 1832, British astronomer Thomas Webb observed a series of flashing dots and dashes that were similar to Morse code. On October 20, 1824, European Moon observers saw alternating blinking lights, occurring continuously throughout the night, close to the Aristarchus crater. In 1873, after carrying out a comprehensive investigation of the flashing lights, the Royal Society of Britain announced that the lights were being emitted by extraterrestrials attempting to signal Earth. Ken Mattingly, who was the Command Module Pilot during the Apollo 16 moon mission, described seeing unexplained flashes of light on the far side of the Moon, during two consecutive orbits. Some astronomers speculate that the flashing is a type of code. Some have even suggested they are akin to a form of Morse Code, with the idea being that a message a Morse Code would be received much faster than radio messages between the Moon and Earth. Could it be that there is someone on the Moon attempting a signal? Might it even be a distress signal? We can only speculate on what someone may be trying to tell us. Were they trying to let us know of their existence? Or could it have been some sort of warning?

There have been other events on the Moon that appear to be messages to Earth as well. The following paragraphs are from my book:

Charles Fort (1874-1932) was a popular author and researcher whose specialty was anomalous phenomena. Fort spoke of moon inhabitants attempting to signal Earth. In his work titled, *New Lands,* Fort spoke of fluctuating geometric shapes being seen in the Linne crater. He believed this was a way that lunar inhabitants might be attempting to message us.

In his book, *Secrets of our Spaceship Moon*, ufologist Don Wilson writes of a strange Moon signaling occurrence out of Japan. "One of the strangest of all such lunar reports comes out of Japan, where *Mainichi*, one of Japan's largest newspapers, reported the unusual discovery of Dr. Kenzahuro Toyoda of Menjii University, who, while studying the Moon through a telescope on the night of September 29, 1958, spotted what appeared to be huge black letters, so pronounced they were easily discernible. The letters seemed to form two words: PYAX and JWA. No one to this day knows what these letters on the Moon mean or can give an explanation of the experience.

[In] NASA image No. 14-80-10439, there is an enormous feature in the shape of the letter "S." It unmistakably looks as if it were made by artificial means. Perhaps it is being used as a symbol that has an unknown message, and again, directed towards Earth.

Radio signals have been picked up in several areas of the Moon in the past. They were detected and reported in the Moon's vicinity in the years 1927, 1928, 1934, and 1935. In 1935, two scientists by the names of Stormer and Van der Pol picked up radio signals both on the Moon and in the area around it.

In 1956 several observatories picked up a signal, that sounded as if it could have been a coded message that was being emitted from the Moon. The code was unable to be deciphered. One wonders if these were extraterrestrials signaling each other, or perhaps were signals meant for Earth.

There have been reports of a strange reoccurring black line moving vertically across the Moon. People have witnessed this phenomenon for years from California's Mojave Desert to the UK. It has been seen both with telescopes and binoculars, appearing to be present most often during a full or super moon... Is it possible that native lunarians have found a way as a whole to signal Earth that there is someone there?

Mars, Clues that We Are Not Alone in the Universe

Mars has a past connection to Earth, and it is one that tells us that we are not alone. Thanks to NASA sending up probes to explore the red planet, we now have an array of images showing what lies on certain areas of the surface of Mars. The images are astounding! There is no denying from the pictures that something occurred in Mars' distant past. The Cydonia Institute is comprised of a team of investigators that study strange constructions on the surface of Mars in the Cydonia region. Many people know of the famous *face* of Mars. This feature has had much controversy surrounding it with it being seemingly proof of an ancient civilization. Close to the face of Cydonia, there is a conical pyramid. It is thought that there may be a connection between the two formations. It appears that the Cydonia Institute, as well as several independent researchers, have discovered a great deal of evidence that shows that there are also ruins on Mars from an unknown civilization. Aside from the Face, researchers have spotted several strangely shaped constructions including pyramids, intact buildings, ruins of buildings, as well as items strewn about the surface that appear to have been in a war. All of which are compelling evidence that an ancient civilization once existed on Mars, and possibly still does today. There are also reports of extraterrestrials on Mars today, stories of Martians and humans working together, UFOs seen on Mars, and humanoids being captured in images of Mars. As I have stated previously, there is a theory that there was a conflict that may have involved Mars, the Earth and perhaps even the Moon.

Phobos

The UFO Magazine: UFO Encyclopedia states, "Phobos is one of the moons of Mars, which according to Soviet Col. Marina Popovich and in the opinion of Soviet scientists, is an artificial structure, and hollow as well." It appears that we may have been sent a very strong message from extraterrestrials from either Mars or Mars' moon Phobos via the Soviet space probe *Phobos 2*. The Soviet Phobos Program consisted of two unmanned probes sent to study Mars and its two moons, Phobos and Deimos. Launched on July 7, 1988, *Phobos 1* functioned normally until it lost contact on September 2, 1988. The failure of controllers to regain contact was reportedly because of a radio command error. *Phobos 2* was launched on July 12, 1988. It was successful in exploring Mars's atmosphere and surface, returning 37 images of the moon Phobos with a resolution of up to 40 meters. On one of the images what looked to be a UFO could be seen sitting on the surface of Mars. At some point during the mission, as *Phobos 2* neared Phobos the probe was obliterated. When the destruction of *Phobos 2* occurred those watching the mission and others on the ground believed it to have been the result of alien intervention. It appears that someone on Mars did not want the *Phobos 2* probe near there. The Russians later stated that it was a "huge" cylinder shaped, fifteen-mile "UFO" that struck the probe, destroying it. There is even an image confirming it. There are those that believe that extraterrestrials were sending us a message to stay away from Mars (or perhaps Phobos?).

Was the destruction of the Russian probe a message that we are not welcome on Mars or was this about Phobos? Did someone not want images sent back to Earth? Is the fact that *Phobos 2* had an extraterrestrial encounter a sign that extraterrestrials are working in different areas of the Solar System? Do they not want us to know about it?

Soviet Air Force colonel Marina Popovich went on record stating that Mars' moon Phobos is an artificial construction. She also believed it to be hollow. This is very interesting since some people think the same of Earth's Moon. Marina Popovich's credentials are outstanding. One article referred to them as, "second to none." She graduated from the Leningrad Academy of Civil Aviation, and she became a military test pilot first class. During the height of her career, she set over 100 aviation records. In other words, *she is a highly credible source!*

It was postulated that Phobos is hollow by Joseph Shklovskii who was a member of the prestigious Soviet Academy of Science. Shklovskii calculated from the estimated density of Mars' atmosphere, and the acceleration of Phobos, that it must be hollow. This data seriously makes one question what is going on in our Solar System, since Earth's Moon is believed to be hollow as well. If so, are there other planetary bodies out there that may be artificial? What's more, do they have inhabitants living inside of them? Are there entire cities located within these objects? If not cities perhaps there are bases with extraterrestrials on a mission, or some kind of assignment for their home world or one of the purported galactic councils. These are unexpected signs of life in the universe that humanity would not have come to research were it not for the space agencies sending out space probes and spacecraft. It certainly gives us something to ponder and requires further investigation. These are interesting *clues* that let us know that we are not the only intelligent species in the Universe.

I would like to add too that there have been many cylinder shaped objects observed around Earth and the Moon. Is there a possibility that there is a common race of beings connected to all three celestial objects (Earth, the Moon and Mars) given that these craft seem to be the same in appearance?

A Monolith on Phobos

The information about Phobos becomes even stranger as we explore further. An incredible discovery was made on Phobos. It is a monolith. It appears to be purposefully designed to be seen and is thought by some to be a message to the galaxy that either there is someone there, or that someone once visited leaving their mark. Of course, there are some that believe that this monolith may be a natural formation. However, according to some experts, there is a very real chance that it is artificial. If indeed this is true, then quite possibly the monolith was designed for the specific purpose of serving as a sign for others, and is a message to others passing through the galaxy that they are there or were there. Perhaps too it means, *keep away!*

In an interview with C-SPAN, former astronaut Buzz Aldrin, the second person to step foot on the Moon during the *Apollo 11* mission, stated, "We should visit the moons of Mars. There's a monolith there; a very unusual structure on this little potato-shaped object that goes around Mars once every seven hours. When people find out about that they are going to say, "Who put that there? Well, the universe put it there, or if you choose God put it there." *Or perhaps it was extraterrestrials sending a message that put it there!*

Signals from Space

Has humanity received messages from extraterrestrials from space? Some believe we have. Our extraterrestrial history has several of what are believed by some to be attempted communications from other intelligent beings in the universe. These have been verified by astrophysicists, astronomers, various scientists, and other experts in the search for intelligent life in the universe. What have scientists encountered? The following are historical accounts of some of what has happened over the years by way of communications from extraterrestrials.

A Message from Another World, Nikola Tesla

It is said that Albert Einstein (1879–1955) was once asked how it felt to be the smartest man alive. Purportedly his response was, "I don't know, you'll have to ask Nikola Tesla." The remarkable Serbian American inventor Nikola Tesla (1856–1943) has been hailed as one of the world's most prolific, innovative engineers and inventors of the nineteenth and twentieth centuries. He is best known for his contributions to the design of the modern alternating-current (AC) electric system, the predominant electrical system used across the world today. He also created the "Tesla coil," which is still used in radio technology. Tesla firmly believed that we are not alone in the universe. Hailed as one of the world's greatest inventors, it is no surprise that he lays claim to being the first human to make contact with extraterrestrials on another world. Tesla had been sending signals into space to reach other intelligent beings in the cosmos. A very interesting occurrence happened one night in the summer of 1899. As he was alone in his laboratory in Colorado Springs working on his "magnifying transmitter," Tesla detected a sequence of mysterious rhythmic signals that he referred to as "counting codes." In an article published on December 10, 2009 in the *Letters of Note* newsletter, it states, "Having just detected cosmic radio signals for the first time, Tesla immediately believed them to be attempted communications from an intelligent life-form on either Venus or Mars."

In the February 9, 1901 issue of *Collier's Weekly*, Tesla recounts the events of that night in an article he published titled "Talking with the Planets." Tesla writes:

> My first observations positively terrified me, as there was presenting them something mysterious, not

to say supernatural, and I was alone in my laboratory at night; but at the time the idea of these disturbances being intelligently controlled signals did not yet present itself to me. The changes I noted were taking place periodically, and with such a clear suggestion of number and order that they were not traceable to any cause then known to me. The nature of my experiments precluded the possibility of the changes being produced by atmospheric disturbances, as has been rashly asserted by some. It was sometime afterward when the thought flashed upon my mind that the disturbances I had observed might be due to an intelligent control. Although, I could not decipher their meaning, it was impossible for me to think of them as having been entirely accidental. The feeling is constantly growing on me that I had been the first to hear the greeting of one planet to another. A purpose was behind these electrical signals.

In 1900, the Red Cross asked Tesla to predict humanity's greatest possible achievement in the next century. The following is a transcript Tesla's reply:

> To the American Red Cross, New York City.
> The retrospect is glorious, the prospect is inspiring: Much might be said of both. But one idea dominates my mind. This — my best, my dearest — is for your noble cause.
> I have observed electrical actions, which have appeared inexplicable. Faint and uncertain though they were, they have given me a deep conviction and foreknowledge, that ere long all human beings on this globe, as one, will turn their eyes to the firmament above, with feelings of love and reverence, thrilled by the glad news: "Brethren! We have a message from another world, unknown and remote. It reads: one... two... three..."
> Christmas 1900
> Nikola Tesla

We can only wonder what these signals meant. What were the extraterrestrials trying to tell us? If the signals came from Mars, could these have been the same beings that put the monument on Phobos? Are they the ones that destroyed the *Phobos 2* space probe?

On January 9, 1901 the *Colorado Springs Gazette* had this to say of Tesla's ambitions regarding communication with another world: "Mr. Tesla now firmly believes that with improved apparatus it will be quite possible for the people of the earth to communicate with the inhabitants of other planets."

The Wow! Signal

In humanity's attempt to locate extraterrestrial life in the universe, we have sent out signals and continuously monitor radio waves. The question is, have any of them been answered? There is one that we know of that some consider to be the most credible proof of there being other intelligent beings out there. On August 15, 1977, Ohio State University astronomer Dr. Jerry R. Ehman, while searching for extraterrestrial life, heard a 72-second radio signal that came from the Sagittarius constellation which is located at the center of the Milky Way Galaxy. The signal was heard on a frequency not used on Earth, as it is allocated for astronomical purposes only. Thrilled by the discovery, Dr. Ehman circled the signal on the computer printout, and wrote an enthusiastic, "Wow!" beside it. Afterward it came to be known as the "Wow!" signal. The Wow! signal is remarkable too because the area from which it originated is an empty region of space. Although astronomers have been listening for the signal for several years now, it unfortunately has not been heard again. Some speculate that the transmission may have come from an extraterrestrial spacecraft or even a probe that had been passing through the area, a thought that is very exciting!

Signals from Cassiopeia

Cassiopeia is a large constellation located in the northern sky. It was first cataloged by the 2nd century Greek astronomer Ptolemy. Nicknamed the "W" constellation due to its W shape, it is the 25th largest constellation in the night sky. It is believed that there are beings from Cassiopeia that are attempting to communicate with Earth. In a video titled "Hidden in Plain Sight: Some things Public MUST NOT KNOW... Jordan Maxwell's Fond Farewell Lecture," the distinguished author and researcher Jordan Maxwell stated that our government for the past hundred years has been receiving messages from someone in Cassiopeia. He stated that the problem is that we do not know how to interpret the messages. He stated that they are intelligent messages, and he believes sincere efforts to communicate with us, but we don't understand. He believed that alone is something to be concerned about.

Since it has been so long that these messages have been continuing, one wonders if they are on some kind of recording system that is on a loop being repeated. Is it a hello? Is it a group of beings that are attempting to see if there is other life in the universe, just as we are sending out signals? Or is there something more dire than that, a signal for help perhaps. *Or is it a warning?* We can only hope that there are those that are working on answering this communication.

A Cry for Help from an Alien World

It is sad to think that there are civilizations out there that may be dying. There are civilizations in our galaxy at all levels. Some are just beginning, and some are ending. Others are in between. Civilizations in the galaxy come and go, just as they have on Earth, although some seem to flourish and thrive forever, just as some of our oldest civilizations on Earth. We have an example of this transcience in a purported SOS call from an unnamed dying planet. The civilization on this planet wasn't very old when they sent this signal. This world was the equivalent more or less to Earth's modern age, with the exception of having very limited intergalactic travel abilities. However, they were in a similar situation in what some propose could be Earth's future, given what we see happening here today. What appears to be the downfall of the planet did not come through natural means, but through what seems to be irresponsibility and negligence. The planet was in ruin; there were wars, diseases, and atomic weaponry. As a result, their world was dying. They needed help from someone, anyone. They sent a mathematical, digital message into space hoping that there was someone that could do something…anything. Sadly, they did not have the means to evacuate their planet.

In 2017, the Ministry of Defense of the United Kingdom declassified its national archives corresponding to a "seventh lot" on UFO documentation. One of the files contained an article from the *Weekly World News* published on September 15, 1998 (in volume 19, superscript 51). The article states that there was a signal from space that was picked up in January 1998. It took years before the complex mathematical transmission could be decoded. The article states: "NASA experts claim to have intercepted an intergalactic distress call from an extraterrestrial civilization that had already reached its ceiling, and that it was really dying when the saber-toothed tigers were still roaming the Earth."

According to the article, the Russian chief of General Staff of the ex-soviet Armed Forces, Viktor Kulikov, disclosed that in 1998 NASA's radio telescopes intercepted a signal from the Andromeda galaxy (the nearest major galaxy to the Milky Way). In 2011, NASA deciphered the transmission and found it to be a desperate cry for help from an extraterrestrial society on a doomed planet. By the time we received it, it was too late. The civilization had already peaked and was actually dying, during our ancient times. According to the article this occurred 80,000 years ago.

(*Author's Note*. The paper that the article comes from is not known as the most reputable source. What is strange about it is that it was discovered in the United Kingdom's declassified files, which indicates that someone believes this account to possibly be true. There are quotes in the article from a Russian chief of General Staff of the ex-soviet Armed Forces, Viktor Kulikov. I performed a quick search online and he comes up. He has been referred to as a highly placed NASA source in Houston, Texas, and was heading a United Nations research team from a state-operated observatory 50 miles northwest of Moscow at the time. In trying to get to the bottom of this incredible story, this author found there is some validity to this account. As always, I believe all information should be considered in our journey of discovery of our ancient origins and our extraterrestrial past and connections. It is in the end, *one strange tale*.)

Crop Formations (also known as Crop Circles)

In 1972 as two men sat upon a hill, they witnessed something incredible. A circle was forming in the crops below them. Since that time, there have been over 9,000 crop formations seen around the world. One of the ways that we are being reached by extraterrestrials is by way of crop formations (also known as crop circles). For years they have been a source of mystery, intrigue, and amazement, with patterns materializing in the English countryside, and other places around the planet every year. These spectacular formations are well known, yet no one knows their origins. They appear to be made by intelligent beings from another world that possess technology that we know nothing of. Seemingly, these beings are attempting to communicate with us, yet our world for the most part is ignoring them. That is a sad state of affairs. One would think that there would be regular governmental discussions and an attempt to decipher all of these messages on a worldwide scale. Obviously, this is not the case. However, these crop formations have become a part of our extraterrestrial history.

Crop formations are a modern-day phenomenon. When they appear, they are photographed, and there are people that walk through them and examine them. As a result, there is no questioning their existence. To narrow down a time frame as to when these formations began, investigators viewed hundreds of aerial photographs from archeological investigations taken from the 1940s through the 1960s. They found no evidence of crop formations prior to 1972. That was the year when two men by the names of Arthur Shuttlewood and Bryce Bond, while seated on a hill one night, observed via the moonlight the large circle slowly materializing on its own in the crops below. Since that time, there have been over 9,000 accounts of crop formations. They are located mainly in the UK, however, they have also formed in several European countries, the United States, and Canda.

Crop formations are unequivocally spectacular in their perfect, highly complex, symmetrical designs, and exact measurements. *They appear overnight!* How they are created and by whom is a mystery. Over the years they have become increasingly multifaceted and sophisticated, and they are massive! They often span hundreds of feet across, with some having been as large as three football fields combined.

Evidence that Crop Formations are Made by Extraterrestrials

There are those that have attempted to debunk crop formations. When looking to determine if a crop formation is an authentic one, investigators look at the geometry, the precision of the way the crops lay, and the scientific results from tests performed. In other words, there is science at work here. People are not just recording the formations from the air as some might imagine. Investigators are on the ground looking into these enormous illustrations. According to *The UFO Magazine: UFO Encyclopedia* by William J. Birnes, crop circles are defined as, "Elaborate designs formed in wheat and grain fields, which have been discovered in England, Australia, eastern and western Europe, Japan, Canada, and the United States." One sources gives the number of countries in which crop formations have appeared as 50. Inside of these enigmatic designs, the stalks of grain are laid flat, most often in a spherical or flowing arrangement. An interesting fact is that eighty-five percent of all crop formations have appeared in England in a focused area approximately 20 miles from Stonehenge. However, they do materialize year after year around the world in various types of grain fields including wheat, rye, barley, and rapeseed, and with patterns of all kinds. Another interesting fact about crop formations is that they appear in different types of weather. Therefore, atmospheric conditions have no effect on whether or not the circles can be created. There have also been reports of formations being created during the day, although for the most part, they are created under the covert darkness of night. Perhaps there is a reason for this that we do not understand. Interestingly, if not alarmingly, the number of formations is said to be increasing around the planet. What could the reason be?

Perhaps one of the reasons that more people do not take crop formations seriously is because they believe they are man-made. However, there is enough evidence to be sure that humans are not behind these creations. There are examiners, researchers and investigators that have looked at these formations and have given us their written statements on the phenomena in books, articles, and documentaries. There are also the intricacies of the creations of some of these designs and how they are formed, which frankly is beyond anything we could do here on Earth. We should ask ourselves, "If this was an elaborate hoax, then to what end?" Crop formations have been going on for years, all over the world. If it is a hoax then it is an expensive one. Take in some of the facts and information below and consider whether they are human made or created by otherworldly intelligences.

The UFO Magazine: UFO Encyclopedia states:

> The stalks of grain involved in crop circles all exhibit cellular changes and an electromagnetic resonance that extends from the center of the crop circle design outward to the unaffected area, diminishing in resonance as it extends. Crop circle stalks have expanded nodes and have been bent up to a 90-degree angle with no breakage. Although many have tried, no one has discovered an earthly process that can duplicate these cellular changes. Crop circles have a strong magnetic field in and around them, which is measurable. Many also exhibit strange

patterns of radioactivity in which the level at a given spot will fluctuate. According to the laws of physics, this is an impossibility since levels of radioactivity are thought to be constant.

The award-winning journalist and author Jim Marrs wrote about crop formations in his book *Alien Agenda* (pages 276-277). States Marrs:

> Circles apparently are created in a matter of seconds, since the longer it would take to press stems to a horizontal position, the more the likelihood of damage." "Very few of the circles—perhaps only 2 percent—are perfectly round. Many are elliptical and others oblate. Researchers saw this fact as a strong argument against the circles being a creation of nature, which generally acts with strict geometrical precision." "Circles never overlap the borders of the fields and appear to take into account existing features such as tractor tracks and pathways, adding to the idea of intelligent control.

In the book *The Missing Lands: Uncovering Earth's Pre-Flood Civilization,* author/researcher Freddy Silva writes:

> [A] rural field named Longwood warren, near the English town of Winchester, hosted an exceptional 240-foot diameter crop glyph, a replica of the inner solar system right down to the planetary orbit ratios around the Sun, each indicated by a majestic sweep of thin, barely eight-inches wide rings made of sanding plants; a necklace of sixty-seven grapeshot circles plus three outlying circles represent the asteroid belt, that thick ring of debris orbiting between Mars and Jupiter. The information is 99 percent accurate, so whoever was behind this artwork is proficient in astronomy not to mention geometry, mathematics and sound because Euclidean theorems and diatonic ratios are concealed in its design matrix.

The Only Planet of Choice, by Phyllis V. Schlemmer and Palden Jenkins, states, "In a couple of the circles last year [1991], some researchers detected radioactivity of a particular kind which is not found on Planet Earth."

Some people have witnessed glowing balls of light around the formations. Some have stated that once these balls of light disappeared, they located a crop formation. In the documentary *Crop Circle Theorist Thinks the Truth is Out There*, Andy Thomas, who is a researcher of mysteries, the paranormal and crop circles, talks about his experience with balls of light in the area in which a crop circle appeared. "I was with a group of two other colleagues, and we were up on a hillside looking down over a field with Crop Circles in it and we saw three of these small glowing balls of light. So, I have seen it for myself, and I know it's there. We cannot say what they were, but they would appear above the field and then suddenly just fly away." Thomas also stated, "It may well be that we are being visited by other intelligences…maybe they are trying very gently to make people aware of them in a way that doesn't create fear."

Of course, we can only speculate as to why these formations have grown to an even greater degree of complexity, with even more beautiful, elaborate designs than before. With all this evidence, we can safely assume that someone out there is attempting to tell us something. *But what?* There was even one formation with the face of what appeared to be an alien being.

What is astounding to this author is the way that the masses have ignored this phenomenon. It is as if people are scared or simply in denial. How can the world not see the importance and perhaps even the "urgency" of crop formations in our world? From looking at the images of these pictures, it appears that extraterrestrials have become even more desperate in their attempt to communicate with us. One thing that we should consider is whether those creating crop formations are answering the signals that we are sending into space? Earth's messages into space may be being answered in the form of these formations and no one is listening, and no one is attempting to decipher these messages.

Award winning investigator and journalist Linda Moulton Howe recalls a tale in a "Mysteries Outpost TV" interview on May 30, 2018 where she states that around 1996, "I was shown videotape in England by a man who spent endless nights with good film equipment on tripod, did it professionally trying to capture lights that would be making crop formations…He showed me a videotape in England that showed six balls of light moving in patterns between two hills, and there was a crop formation up on one hill." We cannot know what this particular group of extraterrestrials are thinking of course. What we can assume from these formations is that someone out there in the universe is watching and listening to us. They are paying attention to us. They obviously know Earth's typography. They search for a large enough area to place their messages in the form of large formations, such as circles and pictographs. They are using Earth's fields of crops as message boards. This group of extraterrestrials appear to have decided to send us messages in the form of these vast formations most likely of course because we cannot miss them, and we cannot ignore them. The question is, *what are they trying to tell us?*

Crop Formation Hypotheses

There are four hypotheses as to why extraterrestrials may be placing crop formations on Earth.

1) To let us know of their existence
2) To communicate with us
3) Responding to messages sent from Earth
4) To warn us of a danger

The Arecibo Message: Did Someone Answer in a Crop Formation?

The Arecibo message is an interstellar radio transmission carrying basic information concerning humanity and Earth. It was the first attempt of CETI (Communication With Extraterrestrial Intelligence), a branch of SETI (the Search for Extraterrestrial Intelligence). CETI focuses on composing and deciphering interstellar messages that theoretically could be understood by another technological civilization. The message was transmitted into space towards the star cluster M13 on November 16, 1974 by the Arecibo Radio Telescope in Puerto Rico. The signal, transmitted at 2,380 MHz lasting 169 seconds, delivered an effective power of three trillion watts. It was the most powerful human signal ever broadcast into space. A method that was initially proposed by American astrophysicist and astrobiologist Frank Drake (Drake's cryptogram) was used to encode the communication, which was comprised of a string of 1,679 binary digits. It is thought that perhaps an intelligent extraterrestrial race out in the ethers that intercepted the message, and attempted to decode it, would understand that 1,679 is a multiple of two prime numbers, 23 and 73 (mathematics, as a universal language).

The SETI Institute Website states:

In 1974, the most powerful broadcast ever deliberately beamed into space was made from Puerto Rico. The broadcast formed part of the ceremonies held to mark a major upgrade to the Arecibo Radio Telescope. The transmission consisted of a simple, pictorial message, aimed at our putative cosmic companions in the globular star cluster M13. This cluster is roughly 21,000 light-years from us, near the edge of the Milky Way galaxy, and contains approximately a third of a million stars.

The broadcast was particularly powerful because it used Arecibo's megawatt transmitter attached to its 305 meter antenna. The latter concentrates the transmitter energy by beaming it into a very small patch of sky. The emission was equivalent to a 20 trillion watt omnidirectional broadcast, and would be detectable by a SETI experiment just about anywhere in the galaxy, assuming a receiving antenna similar in size to Arecibo's.

The message consists of 1679 bits, arranged into 73 lines of 23 characters per line (these are both prime numbers, and may help the aliens decode the message). The "ones" and hzeroes" were transmitted by frequency shifting at the rate of 10 bits per second. The total broadcast was less than three minutes. A graphic showing the message is reproduced here. It consists, among other things, of the Arecibo telescope, our solar system, DNA, a stick figure of a human, and some of the biochemicals of earthly life. Although it's unlikely that this short inquiry will ever prompt a reply, the experiment was useful in getting us to think a bit about the difficulties of communicating across space, time, and a presumably wide culture gap.

Shockingly, the message was answered! States author David Darling, PH.D., in his work *The Extraterrestrial Encyclopedia: An Alphabetical Reference to All Life in the Universe,* "Scientists are inclined to believe that mathematics and the mathematical rules that underpin nature are universal, so that all intelligent races in space would have at least this much in common." In theory, the message can reach possible recipients *only* after 25,000 years. However, astonishingly, the answer arrived much earlier than expected in

2001. The response was answered in two crop formations left overnight in the same field, in close proximity to each other. They were also made differently than other formations that have been seen over the years, which leads this author to conclude that there may be more than one group of extraterrestrials using the world's grain fields to relay messages. If we think about it, it is a simplistic way for more people to become aware of the message as opposed to signals only being received by authoritative agencies, where such information can be kept hidden from the public.

The formations appeared in the field next to the telescope of the Chilbolton Observatory in Hampshire (Great Britain). Right away cynics sought ways to discredit the formations by stating that they could not have been created by extraterrestrials in response to the Aricebo message because not enough time had elapsed for the signal to have reached a civilization in space, let alone there being time enough for an answer to have been received. The problem is that the Arecibo message radio signal travels at the speed of light. The message was sent in 1974. A response was received in 2001. Therefore, the message covered a distance of only 27 light-years. This was the reason that it was believed that the formations were created by hoaxers. In other words, some believe that the incredible notion of an answer to a message that *we* sent from Earth could not have been real, and that it was all a very clever hoax! But, not so fast! We started this chain of events by sending a message aimed at extraterrestrial civilizations in space, and for whatever reason, we were answered. This author contends that it would have been prudent for us to pay attention and listen to the message. It would also have been smart for us to have responded!

Experts were able to decode the messages. The answers received in the crop formations from the extraterrestrials that intercepted the Arecibo message were astounding! They found the answers were virtually the same as ours with a few notable differences. Whereas life on earth is carbon based, this group of extraterrestrials are silicon-based lifeforms, according to their data. The number of chains in their DNA is over four billion. Also, there are 12 billion people on their world. Since the rest of the information was so similar to ours, we can deduce that they are humanoid.

Science does not think out of the box. That is *our* job, dear reader, and thus this book. So, what could have happened in what was basically an experimental plan in sending a powerful message

149

to extraterrestrials somewhere in space, that was thought would take a very long time (if ever) to receive an answer in return? How could we have possibly received an answer back so soon? My answer is, we do not know what is out there. We do not know if there are extraterrestrials about, where they are, who they are and what kinds of technology they have. We do not know or understand the capabilities of beings that are hundreds if not thousands of years ahead of us in science and technology. In continuing to think out of the box we need to entertain all the possibilities.

Perhaps Vicky Verma, a staff writer for the How&Whys, website put it best in her article titled "Message Sent Into Outer Space In 1974 In Search Of Aliens Got Reply In 2001." Verma writes:

> There may be several explanations. First, the recipient was within 14 light—years, so it managed not only to receive the message but also to send an answer. What if a star system with a potentially inhabited planet was located on the way to M13? Another option is that highly developed races may have quantum transmitters in different parts of space. As it is known, due to quantum entanglement, information can be transmitted instantly at any distance. It is possible that one of these stations caught the radio message and transmitted it to the recipient with lightning speed into the depths of space.

The Crabwood Alien Formation

One of the most shocking and amazing crop formations to date is the Crabwood Alien Formation. This formation leaves no doubt that the crop circles and formations are being created by extraterrestrials. The image depicts a humanoid extraterrestrial that is holding a large disc shaped object. It materialized in a wheat field in Winchester, in Crabwood, England on the night of August 16, 2002. The formation itself is massive. It was estimated to be hundreds of feet long. The method used to produce the formation was different from the others. In this image horizontal lines of contrasting height were used, which reportedly has not occurred in any other formations. Even though the image is certainly startling, the most intriguing element is the message. The message was located inside of the large disc shaped object. Paul Vigay, a leading expert on UFOs and crop circles studied the formation

The Crabwood Crop Circle in 2002.

and discovered a message encoded in ASCI binary code. Vigay concluded that the communique started in the middle of the disc and expanded out and towards the perimeter. The message says, "Beware the bearers of false gifts and their broken promises. Much pain, but still time. There is good out there, we oppose deception. Conduit closing. (Bell Sound) Believe."

There are many speculations when it comes to this formation. Most assume it to be a message for humanity. Some believe that it is a warning to not trust other groups of extraterrestrials that may be promising something to us. No one knows for sure. It has even been proposed that the message could be for other extraterrestrials that are here. The takeaway from this is that we understand clearly that our world is monitored. Are we to understand from this message that humanity may have help from other groups out there in the event that we find ourselves in trouble, since they seem to be attempting a warning here? We can only hope! In any case, this crop formation is one of the most important accounts in our extraterrestrial and galactic history because it is a form of clear evidence that others are out there. _So we are not Alone ..._

The Eltanin Antenna, The Antarctic

One of the most interesting clues that extraterrestrials may be watching humanity may have been found at the bottom of the sea at around 4,000 meters in Antarctica. I am speaking here about a relic that is known as the Eltanin Antenna. The Eltanin Antenna is an object that was discovered and photographed on the sea floor by the nearly 2,000-ton icebreaker known as the

151

The Eltanin Antenna photo on the left and an artist's reconstruction.

Eltanin. While collecting sample cores and photographing the seabed west of Cape Horn, the Antarctic oceanographic research ship USNS *Eltanin* on August 29, 1964 captured the first image of the Eltanin Antenna. It is interesting that this item was found in an exceptionally isolated, freezing, and secluded area of Earth, as if it were purposefully placed in an area that people do not often visit. Some wonder if its placement in that part of the world was intentional since the object has all the characteristics of being artificially made. Still, it's presence poses questions, such as, how would a piece of equipment be placed so perfectly at the bottom of the sea floor? And by whom? Investigators also question what it is, and what its purpose may be.

When it was first spotted, scientists had no clue as to what it could be as pointed out by Brad Steiger in an article in *Saga Magazine* in 1968, stating that the item is, "an astonishing piece of machinery… very much like the cross between a TV antenna and a telemetry antenna." Some have speculated that the Eltanin Antenna may have a connection to the Black Knight Satellite (a large object in a polar orbit, believed by some to be an artificial alien satellite). It is thought that the Eltanin Antenna and the Black Knight Satellite may be sending transmissions to each other. Others hypothesize that the mysterious object is a type of extraterrestrial technology that was intentionally placed in a distant and lonely spot to inconspicuously transmit signals to extraterrestrials. But of course, this is all speculation. Scientists have attempted to explain the object away by likening it to a sea sponge, as it vaguely resembles the *Cladorhiza concrescence*. However, that theory was discarded when it was pointed out that the Eltanin Antenna is geometrical and encompasses distinct angles and forms. Right angle, straight lateral branches in natural organisms are not believed to be achievable. The *Cladorhiza concrescence* sea sponge does not exhibit these characteristics. Additionally, the *Cladorhiza concrescence* exists in groups. It is a species of marine life that reproduces very fast. They multiply by a piece of the sponge detaching then falling to the bottom and fastening to the seafloor, and then producing more of its kind. A new group quickly forms. There was nothing like this located near the Eltanin Antenna. The object was solitary. Furthermore, the photograph of the article was taken at a depth of exactly 25 miles, deeper than sponges grow. Moreover, the object appears to be too large and easily seen, as well as flawlessly structured, for it to be an organic sponge. Some researchers have concluded that the item may be man-made and landed there due to an accident involving a ship or some other mishap. It has even been suggested that it is a naval antenna perhaps from a ship sinking. While that could be the case, the chances of that resulting in the antenna standing precisely in an upright position is extremely small. After considering all these scenarios, some are now asking if the item was placed there by extraterrestrials. Is this a device used to monitor Earth and humanity? We are being watched. There is no question. One wonders what type of technology is being used by otherworldly intelligences to surveil us, and if they have placed devices around the planet such as the Eltanin Antenna for this purpose.

So then, what is this object that has been dubbed the Eltanin Antenna? All we know for certain is that it is not a plant, and it is not one of ours. With all our advancements in technology, humanity does not yet have oceanic machinery that is able to dive to such freezing, watery depths. There is talk of extraterrestrials coming to save humans in the event of a catastrophe. Is this a way of monitoring Earth's oceanic movement, tectonics and so forth? One wonders.

A Transmission from an Extraterrestrial Named Vrillon

On Saturday, November 26, 1977 at 5:10 pm, during a live broadcast in the U.K., an inexplicable event happened that is still being talked about today. As people settled in at home for the night and tuned into the evening news, the broadcast was suddenly

153

interrupted. Replacing the voice of the newscaster was that of an unknown, unseen person that was speaking in an authoritative manner. He identified himself as Vrillon, a member of the extraterrestrial group known as the Ashtar Galactic Command. He was their representative. His voice was powerful and his message enthralling. Shocked people listened to the extraordinary transmission. Vrillon basically stated that humanity needed to abandon its warring ways and become a peaceable, nonviolent people before it was too late.

Vrillon's Message:

This is the voice of Vrillon, a representative of the Ashtar Galactic Command, speaking to you. For many years you have seen us as lights in the skies. We speak to you now in peace and wisdom as we have done to your brothers and sisters all over this, your planet Earth. We come to warn you of the destiny of your race and your world so that you may communicate to your fellow beings the course you must take to avoid the disaster which threatens your world, and the beings on our worlds around you. This is in order that you may share in the great awakening, as the planet passes into the New Age of Aquarius. The New Age can be a time of great peace and evolution for your race, but only if your rulers are made aware of the evil forces that can overshadow their judgments. Be still now and listen, for your chance may not come again. All your weapons of evil must be removed. The time for conflict is now past and the race of which you are a part may proceed to the higher stages of its evolution if you show yourselves worthy to do this. You have but a short time to learn to live together in peace and goodwill. Small groups all over the planet are learning this, and exist to pass on the light of the dawning New Age to you all. You are free to accept or reject their teachings, but only those who learn to live in peace will pass to the higher realms of spiritual evolution. Hear now the voice of Vrillon, a representative of the Ashtar Galactic Command, speaking to you. Be aware also that there are many false prophets and guides operating in your world. They will suck your energy from you – the energy you call money and will put it to evil ends and give you worthless dross in return. Your inner divine self will protect you from this. You must learn to be sensitive to the voice within that can tell you what is truth, and what is confusion, chaos and untruth. Learn to listen to the voice of truth which is within you and you will lead yourselves onto the path of evolution. This is our message to our dear friends. We have watched you growing for many years as you too have watched our lights in your skies. You know now that we are here, and that there are more beings on and around your Earth than your scientists admit. We are deeply concerned about you and your path towards the light and will do all we can to help you. Have no fear, seek only to know yourselves, and live in harmony with the ways of your planet Earth. We of the Ashtar Galactic Command thank you for your attention. We are now leaving the plane of your existence. May you be blessed by the supreme love and truth of the cosmos.

He spoke eloquently and genuinely.

This incident has been examined by a number of researchers of anomalous phenomena, as well as ufologists. While some believe it to have been a hoax, some maintain that the technology of that period would not have enabled such an event to take place. In addition, no one ever came forward to claim the incident, and no one was ever accused of pulling a prank. There are those that believe that the Ashtar Galactic Command successfully found a way to communicate, on a large scale, a very important message that had to do with the welfare of humanity, Earth, and those in the galaxy around us. Some believe that the Ashtar Galactic Command was attempting to convince humanity to set aside its warlike ambitions, especially during that period when the Cold War between the West and the USSR was especially tense.

The idea of humanity finding a peaceful way of living has been at the forefront of other purported extraterrestrial communications to Earth for years. Humanity's violent ways and ignorance when it comes to nuclear weaponry is apparently of great concern for extraterrestrials within the Milky Way and is one reason some believe they may be monitoring Earth. This may also be the reason that UFOs are often seen around military installations, and why they were present during the Apollo missions to the Moon. According to reports, extraterrestrials have informed Earth's governments that they are concerned that if we continue along the path of nuclear weaponry that it could have a rippling effect throughout the galaxy. They have also stated that they are not going to allow all life on Earth to be destroyed. In this message, it appears that the Ashtar Galactic Command was putting humanity on notice to sort themselves out and prepare to take our place in what is believed by many to be a peaceful galactic community. Given what has been written about the Ashtar Galactic Command, this message was likely "transmitted" from a mothership located near Earth. That is, according to sources, where the Ashtar Galactic Command is operating from presently.

Deep Space Transmissions

In 2014, the U.S. National Security Agency (NSA) released formerly classified UFO files into the public domain. Two of the reports located within the files are authored by Dr. Howard Campaigne, a prominent cryptologist that worked for the United States government. The first of the documents is from the *NSA Technical Journal* Vol XIV, No 1 with FOIA Case number 41472, titled "Extraterrestrial Intelligence." In the document, Dr. Campaigne presents a series of 29 communications that were received from deep space. This declassified report verifies that we are not alone in the universe, that there is intelligent life out there, and there is an extraterrestrial presence in space that has been attempting to make contact. The second document is titled, "Key To the Extraterrestrial Messages." Both documents are of extreme importance as they relate to one of the most significant times in Earth's galactic history where we have a high office confirming that direct messages were received from otherworldly intelligences. Although the files were officially declassified in 2004, they were not accessible to the public until 2014. Therefore, most people are unaware that these documents exist and are free to review by interested persons.

What do the messages tell us? Some of the messages are mathematical equations. Also, there is a listing of all the elements in the Periodic Table. Reportedly, during his presentation, Dr. Campaigne pointed out that there are "words" that they were able to interpret, and other "words" they do not comprehend. Dr. Campaigne's reports are as follows:

Extraterrestrial Intelligence
By Howard H. Campaigne
https://media.defense.gov/2021/Jul/13/2002761381/-1/-1/0/ET_

INTELLIGENCE.PDF

Key to The Extraterrestrial Messages
By Howard H. Campaigne
https://media.defense.gov/2021/Jul/13/2002761374/-1/-1/0/
KEY_TO_ET_MESSAGES.PDF

Authors Message: My reason for presenting the information in this chapter is this: I wanted to show on a small scale that we have signs, signals, and clues on Earth and in the universe to show that we are not alone. Small evidence helps people to see the bigger picture. Unfortunately, all cannot be placed in this one chapter. Also, I want people to understand that extraterrestrials have been trying to make contact in the various ways and means available to them. What you see here is a very limited amount of what is actually going on out there.

What is the message from the extraterrestrials to us other than we are not alone? The message is that we need to affect change on Earth before it is too late. The message is to be a peace loving, harmonious race, and to set aside atomic weaponry. If not, there could be dire consequences for the people and all life on Earth. We could destroy ourselves and life on this planet. Their concern is also for those in the surrounding areas of the galaxy. They have stated that our actions also affect them.

In the end, they are warning us about who we trust. That message is a mysterious one. Perhaps, somewhere out there, some negotiations are going on with Earth and extraterrestrials that we are not privy to. *Who knows?* However, the message is real, and it is clear. Be careful who we trust.

Chapter Seven
In the Skies Above: UFOs

"For many years I have lived with a secret in a secrecy
imposed on all specialists in astronautics. I can now reveal
that everyday in the USA, our radar instruments capture
objects of form and composition unknown to us. And there
are thousands of witness reports in a quantity of documents
to prove this. But nobody wants to make them public."
—Gordon Cooper, NASA Astronaut, Mercury-Atlas 9
and Gemini 5

There is no shortage of strange events when it comes to Earth's skies. People from all walks of life, from all over the world have witnessed baffling, inexplicable UFOs in the skies. It is obvious that someone or something is behind these mysterious events. The question is, "Who is causing all the commotion?" Many researchers agree that these strange happenings are evidence that Earth is being visited by extraterrestrials. *The UFO Magazine, UFO Encyclopedia* tells us that a UFO is: "A flying object which cannot be identified by its observer and whose definition still defies identification after it has been studied by others. Once the object is identified, whether as a plane, flying saucer, or natural phenomenon, then it is no longer unidentified."

However, it appears that this basic definition has morphed in the past few years. A more modern definition taken from Dictionary. com under "UFO" tells us one is: "any unexplained moving object observed in the sky, *especially* one assumed by some observers to be of extraterrestrial origin." This tells us that in most cases today, when someone refers to a UFO, they are postulating that it is of extraterrestrial origin. Simply put, when most people see UFOs they believe they are most likely looking at a spacecraft being flown by beings from other worlds. Additionally, a new acronym has been entered into the mix. It is the term UAP. This term is so new that I could not locate it in any of the four UFO encyclopedias in my personal library. The online Collins English Dictionary offers this definition: "unidentified aerial or anomalous phenomenon." Simply put, in the minds of some, UFO is now an old school term. It has been rebranded to ward off a stigma attached to the UFO acronym. This is because people see those that research and believe in the phenomenon as tin-foil-hat-wearing kooks. Now that the governments of the world are talking about them, now that classified documents have been released by several governments the world over, now that UFOs are being seen more readily in the skies all over the world, now that cameras are everywhere and capturing images of these...I will just say it like it is. They are *spacecraft*. Those that believe in the phenomenon are gaining more respect...even if it is begrudgingly.

UFOs have been witnessed and reported throughout history, going all the way back to the ancient world. Seen all over the globe, they have become a serious topic, with several governments now investigating and speaking out publicly about the phenomenon. Some have even gone as far as creating task forces to examine reports of sightings of UFOs. For many governments, they have become a national security matter and the militaries in some cases have been put on alert and instructed to report their experiences. It turns out that there have been plenty of sightings by military personnel over the years that are just becoming known to the public. We also have documents now available from world governments that have been released to the public domain. Is this a way that governments are attempting to inform the public that we are not alone in the universe? *Is this finally happening?* Some believe that due to the release of classified documents on UFOs, that soon we will indeed be told by the governments that extraterrestrials exist, that we are not alone, and that we have been visited by extraterrestrials for many years.

Scientists too have weighed in recently on who or what UFOs are. Like the governments, some have taken a keen interest in the topic and are convinced that UFOs are related to extraterrestrials. In fact, a recent study published in the journal *Humanities and Social Science Communications*, stated that, "more than 10 percent of scientists believe that UFOs could be alien objects." The study also stated, "a survey of more than 1,400 academics in the US by researchers at the University of Louisville asked experts about their views on unidentified anomalous phenomena (UAP— the new term used for UFO). Amazingly the survey revealed that a fifth of scientifically minded experts have either seen, or someone they know has seen, a UFO." This shows how much we are growing as a society when it comes to the UFO phenomenon.

It shows that people are paying attention and taking the subject more seriously. This is especially true given the many accounts of witness testimony from all over the world to this phenomenon. People are waking up to the reality that something is going on, and that is that some intelligence is controlling these UFOs and it isn't anyone on Earth.

In fact, many different types of UFOs are seen around the globe daily, and the numbers are increasing. To put the pieces of the puzzle together, we need to be in the know. We need to know what happened in our past regarding UFOs. As stated above, the term UFO means "unidentified flying object." Often when people refer to seeing a UFO they mean that they saw a spacecraft. Granted there are hundreds of unidentified flying objects in the sky. These can be anything from the proverbial weather balloon, satellites, space debris, drones, and more. However, in many cases, the observer has witnessed what they are able to describe as a spacecraft. In this chapter, I am referring to the UFO-spacecraft phenomenon. Regarding the UFO phenomenon, I believe that we should be asking questions such as, "Why are we seeing so many UFOs in the skies today?" "Why have the sightings increased?" "Who is driving them?" and "Why are they here?" Is the reason they are here on such a large scale because humanity is now ready to know about them? By showing us their spacecraft, are extraterrestrials slowly assimilating us to the idea that we are not alone in the universe?

There are accounts of people seeing ships in the skies that appear to be even closer in proximity to Earth than before. There are UFOs entering and exiting large bodies of water, ships landing, and there are even reports of invitations from extraterrestrials to go aboard their spacecraft. Some claim to have been taken on trips on some of these craft. Does this sound crazy? *Maybe.* Some stories could be fabricated, of course. However, are all these people, over so many decades, that have reported these experiences faking them? *No.* Reports such as these go back thousands of years. As has become my mantra, "If just one of these stories is true, then we are not alone in the universe and we are being visited." I come from a place of skepticism, choosing not to believe everything I read or am told. However, I do not believe that all close encounters with extraterrestrials and their craft are falsified tales. I do believe in the saying that sometimes, *"the truth is stranger than fiction."* One thing is for sure, the controllers of these UFOs are watching us. We just may be entering a new age where soon we will learn on a global scale that Earth has neighbors in the galaxy and beyond. I have to say too, it seems that because there appears to be an increase in sightings, and there appears to be an uptick in conversations in the media about UFOs, there may be an underlying reason that now, in this time in history, this is all occurring.

UFO History

The term "Unidentified Flying Object" (UFO) was coined in 1953 by writer Donald Keyhoe in an article in *Air Line Pilot Magazine*, in reference to reports from the United States Air Force. Before then the term "flying saucer" was popular. As stated above, some may be very surprised to learn that UFOs have been around *throughout history*. There is a lot of weight behind that statement. This is not something that should be skirted over. If they have been around throughout history, we need to ask *why*? This is important information for us to know. This is not something that we were taught growing up, which something we should question as to, "*Why*?" One would think that this is important information for us as a global community to be aware of and educated about. What would the reason be for this information to be kept from us? Has not knowing stagnated us as a species? Could this lack of information have contributed to the state of the world today? Would things have been different had we known the truth about our true galactic history?

Looking into events in our history, it appears that nonhuman, advanced intelligences have been watching this world since the beginning. Who are they? Are they the seeders? Are they the creators? Or are they others? Why is it that they are not making their presence known to the world in a straightforward fashion? Or have they? Perhaps, they have contacted us through Earth's governments, and we were as a global society not informed by the powers that be. *Yet*. UFOs are being seen across the globe more frequently today. *Why*? There is something going on. Perhaps it is because we have reached a point in the history of humankind where it is time for us to know. In ancient times, they sometimes appeared during times of war and on other occasions where it appeared that help was needed. Maybe that is the case in our present day. They are still here. People all over the world are recording UFOs, and questioning what they are seeing in the skies. The governments, most likely fearful of security issues, are beginning to get involved. What some people including those in authoritative positions may not be aware of is that Earth has a history of UFO sightings and encounters.

Perhaps for us to better understand them, and discern what is going on with UFOs today, we need to study our UFO history. It is a history that we were never taught in school. It is a history that has been distorted. As we are maturing as a global society, we are beginning to understand more about ourselves and our past, and this is one more area to focus on. We should ask ourselves too, are some of the UFO sightings designed by extraterrestrials to give us a message that we are not alone? Did they know that the incidents of the past would be recorded, and we would be reviewing them today? Were they a warning for the future? Were they preparing us for the future when they would introduce themselves? Is that time now? *I wonder.* Perhaps they are here now, because this is our time to know, in order to prepare for our future. Once the entire world knows that we are not alone in the universe, and that they are here, Earth *will be a very different place.*

Food for Thought: Unless you are someone who has seen a UFO, you should understand that you have gone your entire life without direct knowledge that UFOs/extraterrestrials are here, and always have been. Many people have come and gone without knowing. Unbeknownst to most, UFOs are a part of Earth's history. When the Roman Empire was in full bloom, they were here. During the Crusades, they were here. When Columbus crossed the Atlantic, they were here. During the American Revolution, they were here. During the American Civil War, they were here. During both World Wars, they were here. During the September 11 attacks, they were here. They have been here during humanity's entire existence and for all the major events in Earth's history! They have been here throughout your life! Understand too that when I say UFOs, I am referring really to extraterrestrials. People tend to hear the term UFOs, visualize the craft, and forget that there is someone, a physical being, operating the spacecraft. We can only guess what they may be thinking during the upheavals on Earth.

UFOs and History

Throughout the ages, there have been UFO sightings all over the world involving people from various cultures, countries, races, and religions. In fact, history is full of accounts of UFOs, many of which are similar in their descriptions of what we are seeing today. Others are new and have never been seen before. Just how far back can we trace UFOs visiting Earth? Believe it or not, UFOs can be traced back to the cradle of civilization. Records of them can be found in ancient Sumer (c. 4500—c. 1900 BC), Mesopotamia, Egypt and others. As we can imagine, these were advanced spacecraft capable of far-reaching space travel. The Bible book of Ezekiel tells of an account known today as "Ezekiel's Wheel." It is one of the first recorded public UFO sightings! In the Temple of Seti I in Abydos, Egypt, there are mysterious carvings on the wall that resemble modern day aerial craft such as airplanes and helicopters. Even though we have lost a good amount of our history, we still have evidence by way of ancient writings, artwork, hieroglyphs and more that they were here in the past. Although there are too many tales to incorporate into this small space the following are a few such recorded UFO sightings.

Early UFO Sightings

UFOs in early history (and in various epochs of time) were comprehended and interpreted depending upon the beliefs of those observing the phenomena. Therefore, UFOs were often regarded as signs from God or the gods, as well as omens, magic, supernatural forces and more. The earliest report of a UFO comes from China, where a drawing carved into a rock dating back 47,000 years was discovered. Other early accounts can be found among a variety of cultures from our ancient past that painstakingly documented what they were witnessing. Some recorded them on stone and the walls of tunnels and caves. As time moved forward, we find them in ancient writings, scrolls, papyri, and all manner of records often chronicled by historians that went through great lengths to document the details of these events as best they could with what they knew, and what they had to work with by way of their knowledge of the universe, as well as their belief systems. It appears as time has progressed to today, we are finally understanding that what we are seeing in the skies are spacecraft that are controlled by nonhuman intelligences, or simply put, beings from other worlds.

The ancient world is filled with accounts of incidents involving UFOs. There are numerous historical documents and verbal accounts from various cultures that offer testimonials about the phenomenon. They have been variously described as traveling,

164

hovering, and landeding. Some UFOs appeared to have been observing battles on Earth. There are so many that they simply cannot all be placed in this one volume. However, it is interesting to look at some of the accounts. The following are a few highlights of UFO incidents in our distant past in different parts of the world.

Arabia

In 1479 there was a UFO seen by witnesses flying over Arabia. The historian referred to this as a "large comet." Those that saw it reported that the object had several sizable windows. There was no word as to whether they could see extraterrestrials behind those windows.

China

The earliest recorded sighting of a UFO was discovered in July 1961 in the Hunan province of China. It was discovered by a Professor of Archaeology at the University of Peking, Professor Chi Pen Lao, during an excavation. The image was carved in stone and dates to the time of the Neanderthals, some 47,000 years ago. Chi Pen Lao also found drawings on an island in Lake Tung Ting, where he had come across an underground cave system. The tunnels within the cave were at a depth of 105 feet. He reported that the tunnels walls were glossy with a texture that was smooth to the touch. The tunnel walls were filled with drawings depicting animals being chased. The strangest part of the pictorial are the beings seen above the animals. These humanoid beings are flying on a type of spacecraft, described in the account as a "flying shield." The beings are holding weapons that are aimed at the animals. Peculiar too is they are portrayed wearing contemporary clothing, including jackets and pants. Could this scenario be something akin to cattle mutilations? Animal abductions? Or simply the herding of animals? Whatever the artist is attempting to portray seems quite unusual for that period.

Egypt

Given that the ancient Egyptians are believed to have had connections to the cosmos and were an advanced civilization that some researchers hypothesize was started by extraterrestrials, it is not surprising that they witnessed UFOs in their skies in ancient times. In fact, in one Egyptian record, the *Tulli Papyrus*, we find what is said to hold the earliest record of the witnessing of a convoy of UFOs. The incident purportedly occurred around 1480 BC, during the reign of Thutmose III. According to the account, this was a massive UFO sighting. In a separate account, in 373, Saint Athanasius of Alexandria (c. 293—c. 373) wrote a biography about Saint Antony titled *The Life of St. Antony*. In the section of the book titled "A Disc in the Desert," Saint Athanasius writes about an experience that Saint Antony had involving a UFO. It states:

> Yet once more the Enemy (Satan), seeing (Antony's) zeal and wishing to check it, threw in his way the form of a large silver disc of silver. Antony, understanding the deceit of the Evil one, stood and looked at the disc and confuted the demon in it, saying, "Whence a disc in the desert? This is not a trodden road, and there is no track of any faring this way. And, it could not have Fallen unnoticed, being of huge size.

As was common back then, and still is in some religious thought today, UFOs were seen as objects of the devil. The people of that time had no other reference for the strange things they witnessed in the skies. If they had understood the true meaning behind the UFOs, the fact that there were people from another world visiting them, would they have accepted them? Or would there have been, just as we see today, denial of what is right in front of them? Is this reaction the reason that extraterrestrials did not make themselves known during that period? Is this why they have waited for so long to tell us who they are, where they come from and why they are here? Are they waiting for a time when they will be accepted and not opposed by religious dogma making them out to be evil, and quite possibly causing an uprising among the world's civilizations?

France

Charlemagne of France (also known as Charles the Great) had several encounters with UFOs. He was so plagued by UFOs in the area that according to the popular book *The Gods of Eden,* authored by William Bramley said, "UFOs became so troublesome in the eighth and ninth centuries that emperor Charlemagne of France was compelled to issue edicts forbidding them from perturbing the air and provoking storms." As in other accounts from the Middle

166

Ages, several of the chronicles from Charlemagne's reign list witnesses that had observed UFOs, referring to them as "shields" in the skies.

England

In 1290 in Yorkshire England, there was a UFO sighting that frighted a group of monks while they were dining. William of Newburgh's records gives this account: "The abbot and monks were at a meal, when a flat, round, shining, silvery object flew over the abbey and caused the utmost terror." In another incident, a gentleman by the name of Thomas Short, on December 9, 1731, recounted seeing a UFO in England. His report described "a dark red cloud, below which was a luminous body which emitted intense beams of light. The light beams moved slowly for a while, then stopped. Suddenly, it became so hot that I could take off my shirt even though I was out of doors." This account is interesting in that unlike others, there is an actual physical reaction to the presence of this UFO.

France

On November 1, 1461, the French Duke of Bourgogne wrote about a UFO that was seen in France. He stated, "An object appeared in the sky over France on the night of November 1, 1461. It was as long and wide as a half moon; it hung stationary for about a quarter of an hour, clearly visible, then suddenly spiraled, twisted and turned like a spring and rose into the heavens." From the 1500s, in the Collegiale Notre Dame in Beaune (a church), hangs a picture of the virgin Mary. In the same picture, in the background, is what appears to be a saucer shaped spacecraft. Some ufologists and ancient alien proponents maintain that this is an indication that UFOs were around very far back in history, were seen by witnesses that then incorporated them in art, and may have been influencing religious ideas. In the fifteenth century, artist Ghirlandaio created a painting that is titled "The Madonna and St. Giovannino." In this picture, the Virgin Mary is shown, along with a UFO that is shaped like a disk. It is flying and appears to be emanating beams of light. This picture lends evidence to the belief of some researchers that UFOs were seen in the skies back then, just as they are today.

Germany

167

In the *Annales regni Francorum (Royal Frankish Annals),* a year by year "state of the monarchy" report from 741-829 AD, in 776 AD, there is an account of events involving UFOs that occurred at the Siege of Sigiburg. The UFOs were described as "two shields red with flame wheeling over the church." It states:

A messenger came with the news that the Saxons had rebelled, deserted all their hostages, broken their oaths, and by tricks and false treaties prevailed on the Franks to give up the castle of Eresburg. With Eresburg thus deserted by the Franks, the Saxons demolished the buildings and walls. Passing on from Eresburg they wished to do the same thing to the castle of Syburg but made no headway since the Franks with the help of God put up a manly resistance. When they failed to talk the guards into surrender, as they had those in the other castle, they began to set up war machines to storm the castle. Since God willed it, the catapults which they had prepared did more damage to them than to those inside. When the Saxons saw that their constructions were useless to them, they prepared faggots to capture the fortress in one charge. But God's power, as is only just, overcame theirs. One day, while they prepared for battle against the Christians in the castle, God's glory was made manifest over the castle church in the sight of a great number outside as well as inside, many of whom are still with us. They reportedly saw the likeness of two shields red with flame wheeling over the church. When the heathens outside saw this miracle, they were at once thrown into confusion and started fleeing to their camp in terror. Since all of them were panic-stricken, one man stampeded the next and was killed in return, because those who looked back out of fear impaled themselves on the lances carried on the shoulders of those who fled before them. Some dealt each other aimless blows and thus suffered divine retribution. How much the power of God worked against them for the salvation of the Christians, nobody can tell. But the more the Saxons were stricken by fear, the more the Christians were comforted and praised the almighty God who deigned to reveal his power over his servants. When the Saxons took to flight, the Franks followed on their heels as far as the River Lippe, slaughtering them. Once the castle was safe, the Franks returned home victorious.

This is just one more account of what appears to be extraterrestrial intervention in human affairs involving religion.

In Hamburg, Germany on December 15, 1547 sailors stationed on ships located in the harbor area saw a brilliantly shining sphere in the sky. Unlike most other accounts of UFOs, this had a physical element to it in that it radiated heat. It was so hot as it crossed over that the sailors had to vacate the ships and seek shelter elsewhere for fear that the ships were going to catch fire. On July 9, 1686, a UFO in the shape of a sphere was witnessed crossing Leipzig, Germany. Two similar craft, only smaller, were seen exiting it.

Greece

The famed Greek historian Diodorus Siculus Timoleon wrote of a trip he took from Corinth to Sicily in 343 BC. Along the way, he spotted several mysterious lights. Interestingly, Timoleon claimed that the lights guided him as he traveled. One wonders why Diodorus Siculus Timoleon was being led on his journey by a UFO. Perhaps extraterrestrials have a hidden agenda, where people on Earth are unknowingly a part of something that the extraterrestrials may be trying to achieve, as there are many individuals throughout history that have claimed to have been led by strange lights.

Japan

Japan had several UFO sightings in the early days. For example, it was documented that on October 27, 1180, witnesses saw what they described as an "earthenware vessel" fly out of a mountain in the Kii Province. This occurred around midnight. It was noted that the vessel left a brilliantly lit trail behind it. In 1271 in Tatsunokuchi, Kamakura, Japan, an execution was scheduled to take place by means of beheading. The victim was a popular Buddhist priest named Nichiren Daishonin. Before the execution could take place, a UFO appeared in the sky above. The account states, "There appeared in the sky, a brilliant orb as bright as the moon." One translation of the event states: "There appeared in the sky an object like a full moon, shiny and bright." Whatever this object was, it evidently frightened the people, who may have believed it to have been a sign from a higher power. Because of the appearance of this object, Daishonin's life was spared.

What's interesting here is that this obvious UFO appeared at a specific moment. When looking at this experience from a more modern perspective, we can deduce that extraterrestrials may have intentionally intervened in this execution for reasons unknown to us. Perhaps it had to do with some extraterrestrial agenda that we do not understand.

On March 17, 1458, five UFOs described as "stars" were seen above Kyoto, Japan. According to the account, the "stars" appeared to circle the Moon and modified their appearance by changing color several times before vanishing. Witnesses were so disturbed by what they had seen that they hid, believing it to be the end of the world. Another incident involving Japan occurred in 1468. A UFO was seen flying out of Japan's Mount Kasuga. Mountains are believed by some ufologists to be convenient hiding places for UFOs. Could Mount Kasuga have been one of those places?

In 1606 numerous UFOs in the shape of spinning balls of fire were seen in the skies over Kyoto, Japan. At that same time, what was described as a "whirling, red wheel," was hovering above the Nijō Castle. It was the home of the first Shogun of Japan, Tokugawa Ieyasu, one of the most influential and powerful men in Japan. Even though the castle was originally constructed to be a residence, and was not to be used for defense purposes, this alarming scenario caused the Samurai guards to be put on high alert for danger. One wonders why the UFOs were hovering over this particular castle. This scenario is reminiscent of present-day reports of UFOs hovering over government buildings such as the White House. Is there a connection? Do the operators of these UFOs have some influence on the leadership of the world, and have they since the early days of history? Is that why they were hovering over the palace of the first Shogun?

On January 2, 1749, three UFOs appeared over Japan. The account described them as looking similar to the Moon. The people took to the streets in fear and discontent wanting answers that no one could provide. They were even rioting, to the point that the authorities were threating to kill people if they didn't settle down. What is even more interesting is that days later, two more UFOs appeared that were described as "two suns." One can again only imagine what the purpose of these UFOs was. One wonders too if they were attempting to incite fear in the people, as they had to have seen what happened there, and then returned to the same area again a second time. *Who were these beings?*

Rome

According to their historical records, there were numerous sightings of UFOs in Rome's history. I should note here that in ancient Rome, the keeping of these records was taken extremely seriously. Ancient historians went through authoritarian protocols before documenting events. It was their desire that all information was precisely correct, presumably for future generations to have an accurate account of what took place in their time. It was only then that they were allowed to insert a UFO incident into the official record. Like the Egyptians, the Romans also documented seeing UFOs that they described as "fiery shields."

During the Dark Ages, following the fall of Rome, as Germanic clans were dispersed throughout Europe, several historical documents describe "flying shields" being seen in the skies. One event that stands out occurred as the invasion of a castle was taking place in 900 AD. A writer for the *Annales Laurisseness*, in which the story was found, wrote, "Those watching outside in that place, of whom many still live to this very day, say they beheld the likeness of two large shields, reddish in color, in motion above the church, and when the pagans who outside saw this sign, they were at once thrown into confusion and, terrified with great fear, they began to flee from the castle." These people were horrified, as they could only relate to these two "large shields," as being signs or portents of something terrible to come. The two "large shields" in the sky were spherical UFOs. Those controlling the "large shields" knew what they were doing. They understood that humanity in those days was totally ignorant in the ways of science and technology. One wonders how long they have waited for us to come into the understanding of recognizing what they truly are.

In another account several UFOs were seen in the skies over Rome in 393 AD. According to the account, during the reign of Theodosius, an enormous glowing sphere as well as several smaller ones materialized above the pastures just outside of the village. According to the account, the strange objects sent residents in the area into a panic. There is no other word about what happened here, but quite clearly this was a large ship, possibly what we would refer to today as a mothership, with perhaps smaller craft exiting it. The Roman writer Julius Obsequens wrote that some of the people had witnessed, "burning globes," while others observed "round shields," in the skies of Rome, both at night and during the day.

In 50 AD in Via Campana, Italy, there was a UFO sighting. According to the account, the witness was the brother of Pope Pius I. The sighting occurred on a day when the weather was sunny and clear. There the witness saw what he described as something resembling "a beast like a piece of pottery" in the sky. It was reportedly nearly one hundred feet long. The top portion was made up of several colors, and beams of light were emanating from it. The craft proceeded to move downward, whipping up dirt as it did so, and finally landed. The witness, in describing the event indicated that as the dirt settled, he saw a "maiden clad in white" standing in the vicinity of the craft. There is no word on what happened afterwards. However, we do have an indication here that there were humanoid extraterrestrials visiting Earth during that period.

This is one of the few accounts where there is an actual extraterrestrial sighting that was recorded in the ancient world. If the galaxy is filled with life, with many of them being humanoid beings resembling humans on Earth, then the ancient world may have had many visitors that they did not know came from other worlds. This is something that we in our modern day have been conditioned to think about due to the science fiction of our time. In fact, as I have mentioned previously, it is said that it is partially through science fiction that we are being prepared for first contact. For the most part, I imagine that many extraterrestrials in history kept their identity hidden as they set about observing Earth and life on it. There are a few times, however, where those that saw something unusual reported it, and the event and details were recorded in historical chronicles. In this case, I presume that it was taken more seriously given the prestige of the person that was witness to the event.

Similarly, in 1453 UFOs in the form of mysterious lights were observed hovering above Constantinople the evening prior to the Turks overtaking it. Oddly, the lights flew straight up at enormous speeds and then divided into several smaller lights. Was there a message in the odd behavior of the lights? Why were they there in the first place? This again sounds like there may have been some interference by UFOs in another conflict on Earth.

Romania

A UFO was spotted in Romania on December 9, 1731.

According to written records addressing this event, the UFO came from the west. It was described as being "blood-red" and massive. It hovered for two hours, eventually splitting in two and then becoming whole again. In the end, it headed west and vanished.

Russia

Three UFOs were seen in Robozero, Russia in August of 1663. It was described as a large metallic disc, and it was seen during the daytime hours. It stayed in the sky for two hours. One witness commented that the sphere shone more brilliantly than the Sun. A farmer by the name of Ivan (Ivashko) Rzhevsky, who saw the UFO, signed a seventeenth century document that attested to the fact that he had witnessed the event. That document still exists today. Rzhevsky stated that on August 15, 1663, between 10:00 and 12:00 pm, a "great noise" resounded over Robozero Lake. This sighting in Robozero became the most memorable UFO event in the history of ancient Russia. The incident is still being talked about to this day.

Sweden

Purportedly in 1766 in Sweden, three UFOs that were described as resembling the Moon were seen in the skies. They were there for four days, before suddenly vanishing. Additionally, in 1766, a UFO was witnessed during the night. Rays of light were seen emanating from it. One can only wonder who they were, and what their agenda was. There are so many questions about this sighting. We don't usually read accounts of UFOs staying in an area for several days. Why did they stay for four days? What were the rays of light being used for? In another UFO sighting documented in early Sweden (date unknown), a bright spherical shaped object appeared in the night skies, hovering as beams of light emanated from it.

Switzerland

Bewildering objects filled the sky in the year 1104 in Switzerland. These UFOs truly stunned the people there. They were described as resembling worms. In fact, the chronicler of this event stated that there were what appeared to be "fiery worms" in the sky. These had to be enormous because he also wrote, "They flew in the air and took away the light of the sun as if they had been clouds." *What were these objects?!* This is a very different description than most UFOs described in sightings from the past or present day.

On August 7, 1566, numerous black spherical shaped UFOs were seen in the skies over Basil, Switzerland. Strangely, these UFOs appeared to be battling. This is a scary scenario to think about taking place anywhere around the Earth. According to a newspaper article written by one Samuel Coccius on the UFOs, "Many became fiery and red, ending by being consumed and vanishing." What's more is that this fight between UFOs was witnessed by hundreds of people. What would cause a battle between UFOs in our skies? Perhaps it was a disagreement that had something to do with Earth. Do we have protectors?

A Few UFO Sightings in the United States in Earlier Times
Aurora, Texas

In the popular film *Cowboys & Aliens,* starring Harrison Ford and Daniel Craig, the characters lived during the 1800s. In the movie, the people of that period were witnessing UFOs in the skies. What the audience may not have realized is that people really were seeing UFOs in that era. Of course, people did not refer to them as UFOs or spaceships or flying saucers. In fact, the term flyer saucer was not used until 1947. They did, however, use the term "airships," as aerial technology had not been established yet. Airships were as close a term as they had to explain what they were witnessing traveling across the skies.

One of the most memorable accounts of a UFO encounter happened in 1897 in Texas, where there are said to have been several witnesses. The entire account ran in the April 19, 1897, edition of the *Dallas Morning News*, stating:

> About 6 o'clock this morning the early risers of Aurora were astonished at the sudden appearance of the airship which has been sailing throughout the country. It was traveling due north and sailed over the public square and when it reached the northern part of town it collided with the tower of Judge Proctor's windmill and went to pieces with a terrific explosion, scattering debris over several acres of ground. The pilot of the ship is supposed to have been the only one aboard, and while his remains were disfigured, enough of the original has been picked up to show that he was not an inhabitant of this world. Mr. T.J.

Weems [of] the U.S. Army... gives his opinion that the pilot was a native of the planet Mars. Papers found on his person evidently the records of his travels are written in some unknown hieroglyphics, and cannot be deciphered... The ship was built of an unknown metal, resembling somewhat a mixture of aluminum and silver, and must have weighed several tons. The town today is full of people who are viewing the wreckage and gathering specimens of strange metal from the debris.

The newspaper article was written by a highly regarded journalist by the name of E.E. Haydon. The article concluded stating, "The pilot's funeral will take place at noon tomorrow." The funeral is believed to have taken place, and the body was buried in a nearby cemetery (today known as the Aurora Cemetery). A stone was used to mark the site of the mysterious extraterrestrial pilot.

This story once again gained attention in the 1970s when a journalist by the name of Bill Case learned of the event. Case attempted his own investigation to gain information on what exactly happened that day in Aurora, and if the story held any truth. Case believed that he had located the grave and is said to have performed tests suggesting there was a small coffin beneath the ground. Case also sought to obtain the rights to unearth the grave. During this process, the stone grave marker disappeared, as well as the contents buried beneath it. Case believed that these were the actions of government officials, that did not want there to be proof of an alien having crashed and been buried in Aurora. The Aurora Cemetery has a plaque on the front gate with a passage that states, "The legend that a spaceship crashed nearby in 1897 and the pilot, killed in the crash, was buried here."

Montana

During the summer of 1865 several newspapers ran a story about a trapper by the name of James Lumley that had seen a crashed UFO. According to the account, Lumley had watched as a luminous object flying through the sky crashed into a forest of Montana. Lumley sought out the crash site to see what had happened and came upon a spacecraft which had been shattered into large pieces. The material of the ship he later stated felt like stone. Some pieces appeared to have alien writing on them in what looked like symbols resembling those of hieroglyphics, that of course, he could not understand. He also mentioned seeing what resembled glass that was also broken into pieces, located around the crash and there was also a mysterious dark liquid, that he thought may have come from inside of the ship.

This is not the first that we have heard of crashed UFOs as there have been accounts of them in our present day. However, this one really makes one think about the controllers of this craft in particular. There was no word on survivors, nor any mention of bodies found at the scene when Lumley arrived. This raises the question of what happened to the pilots of this craft. Newspapers of the day suggested that the pilots could have at that time been wandering around Montana. They even hypothesized as to where they may have been from, which included, in their opinion, either the planets Mercury or Uranus. In any event, one wonders what happened to the extraterrestrials flying the craft Did they wander around Montana as some predicted? Are they still there now? How did they look? Did they blend in, or could they have appeared different from us and made a home here on Earth and remained hidden? Or were they remotely controlled drones sent here on some kind of reconnaissance mission? We can only imagine!

Roswell, New Mexico

The following is one of the most famous UFO stories in history. As the story goes, sometime between mid-June and early July 1947, William "Mac" Brazel was performing tasks on the Foster Ranch, located approximately 75 miles northwest of Roswell, New Mexico. Brazel was stunned to find fragments from what appeared to be wreckage that was strewn across a 200-yard-long area. A day later, he returned to the area, this time with his wife and children and gathered pieces of debris and returned home. On July 5, while driving to the town of Corona, he listened to a news report on Kenneth Arnold's flying saucer (UFO) sightings, for the first time. Two days later, when he was on business in Roswell, Brazel visited one Sheriff Wilcox and informed him about the debris and crash site he had found. He also told him that from listening to the reports about flying saucers, he believed the wreckage could be that of a crashed disk (UFO). Wilcox then contacted one Major Jesse Marcel, who was the group intelligence officer for Roswell Army Airfield (RAAF). As a result, Marcel and a second officer, Counter Intelligence Corps officer Sheridan Cavitt traveled to the Foster Ranch. It was their intention to examine the crash site and collect the fragments from the potentially crashed ship that Brazel had located. The official announcement that was released to the public was that Brazel had found a downed weather balloon. Years later, it was reported that this was a cover story, and what Brazel had discovered was indeed debris from a crashed flying saucer. The Roswell Incident has become legend and people are still debating today about what Brazel found there and if there was a cover-up.

Washington State (the Kenneth Arnold Sightings)

What we would refer to as the "modern age" of UFOs, is said to have officially began with Kenneth Arnold on June 24, 1947. At the time, Arnold was an experienced civilian pilot that had amassed over 4,000 hours in flying over mountainous areas. As he flew above the rugged Cascade mountains in Washington State, he saw that it was an opportunity to search for an airplane that had gone missing in the area. At around 3:00 pm, as he approached Mount Rainier, he saw brilliant flashes of light that lit up the area near his plane. He looked for the origin of the flashes. What he saw next would forever change his life. He witnessed nine glimmering UFOs traveling in a chain-like arrangement. He estimated that they were flying at a speed of 1,600 miles per hour. He would later describe them as flat, disk-shaped objects. The configuration in which they flew extended outwards approximately five miles.

In an article written by Ronald Story in *The Encyclopedia of Extraterrestrial Encounters*, under the heading, "Arnold Sighting," it states, "Arnold was no stranger to this territory, as he had flown in the area many times before. This was one aspect of the sighting that made many people take it seriously. Not only was he a 'solid citizen,' and a respected businessman, but an experienced mountain pilot as well; and he saw something that was truly unusual to him.'" During the initial ruckus when he was first interviewed by reporters, he stated that the objects flew, "like a saucer would if you skipped it across the water." It is said that due to Arnold's description, the media dubbed the objects as, "flying saucers." From that time on, mysterious flying objects seen in the skies were referred to as "flying saucers."

This of course was before the time that the term UFO was used, which came later. I can only wonder if anyone investigated or even wondered who was controlling these objects. We may have been further along in our understanding and knowledge if someone set out to investigate. Interestingly, the date of this sighting was close to the date of the Roswell sighting. Did anyone make the connection between the dates of the Roswell Incident and the Kenneth Arnold case? William Brazel who came across the crash on the Foster Ranch, had heard a report about the saucers on the news while travelling in the car, and may have believed that one of them had crashed onto the ranch. We will never know for sure.

Types of UFOs

Throughout history, there have been several types of extraterrestrial craft seen in Earth's skies. That would indicate that there are several different extraterrestrial groups flying these craft, and we are therefore being visited by not just one, but different races of beings. Even though we do not know who is controlling them, it is quite amazing to look at the various types of extraterrestrial spacecraft seen in Earth's skies.

Cylindrical Shaped UFOs

The cylindrical shaped UFO (also known as cigar shaped) has been observed by witnesses for several years. They have also been spotted on Earth, in space, and around the Moon. In fact, there is one photograph taken by the *Apollo 15* crew that shows a huge cylindrical shaped craft on the Moon's surface. At that time, it was interpreted by officials as possibly being an ancient, crashed spaceship. It led to an inquiry and sparked the *Apollo 20* lunar mission that many believe to be real, and others consider a hoax. They have been described as slow and at times erratic. However, according to reports, they can accelerate when needed. Contactee George Adamski and six friends witnessed what was referred to as an enormous cylindrical shaped craft on November 20, 1952 as they were watching for UFOs in the skies of the Mojave Desert in California. Adamski took pictures of the craft through a tripod-mounted portable telescope. In another report, in 1991 cosmonaut Musa Manarov caught a cylinder shaped UFO on film. The object was described as cylindrical in shape, shiny, and appeared to be rotating as it traveled across space. While crossing over Hawaii during the *Gemini 4* mission, James McDivitt reportedly saw a long white cylinder shaped UFO. He described it as having protruding angular arms. In this case it was flying near his capsule. One wonders if it were there to observe the activities of the *Gemini*

4 mission.

Disk Shaped UFOs

The disk-shaped UFO (also known as flying saucers and saucer shaped disks) are the type of UFO that most people are familiar with. They have been seen around the world throughout history. They are generally described as being circular, thin, and rather flat looking, with the top of the disk sometimes having a dome. There are three specified disk shapes. 1) the flat disk, 2) the domed disk, and 3) the double-domed disk, sometimes referred to as the Saturn Disk. The flat discs were observed numerous times in the annals of ancient civilizations such as Greece, Rome, and Italy, in which they are referred to as "flying shields." Could it be that it is the same group of extraterrestrials flying these disk-shaped objects since the beginning when they were first sighted? Does this mean that the same extraterrestrial visitors have been with us since the beginning of human history? Or is this popular discoid shape only a coincidence, and there are many groups or races with the same type of spacecraft?

UFOs in Light Formations

It is sometimes difficult in the night skies to determine exactly what one is seeing when it comes to UFOs. Some are so close that they can easily be discerned when you witness a large, brilliantly lit sphere in the sky, or perhaps a circular ring of lights, or something that is clearly interpreted. However, on many occasions all that witnesses can describe is seeing lights in the sky. Sometimes it may be what appears as a large lit orb in the sky. There have been cases when some have been described as moons. There are some that are so far away that it is difficult to discern if one is looking at a UFO or simply one of Earth's satellites. There are others, however, that are so strange that there is little doubt that the witness saw something otherworldly. There are numerous accounts of lights flying in formation in the night skies. They are usually overt and seem to have an agenda. These light formations have been observed in various colors. There have been reports of red lights flying in formation at night, orange flashing lights, multicolored formations, bright white lights and more. They move in a variety of patterns and often geometric shapes. One wonders the reason they are showing themselves, and more importantly, *where they are going*. The lights are so brilliant on these UFOs that it is difficult to make out their shape. People sometimes mistake them for drones, flares, lanterns, and balls of lightning.

Witnesses often realize that they are UFOs when they begin to move intelligently with intention, direction, and purpose. They move at varying speeds. Sometimes they appear to hover or float along, and other times move in rapid precision and extremely fast, faster than any craft created here on Earth. Additionally, some of the "light UFOs" morph into other shapes. They have also been observed merging together. They have the ability to disappear from one location, and suddenly appear in another. *Impressive*! One wonders if this is indeed what they are attempting to do, in fact: impress an audience that is watching. Do these objects have a purpose or an agenda that has nothing to do with Earth? Or do they appear as a signal to humanity that we are not alone in the universe? Are they attempting to let us know they are out there and to prepare ourselves for an introduction?

Spherical Shaped UFOs

The spherical shaped UFO is the shape that is most often reported on the National UFO Reporting Center (NUFORC) Online Database. It is circular from all angles. They have reportedly been seen in many different colors. Most are described as metallic, and their maneuvers involve hovering, fliting, darting about, and traveling at great speeds across the sky. They are said to be able to alter their course in a split second.

Triangular Shaped UFOs

Triangular shaped (also referred to as pyramid shaped), black UFOs are extremely common. Whole books have been written about this type of UFO. An observance of this type of craft was reported as far back as the 1500s in the famous Nuremburg, Germany case. In modern times, it was seen in the famous Phoenix Lights mass sighting of the 1990s. They also were the predominant type of UFO witnessed in the Belgium sightings that occurred from 1989 to the 1990s.

Another type of UFO has been placed in the triangular shaped UFO category. That is the tear drop shaped UFO. It is similar to the triangular but not quite. Still, it is sometimes referenced under this category.

Shape Shifting UFOs

Perhaps some of the strangest of all reported sightings of UFOs are those of the shape shifting UFOs. These craft appear one way initially, and then slowly change into another shape, sometimes changing color as well. There is no set size, as some appear rather large, and others smaller. These have been reported in several countries. There is also quite a bit of video being taken of them. The imagery is often beautiful and fascinating to watch as they morph into different forms and hues.

Square Shaped UFOs

Huge square shaped UFOs have been seen in Earth's skies. The first image that comes to mind when it comes to square shaped UFOs is that of the famous *Star Trek* episodes and movie involving a group of hive-minded aliens known as the Borg. They operated a square (cube shaped) spacecraft.

Heat Radiating UFOs

There are a few accounts where UFOs are said to have had heat radiating from them. One of these reports is the one described above from Hamburg, Germany, where sailors on boats in 1547 had to leave their vessels due to a large spherical shaped UFO that was emitting high heat passing over them. It was so hot that those in the presence of the UFO had to seek shelter.

In an account found in the book *Wonders in the Sky: Unexplained Aerial Objects, From Antiquity to Modern Times and Their Impact on Human Culture, History, and Beliefs,* by Jacques Vallee and Chris Aubeck, on the night of September 3, 1965 two police officers were on duty in Angleton, Texas when a large cylindrical shaped UFO crossed overhead. The object was approximated to be 70 meters long and 15 meters high. It had glowing lights on each end of the craft. One was a violet color the other was light blue. Officers Sheriff McCoy and Robert Goode stated that it became so hot that they had to leave the area.

Motherships

A mothership is a large craft that leads and holds smaller ships that are dispatched for missions. There are reports of enormous UFOs that have been seen in the vicinity of Earth, near the Sun and also near the Moon believed to be motherships. In fact, there are several reports around Earth where huge ships were seen with smaller ones exiting from them. Are we being monitored and influenced by beings located on motherships above the Earth? *Is this where some of the UFOs are coming from?*

Elliptical Shaped UFOs

Elliptical Shaped UFOs (also called oval and egg shaped) have been commonly reported and were featured in the famous comedy TV series about an alien that came to Earth, titled *Mork and Mindy*. The alien Mork is seen coming out of an egg shaped spacecraft. While elliptical craft are certainly no laughing matter, we have several cases where people have found themselves close to one. One example is the famous case of Lonnie Zamora, a police officer that worked in New Mexico in 1964. His case is particularly interesting on two accounts. The unusual shape of the craft during a period when disk shaped craft were highly reported; and the fact that Zamora claimed to have seen extraterrestrials from the craft.

V-Shaped UFOs

V-shaped (also boomerang shaped) UFO sightings occur often. However, some ufologists believe that due to the similarity in shape between these unidentified craft and experimental military planes, these sightings can be explained away as people witnessing test flights of military aircraft. However, sightings of V-shaped UFOs occur in more places than just North America. Witnesses across multiple continents have reported seeing either V-shaped UFOs or formations of lights in a V-shaped configuration.

Tic Tac UFOs

The term Tic Tac refers to UFOs that are the color white and are shaped like the popular candy of the same name. These craft are said to possess aerodynamic abilities; they can achieve instantaneous acceleration, are extremely fast, have anti-gravity lift (an object that is free from the force of gravity), they do not have wings or rotors, and do not leave a trail behind (meaning it has hypersonic velocities without signatures). The Tic Tac UFO became widely known when videos of the Tic Tac craft, taken by Navy pilots (based aboard aircraft carriers USS *Nimitz* and USS *Theodore Roosevelt*), were released to the public in 2020. Lieutenant Commander Chad Underwood, of the *Nimitz* filmed one of the Tic Tac UFOs. According to an article titled "UFO Witness: What is the 'Tic Tac' and why did fighter pilot say it committed an act of war?" by Neetha K. for the Meaww website, in an interview with *New York Magazine* (2019) Underwood stated that the Tic Tac was flying in ways, "that aren't physically normal." He went on to say that it was moving from "50,000 feet" to a "hundred feet in just seconds." Which Underwood assured the outlet, "is not possible."

Theories on How UFOs Operate

There are various reports of what UFOs are capable of, and their technology is astounding. Some specialists report that these craft can travel at hypersonic speeds, with an acceleration of 600 g, having no wings or propulsion system. To help us to understand the gravity of this statement, the UFOs have been compared to the F-16 which is an American single-engine supersonic multirole fighter aircraft. The F-16 can only fly at half that speed and at 9 g. One fighter pilot witnessed seeing a UFO descend from 60,000 feet to 50 feet in 0.8 seconds. Some have been reported as noiseless. Others have the ability to go from visible to invisible in an instant. They purportedly too can stop on a dime and take off instantly. In other words, their technology far surpasses anything of this Earth.

A potent statement about how UFOs move comes from the famed scientist and oceanographer, and former Soviet submarine captain, Dr. Azhazha as quoted in the *The UFO Magazine: UFO Encyclopedia, 2003* by William J. Birnes, where he states, "UFOs transmorph, going from saucer shape to cigar shape to a spiral in minutes. They can materialize and dematerialize at will. The craft and occupants are varied and may be from dozens of different sources and civilizations." *Dozens of civilizations!*

In April 2020, the U.S. Navy made public videos of UFO sightings from pilots as they flew over the Pacific and also the Atlantic Ocean while conducting training exercises. In the videos, the pilots can be heard making statements about what they are witnessing while observing the UFOs, stating, "There's a whole fleet of them!" "They're all going against the wind. The wind's 120 knots to the west. Look at that thing, dude!" and still another, "It's rotating!" A part of the excitement seen in the UFO phenomenon is the reactions people have when observing the way UFOs move. Their technology far surpasses our own, so it is often a shock to see them outmaneuvering what we have considered to be the latest and greatest technology. Although, it is certain that much of the discussion as to how these objects are able to fly and maneuver the way they do (extreme speeds, changing direction on a dime, flying straight up, rotating, disappearing in the blink of an eye) are being conducted by the higher echelons, there have been some people that have publicly given their ideas on how these craft may work.

Toroids, and Magnetic Discs

The former Princeton physics professor and NASA astronaut Dr. Brian O'Leary made a very interesting statement regarding UFOs and extraterrestrials before passing away on July 28th, 2011, stating:

> There is abundant evidence that we are being contacted, that civilizations have been visiting us for a very long time, that their appearance is bizarre from any kind of traditional materialistic Western point of view. That these visitors use the technologies of consciousness. They use toroids. They use co-rotating magnetic discs for their propulsions systems. That seems to be a common denominator of the UFO phenomenon, and how they can work, manipulate time and space locally so that they can have their own anti-gravity propulsion and their own field of energy that's isolated gravitational field, electro gravitational field that's different.

It's interesting to note that Dr. O'Leary, who had once been a part of the group chosen by NASA in 1967 known as the "scientist astronauts," had at one time been a skeptic as to the reality of UFOs.

No Wings, No Tail, No Exhaust Plume

Navy pilot Lt. Danny Accoin, in the 2019 History Channel documentary series *Unidentified: Inside America's UFO Investigation,* commented on the UFOs stating they had "no distinct wing, no distinct tail, no distinct exhaust plume."

Trans-medium Technology

As we have seen above, there are many different types of UFOs. Roderic Martin, the host of the popular podcast and YouTube channel, Why the Big Secret, once commented about the way UFOs function stating, "UFOs operate in trans-medium technology where they can come between water, air, space and all these things that we don't have a technology to do."

Faster Than Light Theory (FTL)

Some researchers speculate that some UFOs may be using faster than light gravity drives. The Cambridge Dictionary defines FTL as, "Faster than light. Used in science fiction to refer to travel at a speed greater than the speed of light, or to describe an engine or spacecraft that can achieve this, which according to the laws of physics is impossible." Impossible. *Yet here we are, considering it!* If this technology is being used, then it would be the product of an extremely highly advanced civilization.

Multigenerational Technology

In an interview with Washington Post Live, June 8, 2021 titled "The Washington Post, Transcript: UFOs & National Security with Luis Elizondo, Former Director, Advanced Aerospace Threat Identification Program," Luis Elizondo commented on the topic of UFOs and multigenerational technology stating, "We are quite convinced that we're dealing with a technology that is multigenerational, several generations ahead of what we consider next generation technology, so what we would consider beyond next generation technology. Something that could be anywhere between 50 to 1,000 years ahead of us."

Cloaking Technology

In Hindu legends the vimanas had stealth technology. They were able to make themselves invisible. Today, this is referred to as cloacking technology, and is something only found in fiction. At least we thought. Evidently the ability to cloak may not be just something seen in *Star Trek*. UFOs have been reported as appearing and then suddenly disappearing in the blink of an eye. Some believe that they have cloaking technology. Cloaking can cause ships to become invisible to parts of the electromagnetic spectrum. Could this be a possibility with extraterrestrials?

Hiding Their Ships

UFOs are believed to be around Earth hiding in various ways. The top theories of how they remain unseen are:

185

•In the Clouds. To quote researcher Scott Warring, creator of the popular UFO Sightings Daily website, "it is a well-known fact that not only do UFOs hide in clouds, but they actually created the cloud around them."

•Through Portals. Researchers speculate that UFOs sometimes disappear through portals in space as they travel to another area of the universe.

•Other Planetary Bodies. Another area where UFOs are believed by researchers to be hiding is on nearby planetary bodies (or behind them), especially the Moon.

UFOs and the Moon

Are UFOs coming to Earth from the Moon? It is a theory that has been recited time and again and is one that is not going away. There are many cases past and present where UFOs have been spotted in various areas of the Moon. In fact, several of the Apollo missions had encounters with UFOs. These encounters were documented. UFOs on and around the Moon have been seen flying, hovering, and entering and exiting what appear to be large crevices on the Moon. These UFOs have been seen in various shapes and sizes around the Moon, much like the ones observed on Earth, which leads some to speculate that some of the spacecraft seen in Earth's skies are coming from the Moon. There are theories as to why UFOs may be leaving the Moon and traveling to Earth. These theories include:

•Lunar Inhabitants. These would be extraterrestrials that dwell on the Moon. There is a lot of evidence that someone is on the Moon. These beings may have advanced technology. They may also be leaving the Moon and traveling to other places in the galaxy including Earth, for exploration or even resources.

•Bases on the Moon. Extraterrestrials may have bases on the Moon and travel back and forth. It could be a portion of the same beings' fleet that we see in Earth's skies.

•Beings from Various Other Worlds Visiting the Moon. It has long been theorized that the Moon is a kind of weigh station that beings passing through use as a stopover. Some have even predicted that the Moon is used as a stopover before some extraterrestrials visit Earth. The many different ships seen around the Moon could be the result of this kind of activity. There was even one report of a mothership being seen over the Moon.

In an article written by Steve Omar titled "U.F.O. and Reported Extraterrestrial On Moon and Mars," he tells of a city-ship being seen over the Moon. Omar writes, "During the 1950s many UFOs seen over Earth were tracked back to the Moon by government tracking stations in secret complexes in deserts in Arizona and Nevada and inside underground mountain bases." There are reports of fleets of UFOs seen near the Moon and leaving the Moon. Where are these craft going? Are they coming to Earth?

One day as humanity sets sail for the stars, we may encounter extraterrestrials that have been visiting Earth. After all, we did not get very far into space before we ran into someone out there. Thus far, the UFOs visiting Earth have not posed a serious threat. *Let's hope that it stays that way!*

Notes: The Gerik I am I experienced a first UFO incident, out in Nevadas desert, following the PERseid meteor showers and the then full rising moon, over the nearby mountain Range!! Very shocking in what occurred, I will Never forget A constin see it in my minds eye!! Not far from Carson City! Luckily no one hurt, just Very bad I frightened U.! Probably 1990ish Giantic AND — Sun bright... Some Type of Metalic Craft!

The moon seemed to turn into this alien craft, which moved forward + hung low overhead of us!! After a short period, no sound whatsoever, it then began to move upward further into the sky + disappeared!! My Dad was a former WWII plane Navigator + all he could do, was shake his head in disbelief. None of us talked any further about it. Now - 2024 here in Alaska + Not seen anything here. I know we are not the only existing life, than - out of space.

Chapter Eight
The Cosmic Freeway:
Stargates, Portals and
Wormholes

"There are things known, and things unknown, and in
between are the doors."
—Aldous Huxley

Since the beginning of time, humanity has been curious about the cosmos and what might be out there. With all the evidence given in this book of extraterrestrial visitation, one wonders how it is that they can travel here in the first place. It is obvious that they are using technology that we are not yet capable of. However, one theory is that they are using what we know as stargates, portals and wormholes which are favorite themes of science fiction. Creating stargate and portal openings, or the knowledge of how to traverse a wormhole is far beyond our capabilities thus far. Simply put, a stargate, portal or wormhole is an opening in space that connects travelers to distant realms. In fact, every year there are hundreds of UFO sightings around the world. They ask how it is that there are beings capable of traveling such vast distances through space. One of the areas that provokes skepticism in the belief in UFOs visiting Earth is how extraterrestrials can travel here given the vastness of the Universe (not to mention the energy required for such a journey).

They maintain that if extraterrestrials are coming to Earth from other star systems, other areas of the galaxy, or from another universe, then they must have exceptional methods by which they travel. Methods that are far beyond humanity's capabilities. To quote Douglas Adams, author of *A Hitchhiker's Guide to the Galaxy*, "Space is big. You just won't believe how vastly, hugely, mind-bogglingly big it is." Therefore, as far as most scientists are concerned, travel through the universe is not possible because it would literally take thousands of years to accomplish. According to our science, there is no other intelligent life anywhere near us.

The Milky Way galaxy is approximately 80,000 light years across and is estimated to be 15,000 light years thick. Scientists estimate that there are around 100 billion stars. None of them are closer to us than approximately 1 million light years. Albert Einstein stated there is nothing capable of traveling faster than the speed of light which is estimated to be 186,000 miles per second. Our speediest craft is NASA's *Voyager 1,* which travels at 11 miles per second. At that rate of speed, it would take *Voyager 1*, which was launched in 1977, 73,000 years to reach the closest star. Therefore, there are those who believe that space travel over large distances is not possible.

However, an article from ABC News gave popular physicist Michio Kaku's ideas on the subject. Kaku stated:

> Einstein may have said nothing can go faster than the speed of light, but he also left a loophole... In Einstein's theory, space and time is a fabric... In school we learned that a straight line is the shortest distance between two points. But actually, that's not true. You see, if you fold the sheet of paper and punch a hole through it, you begin to realize that a wormhole is the shortest distance between two points.

Kaku goes on to explain that extraterrestrials could be more advanced than humanity by millions of years. If we look at it in those terms, the idea of extraterrestrials traveling to Earth is not so farfetched. Although, we do not have all the answers, we have theories. One of the main theories concerns stargates, portals and wormholes.

Some researchers believe that extraterrestrials are using stargates as shortcuts through the cosmos. We could liken this to a cosmic highway where extraterrestrials can travel the universe and dimensions speedily and efficiently. Most people recognize stargates from science fiction, as ways to travel between worlds, galaxies and even universes. One show in particular that comes to mind is the hit show *Stargate,* where this technology is depicted. Since it takes thousands of years to traverse the universe, some researchers believe that extraterrestrials may be using stargate technology to reach Earth. Many believe that the idea of stargates should remain in the realm of science fiction. However, from what we have learned about extraterrestrial visitation to Earth in the ancient past, not to mention the plethora of UFOs being seen in our skies today, we should remain open to this possibility. The Definitions website offers this description of a stargate, stating that it is, "A hypothetical device consisting of a traversable portal (typically a wormhole) that can send one to another location light years away nearly instantaneously." In other words, a stargate is essentially a portal to other worlds that allows beings to travel to a different location anywhere in the universe in a matter of minutes. Civilizations elsewhere in the cosmos that are far superior to ours may have been using stargates for millions of years. These beings clearly would have knowledge way beyond our physics, and are able to create wormholes, portals, and tunnels.

What is interesting too is that this technology is being seriously considered among our scientists today. According to an article by the popular Gaia Channel titled "What is a Stargate? Explore the Doorways of the Universe,": "As recently as 2015, NASA admitted to having spent at least a decade researching access points to places outside of our world, our universe, even beyond space and time as we know it." In fact, there are researchers who believe that any advanced extraterrestrials may have had the ability to create such devices for ages. If this is true, then that could possibility explain the plethora of UFOs seen from our ancient past right up until today. In fact, it appears that this cosmic highway has been used for eons of time, created by beings from civilizations millions or even billions of years old.

This is because there are civilizations in the Universe that began their technological development much earlier than us. There are races of beings that have been around longer and those that are younger just beginning. However, the older groups have technology that has been around for eons. This is difficult for many to grasp, and most people do not think about it. Many of the planets out there in the Universe host life. And certainly, several of them have learned how to travel the Universe using the complex designs of space-time and wormholes to traverse the galaxy, and appear in our area of the Solar System, locating Earth.

The Guardian of Forever

Before I get into the information on the cosmic freeway, I would like to share something found on the original *Star Trek* television show, in an episode titled "The City on the Edge of Forever." My focus here is a kind of doorway located on the show referred to as the "Guardian of Forever." *The Star Trek Encyclopedia: A Reference Guide to the Future,* defines the Guardian Of Forever stating that it is a "time portal created by an unknown civilization on a distant planet at least five billion years ago. The Guardian resembled a large, rough-hewn torus about three meters in diameter. It was a sentient device, able to respond to questions, although the sophistication of its programming was so great that it was difficult for humans to understand it." On The Memory Alpha website (a popular website where one can find all things sci-fi including information from old episodes of *Star Trek)*, there is information on this episode. The focus here is on the Guardian of Forever. When looking at the information it really makes one consider our galactic past and what may have been happening in our universe since the beginning, even before humanity's arrival on Earth. This author believes it to be important in attempting to sort out our galactic origins. Today, as we are learning about UFOs, we can consider that they have been traversing the stars and visiting the Earth through stargates, portals, and wormholes for perhaps millions of years. It is interesting to look at the Guardian of Forever, even though it is in a fictional setting. Could something like this be out there? Could there be portals that have been in existence for ages? The Memory Alpha website defines the Guadian of Forever, this way, "The Guardian of Forever is a construct of an unknown, ancient alien race, that functions as a time portal, a gateway to the time vortex that allows access to other times and dimensions. It is located on an ancient planet where the focus of all timelines throughout at least the Milky Way Galaxy converge." Captain James T. Kirk is seen questioning the Guardian of Forever:

Captain Kirk: "Are you machine or being?"

Guardian: "I am both… and neither. I am my own beginning, my own ending."

It should be noted that the Guardian states it is very old, that its age even exceeds that of the Sun's age of 4.6 billion years. Let's keep that in mind as we move forward. One wonders, could such a thing exist? Just how old is the cosmic freeway?

Stargates

The Definitions Website offers this description of a stargate: "A hypothetical device consisting of a traversable portal (typically a wormhole) that can send one to another location light years away nearly instantaneously." Simply put, a stargate is a portal to other worlds, realms, and dimensions. Although stargates are for the most part hypothetical, we are becoming more aware of the possibility that extraterrestrials may have stargate technology and may be accessing them as a means of moving rapidly through space. Perhaps one of the reasons that we are seeing so many UFOs today is because they are coming in via stargates from elsewhere in the galaxy and or beyond. In the past, the term "stargate" has been for the most part associated with science fiction, such as the popular *Stargate* television series. That show introduced many to the term "stargate" and gave people an idea about how a stargate might work if it were to ever become a reality. According to author/researcher Michael Salla, in his ExoNews video titled "Did Apollo 17 Find a Stargate on the Moon?": "Stargates are based on the idea of a traversable wormhole. Wormholes have been deemed to be theoretically possible by top scientists." Some researchers, ufologists and scientists examining the UFO phenomenon believe that this kind of technology may already be a reality for advanced civilizations existing elsewhere in the universe.

In the show *Stargate*, the stargate is a series of circular mechanisms that produce a stable, artificial wormhole that makes travel between two devices nearly instantaneous. The distance traveled could be vast. The idea is basically to enter a gate and arrive at another gate on a different world. For advanced civilizations this idea could be expanded to worlds that could be millions of light-years away. Are there extraterrestrials coming to Earth via stargates? Fantastically, there have been occurrences when people in various places around the world have reported seeing bright lights in what appears to be a displaced tunnel of light. These tunnels have been seen opening seemingly out of nowhere, in various places across the globe. People have claimed to have seen UFOs coming and going from these tunnels of light. Some locations in the United States where stargates have been seen include Arizona and Michigan among others. Many researchers believe that stargates have been here since ancient times and were used by the ancient "gods" (extraterrestrials) to travel between worlds. It appears that this may have been one way of reaching Earth, either by flying through the stargate or in some cases simply walking in. There are tales of stargates around the world today. It is only now that it appears that these devices are coming to light as is the case with so many other things in today's world when it comes to otherworldly phenomena. It is also believed that stargates are still being used by extraterrestrials on the Earth today. I should note here that not only spacecraft pass through stargates. People, creatures, and objects can come through as well. Therefore, we could be seeing beings and other objects coming in through stargates located on Earth. Some believe that the depiction of a *Stargate* in the TV series is a good likeness of what one would look like if they exist. Some believe that it could even have a blue event horizon with the wormhole being the area where people would travel to faraway places.

If stargates are real, then we can only wonder who made them? Stargate builders had to have had an amazing amount of knowledge to accomplish the mammoth task of building a gigantic network of stargates operating throughout the universe.

The following are a sample of areas around Earth that are believed to have Stargates:

Gate of the Sun, Boliva

The Gate of the Sun is a large, rock-solid ancient megalithic stone structure located in Tiwanaku, Bolivia. It is roughly three meters tall and is carved from a block of stone that weighs 10 tons. On it are found mysterious symbols and figures that have astronomical meanings. The Sun God, Viracocha (the god of creation), is in the middle with sun rays emanating from his head. According to legend, Viracocha "appeared" in Tiwanaku and made it "the place of creation." Other figures bear a likeness to humans but appear to be a cross between human and other creatures. Some have wings, while others have curved tails. Still others are wearing what appear to be helmets. Some believe that the Gate of the Sun was once a stargate giving access to another world, which was the land of the gods.

The Stargate of Anuradhapura, Sri Lanka

In Anuradhapura, Sri Lanka in Ranmasu Uyana (the Royal Goldfish Park) there is a star guide which is believed to be able to open an ancient stargate that was once activated. The guide, known as the Sakwala Chakraya which means "the rotating circle of the universe," is located on a stone wall that is mostly hidden between boulders. It is also known as the Stargate of Ranmasu Uyana. The symbols on the chart are believed to be coordinates to unlock the gate, which then gives access to traveling the universe. Directly opposite the star guide are four stone seats. Unfortunately, even though this artifact has been studied for many years, no one is able to decipher the symbols. (*Author's Note*: There may be a reason for that. Ancient stargates were most likely shut down by universal authorities that may not want humanity utilizing them.)

Stargate in Lake Michigan, USA

Shockingly, Lake Michigan is an area where a stargate is believed to be located. While searching for the remnants of sunken ships in the lake in 2007, two scientists by the names of Mark Holley and Brian Abbot located a mysterious stone structure 40 feet below the surface. Believed to be somewhere around 12,000 years old, the structure was dubbed "Michigan's Stonehenge." The scientists also found a boulder that was decorated with a carving of a mastodon. Mastodons are believed to have been extinct for approximately10,000 years. This gives an idea of the age of the carving. This time frame corresponds to a period when both humans and mastodons are thought to have resided together in the Midwest. While scientists believe that the carving is a petroglyph, what is very interesting here, and the reason it is put in the stargate section of this book, is because there are researchers that believe the boulder/carving may be the remains of an ancient portal. The reason behind the theory may be that there have been several strange disappearances in this area. Because of this, the area is known as "The Michigan Triangle." Could there be a correlation between the disappearances and a possible stargate? Let's look at the occurrences.

In 1891, a schooner named *Thomas Hume* disappeared along with its crew of seven while sailing on Lake Michigan. In 1921, eleven people were onboard the *Rosa Belle* when it too vanished. The *Rosa Belle* was later located drifting aimlessly, with no sign of the people that had been onboard. In 1937, one Captain Donner, who was serving aboard the *O.M. McFarland* on Lake Michigan withdrew to his quarters. Quite a while later, a crew member went to awaken him. Alarmed at having no response from the captain, he decided to enter the room. Finding the door to be locked from the inside, he broke down the door. The captain's rooms were empty. All the windows to the quarters were closed and locked. Captain Donner had simply disappeared.

The exact area of Lake Michigan where the Stonehenge-like structure and the boulder with the carving of the mastodon are located is undisclosed to the public. This is part of an arrangement with area Native American tribes that would like to keep the number of visitors to the area down, as there are many who believe that these artifacts are the remnants of an ancient, possibly even a prehistoric, stargate.

Stargate Gobekli Tepe, Turkey

Gobekli Tepe is a Neolithic archaeological site in the Southeastern Anatolia region of Turkey. It is estimated to be around 12,000 years old and is considered the oldest stone temple on Earth. The site is made up of several enormous circular constructions in the form of immense stone columns. Two of the columns are in the center of the circles and appear to construct an entranceway. This entranceway is believed to be the remainder of what was once a stargate of which the ancient society that once dwelled there used as a portal to travel to other worlds.

Stargate, Sedona, Arizona, USA

Sedona is a town in Arizona, USA, known for its spectacular red rock formations. It was once referred to as Nawanda by the Native Americans of the area. They considered Nawanda to have been a sacred city. The red rocks are said to sometimes emanate special sounds, thought by some to be mystical. These rocks are believed by some natives to be able to create vortexes that are able to transport people to other realms. It is in the mountains of Arizona that many believe that there is a portal that they refer to as the "Doorway of the Gods." There one can find a mysterious stone archway that acts like a stargate to other areas of the galaxy. There is a strange tale from 1950 that lends some credibility to the portal idea. It was around that time that treasure hunters came to the mountains searching for gold. They had a local tribesman with them to guide and give assistance. The local man told the visitors a strange tale that dated back to sometime in the 1800s. As the tale went, tribesmen had located an archway as they were traveling through the desert. At some point the men stopped and one proceeded to walk through the archway, vanishing as he did so. The other two, frightened and worried that they were on sacred ground, fled the area. Interestingly, the tribesman reporting this tale admitted to having seen the arched doorway. While he was in the area, a storm approached, and it began to rain. He stated that the sky had become gray due to the storm clouds, however, when he looked inside of the doorway, he could see that the inside was clear blue. He inched closer to it. He observed that the doorway's image of the mountain range was the same, however, the sky was different. He became alarmed at this, and quickly left. As the hunters recounted the tale of this tribesman to others, they stated that the tribesman had liked them and wanted to warn them to not walk into the doorway if they happened to come across it.

Stargate, Sarasota, Florida, USA

Purportedly, there is a stargate located off the coast of Sarasota, Florida. According to legend, the gate is closed and monitored by beings from other realms. Purportedly, some have attempted to open the gate to no avail.

Stargate, Iraq

In the documentary "You Have To See This! Our History Is NOT What We Are Told! Ancient Civilizations—Graham Hancock," author and researcher Anton Parks, the author of *Eden: The Truth About Our Origins*, states, "I believe there are many stellar gateways on the Iraqi territory. Gods could travel through stellar gates like the ones that we see in *Stargate*. I think this is the reason behind the problems that occur there. Indeed, we know very well that today most archaeological studies all over Iraq have come to a halt." There is a theory that at least one stargate was discovered in Iraq. There has been a story floating around about it for years. The backstory to this theory is fascinating! The idea of Iraq having stargates begins with their history with Sumer and the planet Nibiru, that according to Sumerian lore, is home to the gods, the Anunnaki, known today as a superior extraterrestrial race. The Anunnaki allegedly are responsible for creating a stargate that they left behind when they left Earth and returned to their home world. It is believed that there are governments that know of the stargate and there is one story of the gate having been restored. Today, it is believed to be hidden and out of reach of the the world at large. (*Author's Note*: The Anunnaki, according to legend, are on the way back to Earth. One wonders, if this account is true, if any of them will be using this alleged stargate that they left behind).

Stargates were, according to sources, one of the many advanced technologies that the Sumerians were given from the Anunnaki. Some believe that it is one of these stargates that was the cause of the war in Iraq. Some believe that the stargate exist, and that the authorities became aware of it, and sought to locate it. It is said to be located near the city of Nasiriyah. There is also a tale of there being a stargate located in the basement area where Sadam Hussein's palace was located. According to the story, Hussein gathered information about the stargate. News of this supposedly reached the West. The West hoped to prevent Hussein from using this ancient technology and set about to prevent that from occurring.

Stargate, South America

There is a strange story out of South America where people have claimed that a group of extraterrestrials have devised a way to produce temporary stargates. These specialized gates are referred to as "Xendra." They are created with the use of certain spaceships. Simply put, as these extraterrestrials are in their ships, they can open somewhere near them a stargate that will transport a person or objects over vast distances to somewhere else in the universe. A man by the name of Sixto Paz Wells asserts that in 1974 he went through a Xendra. According to the account, he says that he was instantaneously transported to Ganymede (a moon of the planet Jupiter). What is most fascinating from this account (if true) is that there is a race of extraterrestrials out there that have the technology to produce temporary stargates that can send people light-years away to other areas of the universe. If so, then this is amazingly advanced technology. One can see where learning of this type of information might spark secret agreements between worlds to acquire such a technology. It really does sound like something right out science fiction.

Stargate, Stonehenge, Wiltshire, England

Stonehenge is a prehistoric monument located on Salisbury Plain in Wiltshire, England. It is one of the most famous constructions on Earth. There is an ongoing debate as to when the formation was created, and what the purpose of the configuration may be. Conventional historians maintain that it was created approximately 5,000 years ago. However, some scientists believe that the stone formation was there before the first settlements were built in the area (5,000 years ago) arguing that Stonehenge was previously there and completely intact. Stonehenge is believed to sit where 14 ley lines join. Therefore, Stonehenge is thought to be an energy portal or stargate that leads to other worlds. The portal is believed to open at a particular point in time giving people the ability to enter. Case in point, in August 1971, a group of teens thought it would be fun to camp out in Stonehenge. They set up camp, in fact, right in the middle of the formation. The group pitched their tents and settled in for the evening. They were enjoying their time, apparently, when something strange and unexpected occurred. At approximately 2:00 am, lightning started to flash, illuminating the night sky. According to the account, it began raining, and the group ran to their tents for cover. However, a local police officer who was patrolling the area at the time witnessed Stonehenge become engulfed with a strange blue glowing light that seemed to be descending from the sky. During the event, a local farmer appeared, and others came as at this point the teenagers were screaming. There were then several witnesses to this event. The police officer stated that the light was blindingly bright to the point that it was difficult to see anything. People just simply had to close their eyes. At first witnesses assumed that the lightening may have hit one or some of the teenagers. However, as they moved closer in, they saw the tents and belongings of the young people, but no one was there. They had all vanished. This was not something that could be written off, as there were simply too many witnesses, including a police report and the names of those who vanished into thin air: Julia Ashton, Lucas Addams, Sheri Wilson Jr., Daniel Wilson, and Wilma Rupert.

Some of the teenagers kept diaries and notes regarding their trip. Daniel Wilson had written about the trip all the way up to the point where he disappeared. However, it was Wilma Rupert's writings that garnered the most attention during the investigation. Some attributed her writing to having psychic abilities. She stated:

> I knew it would rain. It always rains where the blue glow comes. I see him every night, but I don't tell the guys. I stop seeing only when I'm drunk enough. Once they took my dad to heaven. He managed to tell me that they would not come after me if I was too drunk.

> In the past few weeks I didn't drink, especially when I learned that we were going to Stonehenge. Sheri is very afraid of lightning. I think that the lightning will strike close to us.

It is noisy outside and lightning strikes trees. Sheri is afraid, but she needs to be afraid of another. The blue glow is very close. If someone finds this entry, then demolish this godforsaken place ... [further handwriting is illegible].

Stargate, the Bermuda Triangle

The Bermuda Triangle (also the Devil's Triangle) is famous for mysterious disappearances, including airplanes and ships vanish from the area without any plausible explanation, never to be seen or heard from again. Theories as to why planes and ships go missing there are many. However, a longstanding theory is that there is a stargate operating there that these unaccounted-for vessels are disappearing into. Could it be that what we are looking at when it comes to the Bermuda Triangle is an ancient stargate that has not been shut down? What happens to the people that disappear? Do they find themselves elsewhere in the universe?

Stargates in Space
NASA

As it turns out, the use of stargates appears to be in humanity's future, thanks to the National Aeronautics and Space Administration's research into this area that is taking place today. Information on the research can be found in an article taken from NASA's website titled "Hidden Portals in Earth's Magnetic Field," by Dr. Tony Phillips. The article states:

> A favorite theme of science fiction is "the portal"— an extraordinary opening in space or time that connects travelers to distant realms. A good portal is a shortcut, a guide, a door into the unknown. If only they actually existed....
>
> It turns out that they do, sort of, and a NASA-funded researcher at the University of Iowa has figured out how to find them.
>
> "We call them X-points or electron diffusion regions," explains plasma physicist Jack Scudder of the University of Iowa. "They're places where the magnetic field of Earth connects to the magnetic field of the Sun, creating an uninterrupted path leading from our own planet to the sun's atmosphere 93 million miles away."

Observations by NASA's THEMIS spacecraft and Europe's Cluster probes suggest that these magnetic portals open and close dozens of times each day. They're typically located a few tens of thousands of kilometers from Earth where the geomagnetic field meets the onrushing solar wind. Most portals are small and short-lived; others are yawning, vast, and sustained. Tons of energetic particles can flow through the openings, heating Earth's upper atmosphere, sparking geomagnetic storms, and igniting bright polar auroras.

NASA is planning a mission called "MMS," short for Magnetospheric Multiscale Mission, due to launch in 2014, to study the phenomenon. Bristling with energetic particle detectors and magnetic sensors, the four spacecraft of MMS will spread out in Earth's magnetosphere and surround the portals to observe how they work.

Just one problem: Finding them. Magnetic portals are invisible, unstable, and elusive. They open and close without warning "and there are no signposts to guide us in," notes Scudder.

Actually, there are signposts, and Scudder has found them.

Portals form via the process of magnetic reconnection. Mingling lines of magnetic force from the sun and Earth criss-cross and join to create the openings. "X-points" are where the criss-cross takes place. The sudden joining of magnetic fields can propel jets of charged particles from the X-point, creating an "electron diffusion region."

To learn how to pinpoint these events, Scudder looked at data from a space probe that orbited Earth more than 10 years ago.

"In the late 1990s, NASA's *Polar* spacecraft spent years in Earth's magnetosphere," explains Scudder, "and it encountered many X-points during its mission."

Because *Polar* carried sensors similar to those of MMS, Scudder decided to see how an X-point looked to *Polar*. "Using *Polar* data, we have found five simple combinations of magnetic field and energetic particle measurements that tell us when we've come across an X-point or an electron diffusion region. A single spacecraft, properly instrumented, can make these measurements."

This means that a single member of the MMS constellation using the diagnostics can find a portal and alert other members of the constellation. Mission planners long thought that MMS might have to spend a year or so learning to find portals before it could study them. Scudder's work shortcuts the process, allowing MMS to get to work without delay.

It's a shortcut worthy of the best portals of fiction, only this time the portals are real. And with the new "signposts" we know how to find them.

Black Holes

The *Atlas of Space Exploration* defines a black hole as, "a region in space where the concentration of matter is so dense that not even light can escape." On the matter of black holes, galactic expert and Andromedan contactee and representative, Alex Collier, talked about the subject in a video titled "Alex Collier on the Andromedans." There Collier gave pertinent information on the topic. "My understanding is that all of the conscious spirit that in this universe came through different black holes from other universes in time and space which we simply aren't privy to... We came through another universe, through the black holes to this place that we now call our universe to continue to evolve." The question is, could black holes be multi-faceted. Could black holes be used for travel through the universe on a physical level as well as the spiritual? And are extraterrestrials using black holes to traverse the universe? Is this how we are being visited on Earth by people from other worlds? Most of us know about black holes from science fiction movies. They are shown to be massive, violent, and wildly destructive. They are also invisible, which is even more scary. Still, there is a theory that highly advanced extraterrestrial civilizations have the knowledge and technology to somehow maneuver and manipulate these beasts, giving them the ability to visit Earth.

Black holes are parts of space where the force of gravity is so great that everything in its proximity is sucked in. Scientists believe that up to 100 million black holes are in the Milky Way galaxy alone. Even more interesting is that at the nucleus of most galaxies is an exceedingly colossal black hole. Obviously, we need time for our scientists to figure out how black holes operate. However, one theory about black holes in general is that with the right science and technology, humanity too may one day use them to transport people from one part of the galaxy to another, essentially making them shortcuts through space. Who knows, this just may be the way that Earth has been receiving visitors in spaceships for so long. *Good luck with that!*

Interdimensional Travel

Some researchers have taken a different approach to how extraterrestrials may be traveling here. They theorize that some beings may be visiting Earth by way of "interdimensional travel." To make things easy to understand, interdimensional travel can be defined as traveling between dimensions. It can also be viewed as someone coming from a parallel universe, as is often portrayed in science fiction. This would eliminate the need for traveling vast distances. It is a mind-boggling idea.

Teleportation Technology

Are extraterrestrials using teleportation technology to travel to Earth? This is one of the theories that suggests how they have been arriving in our world over millennia. The idea is not new to us as teleportation was popularized in the television series *Star Trek,* where people, objects and even ships (thanks to *Star Trek: Discovery*) could beam from the starship *Enterprise* to the surface of a planet or elsewhere and reassemble into one piece. There is at least one case that I know of where there is an individual that claims to have come here from a different world to help humankind during this difficult time in Earth's history. This person claims to have been teleported from another world. Of course, that is a science and form of technology (if real) that is far beyond our understanding, but not perhaps for a civilization that has been around for millions of years.

To make things a bit easier to comprehend, *The UFO Encyclopedia* by Margaret Sachs defines teleportation as a "term coined by Charles Fort to denote the hypothetical ability of instantaneous movement of physical matter from one place to another, irrespective of distance or intervening matter. The term means, literally, 'far-carrying.'" Even more interesting, in an article titled "How Quantum Teleportation Actually Works" (March 16, 2017, *Popular Mechanics),* writer Avery Thompson, explains it this way: "There's three different kinds of teleportation: teleportation through a wormhole, or something similar, where your body is simply relocated to another place; the *Star Trek* kind where your molecules are disassembled, beamed somewhere else, and reassembled in the same way; and the philosophy problem kind where your body is scanned and the information is transmitted somewhere else and used to build an entirely new body out of different materials."

Transwarp Technology

Believe it or not, in brainstorming the ways that extraterrestrials may be traveling to Earth, researchers have considered the idea of them having "transwarp" capabilities. The term is one that is sometimes used in the *Star Trek* series. According to the *Star Trek Encyclopedia: A Reference Guide to the Future* by Michael and Denise Okuda, Transwarp is, "In subspace physics, a velocity equaling warp 10, unattainable under normal warp theory. An object traveling at transwarp velocity would theoretically be moving infinitely fast and would therefore in principle be occupying all points in the Universe simultaneously." Simply stated, transwarp would give a spaceship the ability to jump from standing still to any warp speed the craft is capable of, without the need to increase speed by going through the different stages, for example, warp 1, warp 2, warp 3, and so on. In other words, it gives the ship the capability of accelerating instantly. In the *Star Trek* universe, a spacecraft capable of traveling at transwarp could travel much more rapidly than a regular warp speed ship. As I stated before, there are some researchers looking into this possibility.

Wormholes

In an article from Space.com titled "What are wormholes? An astrophysicist explains these shortcuts through space-time," September 30, 2022, by Dejan Stojkovic, wormholes are defined this way: "A wormhole is like a tunnel between two distant points in our universe that cuts the travel time from one point to the other. Instead of traveling for many millions of years from one galaxy to another, under the right conditions one could theoretically use a wormhole to cut the travel time down to hours or minutes." Could extraterrestrials be using wormholes to traverse the universe? It could be. They may have knowledge that is far beyond our physics. Simply put, traversable wormholes would be a way of getting from point A to point B very fast. By linking two wormholes and having the capability of traveling at the speed of light, one could travel the stars quite easily. These cosmic subways could be achieved by an extremely advanced civilization that has been around for thousands or millions of years. Theoretically, it is believed that if a traversable wormhole was used, then a spacecraft passing through would have nearly instantaneous access to any desired location in the universe and beyond. It appears that wormholes have been used by extraterrestrials since ancient times to visit Earth. It also just may be that they have been coming in from outside universes as well.

Humanity and Interstellar Travel, We're Going to Need Help

It goes without saying that given all the theories here, at the very minimum, there are extraterrestrial civilizations that have achieved the means of interstellar travel. In fact, when we consider what it takes for space travel, we cannot even begin to imagine the type of advanced technology needed to accomplish such a feat. Given that humanity is nowhere near interstellar travel, we can understand that most of what we are seeing in the skies regarding UFOs indicates that they are far more advanced than we are. Unfortunately, it will take a great deal of time before humanity reaches the capability of interstellar travel. This was conveyed at the Joint Propulsion Conference in Hartford, Connecticut which was held in the early 2000s. During the conference, space propulsion difficulties were discussed. Scientists examined several ideas for advanced propulsion systems for future interstellar travel. Unfortunately, the calculations revealed that arriving at even the closest star in a human lifetime is unattainable. In the August 19, 2008 article by Robert Lemos titled "Bad News: Interstellar Travel May Remain in Science Fiction," from *WIRED*, the then assistant professor of aeronautics and astronautics at the Massachusetts Institute of Technology stated, "In those cases, you are talking about a scale of engineering that you can't even imagine." What are the reasons for humanity not being able to accomplish interstellar travel according to scientists at the conference? The two main reasons are:

1. Propulsion. Propulsion necessitates enormous quantities of fuel. Shockingly, it would require a minimum of all the fuel on our planet to be able to send just one spacecraft to the closest star.

2. Time. We don't have time. Even using Earth's rocket engines that can achieve the greatest velocity, it would still take 50,000 years to traverse the 4.3 light-years to reach the closest star system

to Earth, which is Alpha Centauri.

In order to accomplish such a feat, Earth's scientists would have to mine the outer planets for the resources needed. We can't even make it to Mars yet. These figures alone tell us what we are up against, and the capabilities of the extraterrestrials flying these UFOs. Although many hope that if contact is ever established, perhaps there will be a sharing of knowledge. If we look into our UFO history from the ancient past until now, it appears that there are extraterrestrial civilizations out there that have had the technology of interstellar space travel long before humans even appeared on Earth. This is how advanced they are. *Perhaps they will share technology?*

Who Controls the Cosmic Freeway?
The Cosmic Freeway, I believe, is an enormous multifaceted web of activity. This amazing throughway spans the entire galaxy, the universe and beyond. Just as on Earth (on a much smaller scale) we have those that regulate our freeway systems, and in the United States we have the Federal Aviation Administration regulating air traffic control, there could be beings that control what appears to be a cosmic freeway. Are there beings that hold ownership over certain stargates, portals and wormholes? Who is to say that this technology can be used by whomever, or whatever race of beings, that so chooses? There could be intergalactic regulations of such activity by otherworldly councils and federations out there that we know nothing of. There may also be those that are not allowed to enter this section of the galaxy or be allowed in from certain galaxies or universes. It is mind-boggling to consider all the different scenarios.

Rips and Tears in Space, Tearing into Other Dimensions and What Comes In
One very bizarre aspect of the cosmic freeway is what can be referred to as "rips and tears in space." There is a theory that we may have let undesirable entities into the galaxy, and near Earth's vicinity, when we set off the nuclear bomb. In other words, we may have entities on Earth today that are not meant to be here, because of something that humanity has done in space. This may be one of the reasons that we have allegedly been warned by benevolent extraterrestrial beings to put down the atomic weapons. They basically said that they are dangerous;

they also insinuated that nuclear armaments have a rippling effect throughout the galaxy. Basically, we were told in a nutshell (when allegedly extraterrestrials met with certain government officials) that we do not know what we are doing, and using these weapons will affect Earth and others in the galaxy. If the story is true and extraterrestrials told this to certain government leaders (many believe this story to be true) then what does that mean exactly? I can only say that we have no idea what is out there in the universe, nor other realms and dimensions. We barely know about our Solar System…and our galaxy.

We are still living in a world where people do not believe that extraterrestrials exist. With all the evidence out there today about UFOs, on a mass scale, the people of Earth do not believe it. We also do not know how everything works out there in the universe. We do not understand the idea of other dimensions, and who or what exists there, and then we set off the atomic bomb. Who knows what we did when that happened? We do not know all the ramifications it may have had in the cosmos. That may be the reason for the report that one of the government officials was visited by extraterrestrials with a warning. Since the time of the creation of the atomic bomb, there has been an increase of UFO activity in Earth's skies. This is the reason some believe we are being monitored. What have we done? Is there more to the story than extraterrestrials coming to save life on Earth? What are the effects of atomic weaponry in the universe? Is there something we don't know in this regard?

It is thought that somehow we may have created rips and tears in space so to speak. It is said that we may have let things into the galaxy that should not be here, things far beyond our imagination. What may come in if we as humans somehow cause a tear in the fabric of space? One person that has spoken out in this area is the award-winning journalist Linda Moulton Howe, who talked about the subject in an interview during the 2018 Ozark UFO Conference. She was interviewed by Mysterious Outpost TV. Howe states:

> And if we tear into dimensions that we know nothing about, this is the other part that was said to me that's chilling, it's very clear that something in the nonhuman category is interfering with minuteman missiles not to launch them, but to shut them down and that there

have been communications about, "you cannot do this, because you do not understand that you're tearing into other dimensions." So, this is the side that was always chilling. If we tear into other dimensions in unleashing an atomic bomb or a hydrogen bomb, what could come from those other dimensions, into our dimension that is never supposed to cross barriers? That has been suggested to me by a person who was in the Air Force and then worked for intel. He said we know, we know Linda, in complete and total ignorance, when we exploded some of the bombs that we have exploded, without realizing what we were doing, we allowed things to come in here that are horrible. In our first atomic tests, it was enough to open up dimensions and let something in here that is supposed to be very dangerous.

What did we let in that is so concerning that there are extraterrestrials visiting Earth that are actively shutting down nuclear missiles to prevent us from causing more damage? Who or what is out there? Well, that is another book. Also, how do we repair any damage we may have caused? Most importantly, are any of the UFOs or aliens seen today coming from a tear in space that we created?

Chapter Nine
From Elsewhere,
Extraterrestrials Among Us

"There are millions of worlds, and we (Tibetans) know that
most of them are inhabited. Those inhabitants may be in very
different forms to those we know, they may be superior to
humans. We in Tibet have never subscribed to the view that
Man is the highest and most noble form of evolution. We
believe that much higher forms are to be found elsewhere,
and they do not drop atom bombs."
—T. Lobsang Rampa

The Fermi Paradox encompasses one of the biggest questions
when it comes to whether we are alone in the universe. It asks,
"If the universe is teeming with life, then where are all the
extraterrestrials and why haven't we encountered any?" Well,
by now you know that this author believes that we encountered
extraterrestrials ages ago. However, for others that do not believe
that we have found life in outer space (or that they found us),
this question still needs answering. So then, where are all the
extraterrestrials, and why haven't we been visited by them or
heard from them? The answer is *we have*. People do not know,
understand, believe, or have the information. There is a lot going
on out there, from what appears to be a constant stream of UFO
sightings from around the world, to people claiming to have seen
or had direct contact with extraterrestrials that include witness
reports from people from all walks of life. I would like to point
out, too, that if you have not witnessed anything of this nature, that
does not mean it is not happening. To quote former astronaut Edgar
Mitchell, who served on *Apollo 14* as the Lunar Module pilot,
and who had a life changing experience when in space, "Read the
books, read the lore, start to understand what has really been going
on, because there is no doubt that we are being visited."

Make no mistake about it, extraterrestrials exist on other

worlds. Some of them are aware of us, and some are not. Many are very powerful and have travelled the galaxy from anywhere from thousands to millions of years. Some live on planets and planetary bodies, some live on megastructures, some are traveling the universe in starships or motherships. Some exist in different dimensions. Many are humanoid. Some are ethereal, and of course there are more that are beyond our imagination. Many of these civilizations are aware that they are not alone in the universe. Perhaps they are even taught this from childhood. Humanity, however, has yet to accept that there are other intelligent beings in the universe. As a world society, we are grossly lagging behind.

Humans fancy themselves to be the highest civilization in the universe when, in reality, it is humanity that is the lesser civilization when it comes to science, technology, and even spirituality. When we watch science fiction shows and we see the amazing extraterrestrials with the state-of-the-art ships traveling the galaxy, such as in *Star Trek,* and see the crew visiting planets where there are civilizations that are not so advanced, we are shocked to see them—that is *us*. It is not the other way around. We are the new, primitive, struggling civilization that cannot believe their eyes when it comes to spaceships and aliens. We are the civilization that does not accept that there are other beings in the universe that are superior to us. *They* are the ones that have already established space travel and are seeking out "strange new worlds." To them, Earth is that strange new world, and we weren't even aware of it. We have it backwards.

Many of these otherworldly civilizations follow what we know as a "Prime Directive" (another term that I have borrowed from *Star Trek* for simplicity). And yes, there is a federation, that I will discuss later in the book. In the *Star Trek Encyclopedia: A Reference Guide to the Future* by Michael and Denise Okuda, the Prime Directive is defined this way:

> The Prime Directive prohibits Starfleet personnel and spacecraft from interfering in the normal development of any society, and mandates that any Starfleet vessel or crew member is expendable to prevent violation of this rule…the Prime Directive was a key part of Starfleet and Federation policy toward newly discovered civilizations but was also one of the most difficult to administer. In most cases, the Prime Directive applied to any civilization that had not yet

developed the use of warp drive for interstellar travel.

Again, we are that civilization. It is not the other way around. Shocking isn't it? The extraterrestrials do not want to interfere in the development of the citizens of Earth. Humanity is just at the cusp of acknowledging that we are not alone in the universe. We are just beginning, after thousands of years of being visited and with a preponderance of evidence, to understand that others are out there. We are just learning that there is life on other worlds, and that some of them are visiting Earth. I am sure that all "new worlds" learning this information go through "growing pains," when it comes to news such as this. Learning that your world is not the center of the universe, nor the most important, is life-shattering information for many.

Extraterrestrials, What are They Like?

If one *truly listens* to what's being said about extraterrestrials out there, the stories, the contactees, the witnesses, the experiencers, and others, we learn that there are many types of beings existing in our galaxy. What we notice most is that many are very much like us. They can be emotional, curious, and some have humor. They are obviously interested in the exploration of the cosmos, as well as maintaining a safe galactic environment. They are trying to survive in the universe just as we are. We need to understand that our space ambitions are primitive compared to where they are. They at one time were at the same stage as we are now. Some of them have been around far longer and have gone through the growing pains of establishing their civilizations from the ground up as we have. They too had to become aware that they were not alone in the universe, just as we are learning. They grew, matured, advanced, and headed toward the stars, just as we are planning to do. Some have been watching us and are waiting for us to join them in the galactic family. Are they benevolent or malevolent? We need to accept that the universe is a mix of good and bad. If it helps, from my research, it is my understanding that there is more good in the universe than bad. It is very much as we see in some science fiction movies such as *Star Wars*. Here in these pages, are a few of what we understand to be extraterrestrials that have been in contact with or have visited Earth.

"I say without equivocation, we are not alone in the cosmos. We have neighbors. We should try to get to understand them, and to cooperate with them."
—Paul Hellyer, former Minister of Defense of Canada

Johann Elert Bode (1747–1826) was a prominent German astronomer. Bode was famous for his popularization of the Titius-Bode law (also known as Bode's law and his two influential publications on astronomy, *Anleitung* (1768) and *Erlauterung* (1778). He believed every important cosmic body, including the Sun, stars, planets, moons, and comets are populated by extraterrestrials. It appears that Bode may have been close to the truth, as it is beginning to look as though we exist in a galaxy full of life. This would explain why since the beginning of history, there have been tales of beings coming here from the stars. It seems that these were not made-up fantasies of primitive people that did not know any better. Yes, Bode and others were right all along. There are others out there and some of them have been coming to Earth.

Just who are these extraterrestrials that have infiltrated our lives for so long? Why are they here? What do they want? What do we know about them? Even though they have been elusive to the majority in the modern age, there are a few accounts from reputable people that claimed to have had direct contact with extraterrestrials. These people come from various walks of life, from ordinary citizens to political leaders. To hear this sounds like something straight out of a movie, but I assure you, it is not, and the stories are extraordinary. People that have had these encounters are often referred to as "contactees," and "experiencers." These contactees have given us a plethora of information as to who the extraterrestrials visiting Earth are. Until the extraterrestrials come forward and introduce themselves to the entire world, rather than just a few, our information about them is still extremely limited. But rather than not discussing the topic at all, let us look at the information that we do have. It does not hurt to listen to it, and determine for ourselves what is real, or true. It is better than not considering the information at all. How else will we ever get started on the journey of knowing and understanding who or what is out there? So, before dismissing people's claims of what they have seen, heard, or experienced by way of extraterrestrials, can't we at least look at the information out there? We can look at what has been told to us from contactees, experiencers, tales from oral traditions, ancient text, writings and documents from history going back thousands of years and connect the dots as to what we know about extraterrestrials.

The following are highlights of accounts, experiences and what we know and understand of the extraterrestrials that are visiting Earth, and others out there in the cosmos. Cosmic mysteries abound! *Let's get into it.*

Scientists' current approximations tell us there are in the area of 100 million galaxies in the observable universe. What is even more fascinating is that as we progress in our knowledge of science and technology, that number could increase. That estimate leaves little doubt that we are not alone and the chances of us being the only intelligent beings in the universe are very slim. Perhaps the eminent astrophysicist and astronomer Carl Sagan said it best when he stated, "The universe is a pretty big place. If it's just us, seems like an awful waste of space." Today, many people agree with this statement. In fact, the number of people that believe extraterrestrials exist is increasing. More people than ever before are taking interest in the subject of unidentified flying objects (UFOs) which are now being referred to by the US government as unidentified aerial phenomena (UAPs), and then there are the unidentified submerged objects (USOs). People are now openly showing more interest in the idea of extraterrestrials and are finally questioning who is operating those UFOs, UAPs and USOs. They are also wondering if they are benevolent or malevolent.

Star Trek—Is Art Imitating Life in Space?

Is art imitating life? Or should I be asking, *"Is art imitating life in space?"* In a story that seems to appear straight from a science fiction movie, we have a true tale of a person who learned about a group of extraterrestrials traveling the galaxy. He learned that this group came from different worlds and are traveling the galaxy in a highly advanced ship. The person was so taken with what he learned that he wrote a television show about it. The show was well-received, and became a worldwide phenomenon, influencing people's views of life in the universe all over the globe. As you may have guessed, this show was *Star Trek*, and the man in the story is none other than *Star Trek's* creator, Gene Roddenberry. Roddenberry helped people to dream of a spacefaring future; one where beings from different worlds come together for the greater good of the galaxy. It was a show that showed people that there

Extraterrestrials from the television show *Star Trek*.

are all types of extraterrestrials in the universe, and that peaceful collaboration together is possible.

According to the story, Gene Roddenberry sat in on extraterrestrial channeling sessions with a woman named Phyllis Schlemmer who was receiving information via telepathy from these beings. It is my opinion and that of others, that Roddenberry found inspiration for *Star Trek* during these meetings. One can only imagine what information he received during that period. According to accounts, the extraterrestrials that were channeling this information were in a ship in Earth's vicinity. They stated that they had a crew that had come from different worlds, and they were traveling the galaxy. It has been speculated that one of the ways that extraterrestrials are preparing humanity for first contact is through the media. If so, then Gene Roddenberry's *Star Trek* is certainly accomplishing that task. In fact, many believe that *Star Trek* was a catalyst for opening people's minds to the idea that we are not alone in the universe.

The *Star Trek Enterprise* was a ship that was designed to explore the galaxy and seek out new life and new civilizations. On board they had personnel from a variety of worlds, working in several professions including science, medicine, engineering, anthropology, history, astronomy, archeology and more. The exploration of other worlds was to introduce them to new extraterrestrial races and to collect data that would advance life in the galaxy. The races on the receiving end of this knowledge would absorb that information into their own education of their understanding of the universe. In a way, the beings on the ship worked as pioneers in the galactic community. They could also use the information to determine if primited civilizations should one day be invited to a galactic federation of planets.

The Extraterrestrial Presence on Earth

There has been talk among ufologists in recent years stating that extraterrestrials are not only visiting Earth in their spacecraft, but some are walking among us. This is not as far-fetched as it may sound. Some believe that humanoid extraterrestrials live among us and have been all along. People have incredible stories to tell about beings they have seen, and people they have met that were not "quite right." Others have stories to tell about how they befriended or were befriended by an extraterrestrial person. Some even admit to being taken aboard ships, given a tour, taken for a ride, and given a message for humanity. These, however, are one on one meetings, as the extraterrestrials have not yet been ready (it appears) to approach the masses of people on Earth. Believe it or not, some of the people that have had these experiences are those with official, authoritative positions on Earth. Several people have come forward putting their reputations on the line to let the world know of their extraterrestrial experience. They are taking a risk to help people understand that extraterrestrials are real and are here.

Allegedly, some extraterrestrials are physically on Earth living among us, some are in ships in the skies, and some have bases in Earth's waters. There are those who claim to have seen alien spacecraft landing and otherworldly beings exiting the craft. The number of extraterrestrial encounters on Earth is numerous! Several books have been written about extraterrestrial and human encounters. In fact, there are many books available today naming the various groups of otherworldly beings that have visited Earth.

Just who are these space people? Where do they come from? What do they look like? You may wonder that if they are so prevalent, if they are here, then why haven't *you* seen them? You may have. To start, there have been reports for decades of sightings and interactions with extraterrestrials. In fact, according to sources, there seems to be a variety of races that have been seen on Earth. Of course, in a world that is basically in denial about the existence of extraterrestrials, it is no wonder that they have gone unnoticed. There is also the fact that they are extremely adept at keeping themselves hidden, and for good reason. Number one, there presence might cause panic among humanity. Number two, they may have agendas that do not include becoming friends with humans. And as I have mentioned before, they may be living under a kind of directive about rules of contact. Perhaps they are only allowed limited contact with certain individuals. We just do not know. *But the stories persist!*

It is likely that there are various extraterrestrial groups that come to Earth on different missions. Some are simply "citizens" of other worlds involved in space travel and for whatever reason, had a need or desire to come to Earth. In many instances they are fulfilling their duties, work and other obligations when coming to Earth. They are sometimes hidden, sometimes incognito going about their business, and then leaving. Therefore, most people are unaware of extraterrestrials (unless someone has an experience with someone from another world or is a researcher on the topic). The majority have no clue as to what is going on out there, sometimes literally right in their own backyards—*until a ship lands right in front of them, which has happened!* Also, it's a big world. We do not hear about all accounts. However, with the spread of cellphones with cameras everywhere, and social media, there is more information on UFOs and other related phenomena being shared. *In fact, it is so busy that it is difficult to keep up with!*

In this chapter, I reference a few of the groups that are believed by researchers, ufologists, and ancient astronaut proponents to be visiting Earth or that have in the past. However, there are groups of extraterrestrials that have visited Earth, that we have no names for. Some just appear to have been passing through. Of course, we have more information on some groups than others. Most of the extraterrestrials appear to be humanoid. This may well be because the galaxy in which we live was seeded or created by the same group of beings, which were similar to us. These humanoid extraterrestrials, according to sources, have some variations on the surface, but for the most part look like us and can sometimes pass for human, to the point that some could pass right by you on the street, and you would not know the difference.

Others maintain that they may even be living and working here. A very good example of such a scenario can be seen in the 2015 movie *Jupiter Ascending*, starring Channing Tatum and Mila Kunis. In the film, extraterrestrials are seen riding on flying craft (similar to a flying motorcycle) by the audience. However, they are cloaked (invisible) and are unable to be seen by humans that are going about their business on the street. *Could that be a scenario on Earth today?* In *Jupiter Ascending* we also see extraterrestrials living in a residence. They had a mission to carry out and were passing as human. It is believed by some that this could be a reality on Earth. The adage that the "truth is stranger than fiction," can be aptly applied here. The other saying, "art imitates life," can also be used here. Could it really be that art is imitating life? Are extraterrestrials living, working, and existing amongst us?

Why They Come—Hypothetical Reasons Extraterrestrials are Visiting Earth
Science

Earth may be considered by people from other planets or other worlds to be a place of interest when it comes to extending their own scientific knowledge. If you have worlds more advanced, it may be a type of situation where they are looking for outside worlds to study. This may especially be the case when it comes to species/worlds with lesser knowledge as to what is going on in the universe. Given the variety of life on Earth, this may be a prime target when it comes to furthering themselves and their own understanding of the universe. Could they be interested in human genetic diversity or the biodiversity of the Earth? There may be any number of areas they may come to Earth to study with the goal of learning and taking information back to their own world.

Exploration

I liken this hypothesis to *Star Trek*. In the original show, actor William Shatner is heard reciting the following, "Space, the final frontier. These are the voyages of the Starship Enterprise. Its five-year mission, to explore strange new worlds, to seek out new life and new civilizations. To boldly go where no man has gone before." When we think of life out in the universe, we are usually considering it from our standpoint. We wonder who is out there. We dream of traveling the universe and, like the *Star Trek* crew, seeking out new life and civilizations. However, we seldom consider if someone out there is also looking into the cosmos and wondering the same thing. There may be others out there that are longing to explore space and are at our level of technology. Still, there may be those that have just achieved the ability to travel to the stars and fulfill their dream of space exploration. It just may be that some of what we are seeing in the skies by way of UFOs, are being flown by space explorers, just as we dream to be. Additionally, they may even remove a few items to take back to their world for study. Just as we have done on the Moon and Mars.

Colonization

Just as we have plans of eventually colonizing other planets, the same could be applied to more advanced civilizations that may be seeking to expand their species and or territories in the universe. We may not be the first with the idea of sending people into space for the purpose of colonization. This may have been accomplished already and is still being done by other civilizations today. Therefore, some may be here on a reconnaissance mission for the purpose of expanding.

Cultural Studies

There may be extraterrestrials focused on learning about other worlds and how the beings on them live. They may simply be interested in learning more about other cultures and civilizations in an educational capacity. Almost like a field trip type of a mission. Just as we visit countries outside of our own, there may be worlds advanced enough to travel the stars and explore other worlds outside of their own, to learn about new species. These extraterrestrials may be studying humanity's lifestyle, traditions, education system, and more.

To Inform Us that We are Not Alone in the Universe

There are various groups of extraterrestrials that are visiting Earth (as seen by the many varieties of ships seen in the skies). They may come to bring humankind the knowledge that we are not alone in the universe.

To Assist Earth

Earth, as we are aware, is in trouble. There are wars, dwindling resources, hunger, the destruction of nature and much more. It may appear to extraterrestrials that we are potentially a dying planet. Could there be beings in the universe that have selflessly come here to assist Earth and its inhabitants? It has been said that some extraterrestrials have an interest in preserving life on Earth before we destroy it. There is also the theory that the Earth was terraformed and seeded and the extraterrestrials that achieved this would like to save their creation. There are also the extraterrestrial groups that assisted humanity in starting civilization at the beginning of history, helping us to advance. In an article titled

"Flying Saucers Come from a Distant World," in the October 24, 1954 issue of *American Weekly*, the imminent German physicist and mathematician Hermann Oberth tells us, "We cannot take the credit for our record advancement in certain scientific fields alone. We have been helped by people of other worlds." Is it possible that the same extraterrestrials that rendered assistance in the past are coming to Earth today?

Rescue Mission and a Preserving of the Species

In some communications claimed to be from extraterrestrials, it has been stated that extraterrestrials are standing by with ships in the event of a global catastrophe. It is their mission to lift off and relocate as many humans as possible. These extraterrestrials are believed to be poised and ready to help should a devastating scenario occur. It is believed that some of humanity will be evacuated and temporarily taken off the planet until the Earth is livable again. This, it is believed, would be a way of preserving the human species.

Earth's Resources

There are those who believe that many extraterrestrials have no interest in helping humanity and that their interest in Earth is purely based on resources that can be extracted from here to be used in some capacity for their own means, such as crops, farm animals, minerals, water and other resources that may be useful to them. The usage could range anywhere from needed items on their home worlds to goods for bartering. There is also evidence of mining on the Moon, and bartering is believed to happen there as well. Could the same be occurring here on Earth and elsewhere in the galaxy?

Nuclear Warfare Concerns

Witness testimonies to UFOs flying close to military bases have led some to believe that extraterrestrials are here to survey what is going on with Earth and our stockpiles of missiles and nuclear installations. They are thought to be keeping a close eye on humanity when it comes to this area. They know what humans are capable of when it comes to the matter of arms and warring, and they are ready to intervene if it comes down to a world war involving atomic weapons. In his book *The UFO Magazine: UFO Encyclopedia*, William J. Birnes writes:

The atomic bomb is one of the reasons, UFO researchers say, extraterrestrials have decided to intervene in our affairs. The destructive nature of these weapons is so immense that a full-scale nuclear war is more than capable of wiping out all life on the planet, an event, according to contactees and abductees, the aliens will prevent by direct intervention and disclosure, if necessary.

Several accounts of UFOs shutting down missile tests have been documented. An example of one of those incidents is the Vandenburg, California event. In September 1964, as the U.S. military was testing a nuclear missile in Vandenberg, an unusual event took place. The missile was intercepted by a UFO in the stratosphere (the second layer of the atmosphere of Earth). It emitted a type of beam, which it used to shoot the missile a few times, disarming it. Dr. Robert Jacobs was a witness to the event. Jacobs reported what happened, giving a description of the details. The incident was investigated by UFO researcher and author Robert Hastings. Hastings examined the connection between UFOs and nuclear weapons.

In another fascinating incident known as the Malmstrom Air Force Base UFO incident, which took place on March 16, 1967, 10 nuclear missiles that were kept in a subterranean bunker were deactivated by mysterious UFOs that hovered above.

Witnesses that consisted of guards and military personnel were shocked to find their installation surrounded by several reddish-orange UFOs in the sky. Panic ensued as they called their superiors for help. As they did not understand what they were looking at, although they knew they were UFOs, and thought they might be under attack. As it turned out, the UFOs were only interested in the nuclear missiles located there, which they promptly disarmed and left. It appears that there really are universal laws in place that we are not aware of when it comes to such issues as atomic energy. For any groups not following those laws, we have no idea what the repercussions might be.

Today, UFOs are often seen around power plants, nuclear-powered vessels, military installations, and as we have seen, they have shown up during atomic testing, and have shut down nuclear missiles. Therefore, it is clear they are concerned with humanity's nuclear capacities including nuclear weapons, nuclear technology, and nuclear capabilities. Many believe that these events, as well as several others with the same outcome, are a warning that we ought not be operating nuclear armaments. It is thought that if we use atomic weaponry, our actions will have widespread consequences, both for Earth's inhabitants and for the numerous beings and lifeforms in the galaxy. They may also be concerned that there could be some bleed-through into other realms and dimensions due to nuclear explosions. As mentioned before, there are also those who believe that when we set off the atomic bomb for the first time, we let something into the galaxy that should not be here. The extraterrestrials may have that concern as well.

Space Travel

There are clear signs that extraterrestrials are paying close attention to what we are doing in the area of our space travel ambitions and endeavors. All the NASA programs as well as the Soviets encountered UFOs during the 1960s to early 1970s. They were clearly being followed. Several were followed into space by UFOs, and there is a prevailing story of UFOs being on the Moon when the *Apollo 11* astronauts arrived. In June of 1982, UFOs were witnessed flying above the Baikonur Cosmodrome (Russian spaceport). To those present, it appeared as if the UFOs were watching the events at the Cosmodrome. Interestingly, is believed that the installation received damage from energy fields possibly emitted from the unknown spacecraft.

Reconnaissance Mission for First Contact

In Earth's galactic history, evidence shows that we have been monitored by otherworldly beings for ages, and for a variety of reasons. One of the reasons that researchers suspect extraterrestrials are watching Earth is to discern when we as a global society will be ready to meet them. The theory is that there are extraterrestrials monitoring Earth and sending information back to their own superiors as they report on our progress and activities. Perhaps it is these beings that will help determine when humankind is ready to know the truth about our galactic history, and when we will be ready for the proverbial first contact.

In Search of Their Own Roots and History (perhaps Earth is a part of that)

This is one of the more complicated theories. As we reach far

221

back into our galactic history, there is the idea that at one point humanity may have reached space travel eons ago. There is a long history of evidence that humanity in ancient times was more advanced and extremely familiar with advanced aerial technology. Some ancient writings, such as the Sanskrit writings of India, told of a time when aerial craft from Earth went to the Moon and beyond. The theory is that catastrophes on Earth happened, and humans were scattered throughout Earth and perhaps even went inside. As a result, some humans took to the spacecraft and headed for the stars to escape. Fast forward a millennia later and we might have human beings existing on other worlds that know Earth's galactic history and humanity's origins. The question is, could some of the UFOs seen in the skies today be a result of events that happened in Earth's past? In other words, are there extraterrestrials out there that recognize Earth as their original home and are visiting?

Hybridizations

Some researchers believe that there is a hybridization program for a species of extraterrestrials attempting to save their own kind by mingling with ours. There are stories out there of women being impregnated and the babies been taking from them by extraterrestrials with access to science capable of achieving such an act.

Manipulation

There are those that believe that humankind is being controlled by malevolent extraterrestrials that are bent on keeping people in the dark and ignorant as to who they are and where they are from. These beings, according to some, are controlling humanity and preventing them from becoming independent, spiritually aware, free thinkers.

Educating Humanity

It is believed that some extraterrestrials are here to educate humanity to the fact that we are not alone but are a part of a galactic community. They are believed to be doing so in several ways. They are believed to be using the media. They are said to have met with some government officials. They select individuals to disseminate information. They themselves are here in human form to educate the masses about their existence. They know that this is very important if humanity is to grow and join the galactic community. They also want to help prepare and arm us in case we come across a future foe. If so, we would need allies. President Reagan once made the statement, "I occasionally think how quickly our differences, worldwide, would vanish if we were facing an alien threat from outside this world." Some have wondered if this remark had a significant meaning to those in the know about such things. Could there be an unknown threat out there, and the extraterrestrials would like to assist us in preparing for it? Is that one of the reasons they are visiting? Are they keeping an eye on things, since they are obviously aware that we are defenseless against advanced technology and otherworldly armaments?

Observing Humanity's Progress

It could well be that advanced extraterrestrials are observing our progress in all areas of our lives. They may be watching to see how advanced we are in the areas of science and technology. Perhaps they are interested in where we stand on the subject and belief in other life in the universe. Perhaps they are watching too in an effort to learn when we will be ready for first contact. Former Israeli Space Security Chief Haim Eshed, a respected professor and retired general, in an interview that ran in Israel's *Yediot Aharonot* newspaper, informed the world that extraterrestrials exist, and they are waiting for humanity to progress before they tell the masses. Eshed stated, "The Unidentified Flying Objects have asked not to publish that they are here, humanity is not ready yet." Eshed also stated, "They have been waiting until today for humanity to develop and reach a stage where we will understand, in general, what space and spaceships are."

According to the article, Eshed was referring to the Galactic Federation. Given Eshed's prestigious past, many consider him to be a credible source and take his words seriously. Therefore, apparently the extraterrestrials do not believe that we are ready to know of their existence. How would they know that if they were not observing Earth? How are they observing us? Surely they have their own systems and advanced technologies to tune in to what's going on here. However, some speculate that they may have "ground troops" here too. This means extraterrestrials that are assigned to Earth and walking and living among us to observe our behavior, learn more about us and report back to galactic authorities. Once they determine that we are ready, perhaps they will decide if we are worthy of being invited into one of the federations. They may also be awaiting a time when we will be less violent, less volatile in our ways of living.

The Creators

It is hypothesized that the creators of humankind may be here observing their creations. The idea that humankind was created by advanced beings and placed on Earth has been circulated for thousands of years. It is being recognized today as a theory to be seriously considered. If true, then it may well be that they are here to watch our progress, even help and assist in our advancement and evolution, perhaps even performing DNA repairs. These might be the extraterrestrials that were initially mistaken as gods and came to Earth long ago to teach humanity how to establish civilization.

To Guard and Protect

There is a theory that in the universe new civilizations may be be under the protection of space councils and fall under their territories. There may be extraterrestrial sentries on Earth that have always been here, keeping us safe from predators, conquerors, asteroids, galactic wars and more. The Earth is a very important planet in the galaxy. It isn't just some random planet in our Solar System, where life accidentally developed. It and all life here is considered unique and special by those on other worlds. This may be due to what some consider to be the intricate and complex forms of life found here. Earth resembles a beautiful piece of artwork that took a great deal of contemplation, planning and time to create. This may be why there are so many tales of extraterrestrials visiting Earth in the past, and why there are so many accounts of UFOs seen today. This may also be the reason Earth may be under special protection, at least for now. This group of beings, I presume, may be on ships above Earth, remaining hidden until we are ready for open contact. These beings are thought by some to look for threats in Earth's vicinity. When they notice there is a danger to Earth, they neutralize it, for the most part without us noticing. For example, there have been tales of asteroids coming dangerously close to Earth with near misses that could have done a lot of damage to life here. In fact, there are some qho believe that the reason Earth is not struck by perilous objects from space more often is due to the assistance of benevolent extraterrestrials. Some reportedly have witnessed meteors exploding in the skies and witnessed a UFO nearby just after a meteor was blown to pieces.

In some cases, it is believed that extraterrestrials assisted Earth by pushing meteors and asteroids away from the planet. It appears that there is a group out there that has an interest in Earth's future.

Ownership of Earth

Earth may have a problem. It is one that is not always considered to be a possibility. There is the idea that there are beings that are so far advanced that they own parts of the galaxy, and they may own the Earth. There are stories and speculations of beings at war in the cosmos, and some who tell a tale of warring over the control of Earth. Could Earth be owned by another species of beings? Not only might there be beings that own the Earth, but some may also have a hand in some things that are going on here on the planet. Believe it or not, there is the idea that Earth may be under the control of unseen beings that have influence in our world. Humanity has not considered all the scenarios that could be at play when it comes to our planet. Earth, believe it or not, may be someone's real estate.

Are We Them?

The theories and speculations are endless as to why extraterrestrials may have come in ancient times and why they may still be here today. Perhaps the most important question is, *are we them?* Are the UFOs seen today controlled by extraterrestrials that placed a colony here long ago? In other words, did human beings come to Earth initially from another world, set up a colony and are now returning to see the result? Are we those colonists and if so, did have we forgotten who we are? Are those coming to Earth today in ship, returning to Earth to check in on their descendants?

Rescue of Other ETs

There are rumors of extraterrestrials that have crashed on Earth. It is often asked where these beings are now. Some have reportedly been killed. However, what becomes of the extraterrestrials that have survived? Could it be that there are stranded extraterrestrials on Earth? Worse yet, could it be that there are extraterrestrial beings being held on Earth? There is some speculation that this is the case. If so, both scenarios might warrant rescue attempts from otherworldly beings. Are there extraterrestrials existing here or being held on Earth and their people are here to locate and/or assist them?

Who's Who in the Galaxy?

So, who is who in the galaxy? What have we learned over all these years with the many purported cases of contact with extraterrestrials? This is perhaps the most shocking part of this book if you are new to the phenomenon. There are people that have come into contact with otherworldly beings as stated at the beginning of this chapter. In some case people have come forward and reported their experiences. Also, there are those that have been compiling such data. It is believed by many today that Earth is being visited by many different races of extraterrestrials. In some cases, these beings have been here physically, and in other cases they have contacted people through creative methods, such as dreams or telepathy. There are rumors and tales that in some cases otherworldly people have interacted with humanity. There are stories of people claiming to have seen UFOs in the skies and watched them land, with beings exiting these mysterious vehicles from the cosmos. There are tales of extraterrestrials having met with governments. The descriptions of these otherworldly people are many. So, what do we know about the extraterrestrials that have visited Earth in the past and that are possibly here now? Who is it that people claim to have seen or interacted with? Who is it that is controlling the UFOs in the skies?

What I have done in this chapter is introduce the ones we know something of. Over the years there have been descriptions from sightings, channelings, encounters, contacts, and more. Of course, we must take this information with a grain of salt. The beings here have allegedly either visited Earth sometime in the past, recently, or somewhere in between. Additionally, there has been talk about which group of extraterrestrials will be the first to officially make contact with humanity. It could be any of the groups below. Time will tell.

Obviously, when it comes to extraterrestrials, the information we have is very limited. However, in this journey of knowledge it is still prudent to look at the information that we allegedly have in attempting to understand our galactic origins. Examples of some of the most well-known extraterrestrial players in our galactic history follows:

__Aghartians__ (also Agharians)
Origin: Unknown

Life Span: Unknown

Current Location: Inner Earth. The Aghartians are an ancient race and, according to legend, established a kingdom-civilization inside the inner Earth eons ago. *Could the crystal city belong to them?*

Physical Features: If they are intraterrestrials and not extraterrestrials then it is believed they may have Asiatic features.

Communication: According to sources, they communicate via telepathy.

Science and Technology: They are superior in their technology in the areas of science and mathematics. They have time travel and teleportation devices.

Special Interests They can manipulate matter on a quantum level.

Earth Agenda and Concerns: They are said to have come to Earth to assist humankind in its advancement.

Universal Agenda: Unknown

Special Notes: They are one of the most well-known extraterrestrial groups out there. They are so popular that stories on them have been done in television shows including *The X-files* as well as *Stargate SG-1*. There is also the possibility that the Aghartians may be from Earth. There is a theory that they may be intraterrestrials from a group that created a civilization inside of Earth in pre-history.

Alpha-Draconians

Origin: Reptilian beings who established colonies in Alpha Draconis. The Alpha-Draconians claim to have originated on Earth (Terra) thousands of years ago. This is a belief that is said to be held by all reptilian races. For this reason, it is believed that Alpha-Draconians would like to take control of Earth.

Current Location: Alpha Draconis

Life Form Type: Reptilian

Physical Features: Reptilian

Characteristics: They are repeatedly referred to as the "bad guys." They have also been called an "abomination."

Belief System: Alpha-Draconians believe they are superior to all beings.

Science and Technology: Advanced

Spacecraft: Advanced. They have been traveling the universe for thousands of years.

Earth Agenda: They seek to control Earth.

Universal Agenda: They have the ambition to control the galaxy.

Special Notes: The Alpha-Draconians do not like human beings. According to a variety of sources about them, they would like to invade Earth. In fact, they would like to take over the galaxy. According to *The KGB Book of Alien Races*, "Being that Terrans have an inbred 'warrior' the Draconians do not want us to attain interstellar capabilities and therefore become a threat to their imperialistic agendas."

Andromedans
Origin: The Andromeda Galaxy
Current Location: Andromeda
Life span: Hundreds of years
Physical Features: Humanoid. Their appearance is almost exactly like human beings, except for having white to light blue skin. Their height ranges from five to eight feet tall.
Characteristics: Highly intelligent. Exceptionally healthy. They require very little sleep. They are generally a peaceful, content and happy people.
Communication: Andromedans are telepathic. When communicating they use symbols.
Social System: They are an ancient race with a vast civilization. They live under a one world government. Their society is crime free. They do not use money or a bartering system, as they do not pay for anything in their world.
Education System: Andromedans attend school from 120 to 150 years. Students are educated in science, technology, and the arts. Their education is comparable to the higher educational degrees on Earth.
Belief System: The Andromedans believe all races are equal. They view their life as an education, and as a means of bettering themselves with the goal of evolving.
Science and Technology: Highly Advanced. In science and technology Andromedans are approximately fifty thousand years ahead of us. They do not regard technology as something to be used as a means of defense.
Special Interests: Art and music (created differently than on Earth).
Earth Agenda and Concerns: The Andromedans are concerned about negative events on Earth, and how our behavior may affect the rest of the universe. They are in communication with certain people on Earth. These individuals are charged with disseminating

information to help prepare humanity for a change in the future.

Universal Agenda: They Andromedans desire a harmonious, peaceful existence for all beings in the universe.

Special Notes: Special thanks to Andromedan ambassador Alex Collier, from whom most of this information comes from.

The Anunnaki

Origin: The Planet Nibiru

Current Location: Nibiru and perhaps some other locations around the galaxy.

Lifespan: Their lifespan is extremely long. They are said to be able to reach up to 50,000 years and sometimes beyond.

Physical Features: The Anunnaki are believed to be a diverse race of humanoid beings. Skin tone, eye color, hair color and facial features vary. Some have been described as having a glow surrounding them. They are much taller than humans and can grow to be up to nine feet tall.

Social System: Their social system is that of a hereditary monarchy.

Science and Technology: Highly advanced. They have been traveling the cosmos for millennia.

Earth Agenda and Concerns: The Anunnaki are the beings that posed as gods in ancient Sumerian beliefs. According to Sumerian lore, they came from the stars and created mankind to act as a slave

Annunaki extraterrestrial gods depicted in Sumerian cylinder seals.

Annunaki extraterrestrial gods depicted in Sumerian cylinder seals.

race. The Sumerians were members of the world's first civilization that flourished, circa 3500 to 2000 BC, in the southern half of Mesopotamia. They spoke an agglutinative, ergative language that was unrelated to any other known language. The writing system that they established (cuneiform) was later borrowed by the Babylonians and Assyrians. The Anunnaki initially arrived on Earth approximately 450,000 years ago from the planet Nibiru (also known as the Tenth Planet and Planet X). They came in search of gold, which they located and mined in Africa. The planet Nibiru itself takes an elliptical path, reaching Earth every 3,600 years. They have been referred to as "gods," "angels," "the watchers," "the Nephilim," and more recently "extraterrestrials." According to lore, there was an argument between the leaders of the Anunnaki. Some wanted humans to have free will, to live their own lives and develop accordingly. Eventually, humans were released, and supposedly this is the reason that humans are free on Earth today. After a conflict among the Anunnaki elite over the future of mankind, the Anunnaki left Earth and returned to their home, the planet Nibiru.

Special Notes: According to legend, the Anunnaki will return to Earth via Nibiru, which some believe will travel near to Earth on its elliptical path in the near future (relatively speaking).

Arcturians

Origin: Arcturus, located in the constellation Alpha Bootes of the Milky Way Galaxy, some thirty-seven light years from Earth.
Current Location: Arcturus
Lifespan: They live to be between three hundred to four hundred

years of age.

Life Form Type: Humanoid

Physical Features: Arcturians can reach upwards from five to six feet tall. They each look very similar to one another. They are slender, have three fingers, and have green to blue skin. They have large, dark, almond shaped eyes. Their eyes are said to be able to see right through a person.

Characteristics: They are an ancient, very insightful, and perspicacious race of beings. They have a reputation for being the most kind and loving beings in the galaxy.

Communication: Arcturians are telepathic.

Social System: They are a peaceful, harmonious society.

Planet Characteristics: Arcturus is said to have lush foliage as well as oceans.

Belief System: They have a vast spiritual awareness. They operate from a place of love that is free from all negativities.

Science and Technology: Arcturians are highly advanced in the areas of science and technology. The renowned psychic Edgar Cayce once stated, "Arcturus is one of the most advanced civilizations in our entire galaxy." Their starships are said to be highly sophisticated and are some of the most advanced in the universe. They have interstellar capabilities and are adept at time travelling.

Special Interests: Vibrational and energy healing techniques.

Earth Agenda and Concerns: The Arcturians are on a mission to assist humanity in its evolutionary advancement. Those that are located within Earth's vicinity are said to be on a gigantic mothership. From there they help humans in their understanding of the universe; however, they do not interfere with our free will. The Arcturians are also acting as protectors of Earth by warding off negative extraterrestrials who would otherwise overtake earth with their advanced spaceships. The Arcturians have transmitted a special message to humans in the form of a book. They channeled this information through Dr. Norma Milanovich who wrote the book *We, The Arcturians*. In an article from the popular website anomalien.com, titled "The Arcturians—The Most Evolved Alien Species in Our Galaxy and Earth's Wardens," it states, "The Arcturians have built bases on our planet, particularly in secluded mountainous regions, but also on the surface of the Moon. From these strategic spots they carry out important operations where they revitalize Earth's energy points that have gone inactive."

Universal Agenda: Peace and unity in the galaxy.

Special Notes: Many Arcturians had contact with the people of ancient India, as well as the Native American tribes. It appears that they can be counted as one of Earth's allies and friends.

Bellatricians

Origin: The Bellatricians are said to have migrated from the constellation of Sagittarius approximately twenty-five million years ago to the constellation of Orion.

Current Location: The Bellatricians are in the constellation of Orion. Their world is found just to the right and above the Belt of Orion. The Bellatricians home is 112.5 light-years from Earth.

Lifespan: Unknown

Life Form Type: Dinoid-Reptoid hybrid

Physical Features: They are described as being bipedal, with shiny scaly skin that comes in a variety of colors. The scales are said to closely resemble those of a crocodile. There is a prominent boney crest that circles the top of the head. There is also a smaller crest that extends up the middle of their back, connecting to the one on top of the head. Their eyes look similar to those of the reptiles on earth, and can be either a lackluster yellow or red. They have wide mouths that extend from one side of the head to the next, extremely thin lips, and sharp teeth. The nose is small, with ears resembling that of a frog. They have long slim arms with slender hands and six long sharply clawed fingers. They have five toes that are also clawed. They have a tail that reaches to their feet. The males are smaller in stature than the females. Their height ranges from eight to 10 feet tall. Their sleep requirement is between five and eight hours a day.

Characteristics: They are said to be a somber, very serious race of beings, and lacking in humor. However, they are known for being highly proficient when it comes to matters of diplomacy. They also excel in the roles of management and governance.

Communication: When speaking, their voices sound rough and coarse, with a deep throaty tone. They also hiss and snarl as they talk.

Science and Technology: Advanced

Spacecraft: Their craft are in the shape of a dew drop. They range from 100 to 400 feet in length. The mothership can be up to 400 miles long. The shape of a mothership has been likened to that of a tadpole.

Earth Agenda and or Concerns: Unknown
Universal Agenda: To bring about change for the good in the Milky Way Galaxy and the universe.
Special Notes: One account talks about the Bellatricians once having worked very closely with Alpha-Draconians. It is said that the Bellatricians seek to make restitution for their evil acts committed in the past.

The Carians

Origin: The Carians are the most ancient extraterrestrial race in our universe. They incarnated into our universe when it was first created and are known as the "master race."
Current Location: The Orion constellation
Lifespan: Unknown
Life Form Type: Humanoid
Physical Features: Originally etheric, the Carians took on the form of a humanoid, but with the face of a bird. They are extremely tall and grow to be somewhere around 12-13 feet tall. **Characteristics:** Carians are highly intellectual beings with a tranquil demeanor, avoiding wars and conflict. They excel in science and philosophy.
Universal Agenda: To travel and explore other worlds.
Special Notes: None

Lyrans

Origin: Lyrans are a serene extraterrestrial race that originated in the Lyra constellation on Vega, the brightest-shining star in the area, and one of the brightest stars visible from Earth. Lyrans are said to be the root race of all humanoid races within the Milky Way galaxy. They played a unique role in the creation of humanity. They are an ancient race believed to have eventually colonized other worlds millions of years ago.
Current Location: Lyra constellation and various areas through the Milky Way galaxy. In fact, it is thought that due to their great age, it is unlikely that any first-generation Lyrans still exist, due to their migrating and colonizing different worlds.
Lifespan: Unknown
Life Form Type: Humanoid
Physical Features: The Lyrans that people are most aware of look similar to a cat. They have yellow, green, or blue eyes, with huge pupils. Their muzzles are short and round. Their ears look like those of lions on Earth. Their bodies are tall with slender,

sometimes muscular, bodies, with skin ranging from light to dark. Their hair is typically light brown or white. They are covered with fur which, according to sources, ranges from gold to reddish brown, and sometimes white. They have tails like that of a lion. They are rather flashy as they enjoy wearing ornate clothing.

Characteristics: They are described as an extremely intelligent race. Even though they are known to be peaceful, there are some factions of them that can be quite ruthless.

Earth Agenda and Concerns: Unknown

Universal Agenda: Unknown

Special Notes: None

Nommos

Origin: The Nommos came from the Sirius system.

Current Location: Their home world is a planet in the Sirius star system.

Life span: Unknown

Life Form Type: Amphibious

Physical Features: They are amphibious beings with the ability to exist on land and in water. They prefer water to land, due to their fish-like tails, which work better in water. However, many of them walk upright.

Characteristics: They are known for their highly advanced use of sound.

Planet Characteristics: Warm aquamarine colored water.

Spacecraft: They landed on Earth in a ship that made a spinning decent when landing.

Earth Agenda and or Concerns: The Nommos came to Earth thousands of years ago and gave advanced information to a tribe of people known as the Dogon.

Universal Agenda: Unknown

Special Notes: None

Nordics

Origin: Pleiades star system

Current Location: Pleiades star system

Lifespan: Unknown

Life Form Type: Humanoid

Physical Features: The Nordics have been described as being very tall and blond, with slanted or almond-shaped blue eyes, with fair skin to a tanned complexion. They are said to be very beautiful and are nearly identical to human beings. Some grow to be up to 12 feet in height.

Characteristics: They are said to be quiet and not very communicative. They are "caretakers," and have only the best intentions. In other words, they are benevolent extraterrestrial people.

Science and Technology: Advanced

Spacecraft: We have at least one story of a rather vague description of a Nordic spaceship sighting. An interesting tale involving the Nordics can be found in the book *Extraordinary Encounters* by Jerome Clark. There Clark writes about an incident involving a farmer that happened several years ago near Linha Vista, Brazil. As the farmer was in the field, he saw what he described as a mysterious spacecraft that was "shaped like a tropical helmet," sitting stationary in the sky. It was so close that he was able to observe a male figure inside of the craft. He also saw someone (an extraterrestrial) standing nearby and realized that another was walking toward him. The farmer was so surprised that he dropped a gardening tool that he was holding. The extraterrestrial appeared friendly, smiling at the farmer as he retrieved the tool and gave it to him. The two extraterrestrials then entered the craft and flew away. What is interesting in this account, besides the obvious experience, is the description of the spacecraft as well as the extraterrestrials that was later given by the farmer. In his report, he described them as having long blond hair, slanted eyes and wearing "brown coveralls." It is interesting that they simply appeared to be observing the farmer, were friendly toward him, and were quiet. The description matched that of the Nordics.

Earth Agenda and Concerns: The Nordics have informed contactees that they are here to observe humanity. They apparently find us to be fascinating due to our individuality, and our determination when it comes to achieving our goals.

Universal Agenda: Unknown

Special Notes: The Nordics have sometimes been seen in abductions along with the Grays. However, those who observed them in these circumstances have indicated that they were in a more authoritative position than the Grays. What's more is that there are those that believe that Nordics are hybrids. It has been stated regarding the Grays that some of them are working in a hybrid program, and that is why humans have been abducted. Could there be a connection? In any event, Nordics appear to be the real deal when it comes to extraterrestrials visiting and or perhaps with some even living on Earth in an experimental or work capacity for their own world.

In an interesting statement, author David McCready in his book *Real Alien Worlds: A Brief Encyclopedia* says on page 209, "Nordics are a good example of how earthly human beings are not the only species to have generally human appearance. Thus, demonstrating that in many ways, earthly human beings have been evolved so as to achieve a relatively common humanoid appearance." Even though this is a side issue, it shows us how humankind may have been developed to resemble other beings in the universe. We are not the first group of humanoids. We are designed to look and be humanoid.

Pleiadians
Origin: Pleiades star system
Current Location: Pleiades star system
Lifespan: Unknown
Life Form Type: Humanoid
Physical Features: The Pleiadians are described as closely resembling Earth's blonde Vikings. Tall, slender, and fit, they look very similar to the extraterrestrial race of beings known as the Nordics.
Characteristics: The Pleiadian civilization is one that is made up of peace-loving, spiritual people.
Science and Technology: Highly Advanced
Spacecraft: They are highly advanced in technology and are adept at interplanetary space travel. They have sleek, state-of-the-art spacecraft referred to as *Beamships* that enable them to travel swiftly through the cosmos. The Pleiadeans also travel via hyperspace allowing them to reach their destination in a short period of time. Pleiadean ships come in different sizes and are used according to the need, destination, or assignment.
Earth Agenda and Concerns: They have been in contact with Earth for a very long time. It is said that they look so like humans that one could be standing next to them and not realize it. President Eisenhower is believed to have met with the Pleiadians, who are interested in humans achieving peace on Earth.
Universal Agenda: Peace in the galaxy
Special Notes: The Pleiadians channeled information through Barbara Marciniak. It was published in a book titled *Bringers of*

the Dawn: Teachings from the Pleiadians (1992).

Sassani (also known as the Shakani). Their name means, "living light."
Origin: The planet Essassani (approximately 500 light-years from Earth near the Orion constellation)
Current Location: The planet Essassani
Reproduction: Created
Lifespan: Approximately 300 years
Life Form Type: Humanoid
Physical Features: The Sassani are said to be a hybrid race comprised of human and Gray alien DNA. The Sassani are described as being around five feet tall, with a light gray skin tone. Their eyes are large and almond shaped, with some being upturned, with nearly always grey irises. They have very large pupils which makes their eyes look completely dark or black. They have large heads, and very slim bodies that are similar to the Grays. Generally, the males do not have hair, while the females reportedly have light colored to white hair. However, being that they are a mixed race, some also resemble humans with hair and eyes that are closer matching those of humankind.
Communication: They once used an ancient language, combined with some Earth languages, however, they eventually evolved to using telepathy.
Social System: They live in a serene, nonviolent world. They reportedly exist in the fifth dimension.
Belief System: The Sassani are known to be a spiritual, enlightened race of beings, that exist in peace, harmony, and love.
Earth Agenda and Concerns: They use channeling to communicate with certain humans on Earth to assist in humanity's spiritual development, and the Earth's ascension.
Universal Agenda: Unknown
Special Notes: The Sassani allegedly were created out of necessity, due to the Grays inability to reproduce. The Grays lost the ability after performing genetic experimentation on themselves, and instead began a cloning program to save the species. Authors Note: This may explain the alien abductions and the physical exams). Much of this information about the Sassani comes from Bashar, a being that is channeled by Darryl Anka (with some additional information coming from Elan and Kayel).

237

Tall Whites

Origin: Unknown

Current Location: Unknown

Lifespan: Their lifespan can reach up to 800 years.

Life Form Type: Humanoid

Physical Features: They have white hair, are tall and slender, with a chalky white skin tone. The way in which they walk is different from humans. This is due to them coming from a world with a stronger gravity pull. They normally wear aluminized jumpsuits that are made to allow them to levitate. The suits are described as being white with a glowing effect.

Characteristics: The Tall Whites are highly intelligent. They are said to be able to process data more speedily than humans. They have weak, brittle bones. If injured, they need to return to their planet rather quickly to heal.

Communication: They communicate via telepathy. They are adept at telekinesis.

Planet Characteristics: They are said to come from a planet that is exceedingly warmer than Earth, where the days are longer. Their sleep pattern is different from humans. They generally sleep for a period of two Earth days, followed by being awake for nearly the same amount of time.

Science and Technology: Highly Advanced

Spacecraft: They are highly advanced in their technology with ships said to travel over 8,000 miles per hour.

Special Interests: Although we do not know why, they have a strong interest in Arcturus. It has been observed that Arcturus, for some reason, is extremely important to them.

Earth Agenda and or Concerns: The Tall Whites were featured in books by retired Air Force weather observer Dr. Charles Hall, who claims they at one time had bases and operated out of Neveda. Apparently, in the 1960s the Tall Whites were taking part in the technology transfer program. Hall states that he had interactions with them in the mid 1960's while working out of the former Nellis Air Force Base, now Creech AFB in Indian Springs, NV. His story was also told in the documentary *Walking with the Tall Whites*.

According to sources, the Tall Whites have been visiting Earth for approximately 3,000 years. This is especially relevant information given the history between humans and Tall White extraterrestrial visitors. Reportedly, tall, white-haired beings were seen in history by various groups all over Africa prior to the appearance of the Europeans. African peoples were so familiar with these beings that they thought the Europeans were these extraterrestrials revisiting them. This is said also to have happened with the people of Central America when Cortes and his Spanish invasion party reached there in 1519. These could be the same beings. They may also have been mistaken for Nordics, who have a very similar look.

Universal Agenda: Unknown

Special Notes: One of the most interesting pieces of information when it comes to describing the Tall Whites is the fact that they are exceedingly weary of humans and avoid them if possible. Most of the information given here is from Dr. Charles Hall's experiences with the Tall Whites.

Yahyel

Origin: The Yahyel are descendants from the Lyran family of extraterrestrial races.

Current Location: Unknown

Reproduction: The birthing process. Pregnancies last from seven-eight months.

Lifespan: 300 years

Life Form Type: Humanoid

Physical Features: The Yahyel are humanoid in appearance and are reportedly genetically related to humanity. As a result, they consider humans to be their relatives. They are said to look very much like humans, perhaps more than any other humanoid race in the galaxy. They are described as having large eyes, with irises that come in a variety of colors. They have tiny ears, slender lips, and only four toes. On average they grow to reach five feet in height. They are a diverse race with varying hues of skin tone, as well as a variety of hair and eye shades.

Characteristics: They are younger than humanity, yet very intelligent and highly spiritual.

Communication: They are telepathic.

Social System: The Yahyel appreciate living life to the fullest.

Planet Characteristics: They live on two planets that are like Earth. However, they have never shared their names or locations in the cosmos with contactees though they have said their home worlds are quite close in interstellar travel to Earth.

Belief System: The Yahyel value harmony, balance, and inner peace as the driving cultural influence behind their civilization.

Science and Technology: They are highly advanced in technology. The Yahyel are said to be careful not to allow their technology to do damage to their world.

Earth Agenda and or Concerns: Out of all the aliens that interact with Earth and possess affection for humanity, the Yahyel are probably the foremost in that category.

Special Notes: Purportedly, it was the Yahyel that were responsible for the "Phoenix Lights" UFO sighting that took place on March 13, 1997 in Phoenix, Arizona, which they are said to have claimed responsibility for. Thousands of people witnessed that event. It is said that this was a friendly way of the Yahyel to introduce themselves, as it has been speculated that out of all of the extraterrestrial groups out there, the Yahyel will be the ones to make first contact with humanity. Their huge display in 1997 has convinced some ufologists that this is a possibility. It is said to be their intention to eventually share with us our galactic history and our origins. They may also be using telepathic abilities to connect with humanity in a sharing of information.

The Zetans (or Zetas)

Origin: Zeta Reticuli star system. They are better known as the Grays. They have a history of contact with Earth going back approximately 60 years (although this author feels that that can be debated). They have been linked to most of the alien abduction experiences reported around the world.

Current Location: Zeta Reticuli

Lifespan: Unknown

Life Form Type: Humanoid

Physical Features: They are described as gray-skinned, short, thin-limbed, slight-bodied, with large hairless heads and large almond-shaped black eyes with no pupils; they have just a slit for a mouth. Their ears are described as a small lump on each side of the head. For clothing, they wear what appears to be tight fitting silver or light blue jumpsuits with a high neck. One interesting note about the Zetans is that they are said not to have any lungs. Therefore, they do not require an atmosphere in order to live. It has also been stated that they have no digestive system.

Characteristics: They are said to be emotionless creatures, lacking in spirituality. They are also believed to be superior in intellect.

Science and Technology: They are believed to be advanced in technology and science, with time travel capabilities.

Spacecraft: They have been seen operating disc-shaped spacecraft.
Earth Agenda and Concerns: They are often seen by witnesses in alien abductions. There is a theory that the reason the Zetans abduct humans is due to the human DNA, which they are believed to be using in repairing their genetic material. They are also believed by some to be manipulating the destiny of humanity through time travel, attempting to change historical events. It has been said that they are humans from the future. This of course could be a deceptive ruse.

Universal Agenda: Unknown
Special Notes: One of the most famous abduction cases involved that of Betty and Barney Hill, a couple who were abducted in the 1960s by the Zetans, and whose case has been well-documented. Betty Hill was shown a star map by the Zetans that abducted her and her husband. This was to show Betty where they were from. Hill later drew a map of Zeta Reticuli when relaying their abduction experience. The Zetas, also referred to as "gray aliens," have become the archetype for extraterrestrial life.

The Watchers
Quis custodiet ipsos custodes? (Who Watches the Watchers?)
   One of my favorite *Star Trek* episodes dealt with the issue of humans (in this case the *Star Trek* crew) being mistaken by the primitive people of the planet Mintaka III for gods. For me, this episode is apropos to mention in this book. The Latin term, "Quis custodiet ipsos custodes?" means, "Who Watches the Watchers?" This is also the title of the episode. In this installment of *Star Trek the Next Generation* (Season 3, Episode 4), the *Enterprise* crew is scrambling to repair the damage caused by people of a Bronze Age level of development seeing them, and their technology, and mistaking them for gods. This is a similar scenario to what occurred on Earth, where extraterrestrials came and, due to their advanced technology, they too were mistaken for gods. Descriptions of these beings are found throughout history. Some may have been accidentally discovered, as was the case in the *Star Trek* episode, while others may have intentionally outed themselves and enjoyed the worship bestowed upon them by naïve humans. Others intearcted with the people, coming to Earth to help humans to progress and develop. It appears that in the beginning there were possibly the seeder/creators of humanity here to watch over us,

perhaps to protect us from threatening malevolent civilizations. Then, too, there is the famous account of the Anunnaki that, according to Sumerian law, created humanity as a slave race and set us free eventually for our own good and to have free will. That, according to legend, did not occur without a fight among members of the leadership of that extraterrestrial culture.

Once humanity was free (if that creation story turns out to be true), or if we were placed here via some other means such as planet seeding, either way, humanity was on its own, Free to develop as they pleased. It is at this point where other races of beings may have come in, or some of the Anunnaki may never have left. Either way, eventually extraterrestrials came to this planet and interacted with a "free will" society of humans.

It appears that humanity is being watched by someone. We always have been. Did all of the extraterrestrials from the beginning truly leave? Are they among us, watching, remaining hidden? As in the case of our ancient past, it appears that they are slowly being outed. Some are good. Some not so much. So, I ask, "Who Watches the Watchers?"

Imperceptible Beings

It is said that the human eye can only see between 430-770-Thz. Our ears can only detect sound between 20Hz-20Khz. These ranges make up a fraction of the total sound and light frequency range. This means there is a lot going on around us that we cannot see or hear. If so, this means that there could be extraterrestrial beings around us, and we would not know it. This author believes that is the case. It is believed that some of the extraterrestrials are ethereal in their makeup and therefore naturally invisible to us. Others are able to use a technology that enables them to hide themselves. This may explain many things going on around the planet. People tend to put every experience with the unseen world under the umbrella of ghosts. Given that our universe is filled with life, there is the distinct possibility that we are being visited by extraterrestrials that are possibly naturally invisible to us or have the ability to cloak themselves. They may be here and freely moving among us, studying us, and we have no idea. This may also explain some of the channeling going on between humans and extraterrestrials. They may not be on some distant planet or cloaked ship, as some believe. They may be right here relaying (hopefully) benevolent messages to humans. As we progress with science and technology, there is a possibility that if they have the capability to be invisible to us, they may be relaying information to us telepathically, and we are not aware of it.

This does sound a lot like science fiction. However, a lot of what we see in science fiction becomes reality. As I have stated before, extraterrestrials may be using the media to reach us, convey information, give us a view of what extraterrestrials may be like. Not to mention space travel, the cosmos and other relevant information we should know before they make an official appearance on Earth. I recall a *Star Trek* original series episode titled "Wink of an Eye," in which captain Kirk and crew are consistently hearing a buzzing in their ears. Eventually, the captain is changed, and he is then able to see people around him that had been invisible and causing complications on the ship. This is something similar to what could be happening today. It could have been happening all along. The following is dialog from "Wink of an Eye":

Kirk: What have you done?

Alien Woman: Changed you. Your crew cannot see us, or any of us because of the acceleration. We move in the wink of an eye. Oh, there is a scientific explanation for it. All that really matters is that you can see me and talk to me…You are accelerated far beyond their power to see. So, they will go on without you.

That episode of *Star Trek* is intriguing because in my metaphysical studies I learned that we are energy and vibrating. It has been said that for us to see those on the "other side," in order for someone that has "passed on" to show themselves, they have to slow their vibration. This is what is going on in "Wink of an Eye." Is this what some extraterrestrials must do to make themselves seen to us? Even more interestingly, is what we refer to as a "soul" really an "extraterrestrial body?"

Also, there is the cloaking technology. According to some science fiction shows, there is technology that can hide not only people, but objects as large as motherships. This is believed by ufologists today to be occurring with some of the UFOs seen in the skies in these modern times. One moment the UFOs are there, and the next moment they disappear, presumably by some through cloaking technology.

Born Ins

In my anomalous studies (ufology, metaphysics and more), I have heard that there is technology and science that may allow a being from another dimension to enter a world in human form, or a form other than what they were before they arrived. Some refer to these beings as "born in." This is perhaps one of the most startling theories about extraterrestrials and Earth's connection. Those that are "born in" come to Earth to assist humankind, or simply to experience life here, or to fulfill a mission. I first encountered this idea through researcher and author Scott Mandelker and his book, aptly titled, *From Elsewhere*. It was a startling, eye-opening book. Here Mandelker had based his thesis on the idea that there were extraterrestrials that had been born into human form and living on Earth. In the process of writing this book he interviewed several people that gave their thoughts and experiences of being an extraterrestrial in human form. Some remembered who they were and had known their entire lives. Some awakened later in life and remembered that they were, simply put, aliens from other worlds. Some had had contact experiences where they were made aware of who they were. As far out as that may sound to many, let me remind you that we have no idea what the "soul," ("astral body," "light body," or whatever name is familiar to you) really is, nor where it comes from. We only know that it is there. That part we have established. It exists.

The born ins may also be the Lightworkers and Starseeds that we hear so much about. Also, the indigo children. All are born in and claim to have come here for a purpose. There are also the walk-in extraterrestrials that exchange souls for the use of a body for the same purposes as born in extraterrestrials.

The Black Knight Satellite (The All-Seeing Eye)

Lastly, in wrapping up this chapter, I would like to talk about humanity being monitored. Some question whether we are being monitored by extraterrestrials and if so, when will this come to fruition? In our galactic history, humanity has been watched. We do not yet know by whom, but there is a preponderance of evidence that we have seen, perhaps through extraterrestrial reconnaissance missions or perhaps they send probes. Maybe both. In the case of what is known as "The Black Knight Satellite," there is speculation that this enormous object that has been witnessed and photographed in space may be a probe sent from a group of extraterrestrials intent on gaining information about Earth. It is so interesting that I thought I would share a bit of information about it here. I should note that this object has posed no threat and is thought by some to be ancient. It is a fascinating object.

In 1953, an American astronomer by the name of Dr. Lincoln La Paz of the University of New Mexico, a pioneer in the study of meteors, spotted a mysterious object orbiting the Earth. After this, there were others who reported seeing something strange in space, and it was discovered that it was the same object as seen by Dr. La Paz. It was then that the U.S. Department of Defense got involved and assigned a well-known astronomer by the name of Clyde W. Tombaugh to investigate the anomalous oddity. Tombaugh was most famous at the time for his discovery of Pluto in 1930. The anomalous object was eventually dubbed the "Black Knight." Today it is known as the Black Knight Satellite, but as some call it "the all-seeing eye." Little is known about the findings of Tombaugh. However, the mysterious object was photographed in December 1957 by Dr. Luis Corralos of the Communications Ministry in Venezuela as he was taking pictures of *Sputnik II* (the Russian satellite) as it passed over Caracas. It was astonishing that the Black Knight had actually been photographed. These were the first pictures of this otherworldly, extraterrestrial object. Officials believed the Black Knight was tracking the Russian satellite, and this is how Dr. Corralos managed to get it in pictures.

The Black Knight was seen again in 1960 by one of the stations that formed the American Air Force Space Surveillance System (the U.S. Navy's dark fence radar system). They detected the object in polar orbit around the Earth and noted that it possibly weighted as much as 15 tons. The world knew that neither the United States nor Russia had the ability to produce a craft of this magnitude during that period in history. The scientists were baffled. This object was larger and heavier than anything capable of being launched with 1960 rockets. They knew that it shouldn't exist, and it certainly should not have been in space in polar orbit, however, there it was! This huge, black, mysterious object sent panic through the United States and Soviet militaries. Officials were scrambling for more information on what it was and what it was doing there. Was it a threat to Earth? This may have been the one time when the two sides may have potentially been working together. Both sides knew that neither of them could place a craft or anything of the kind into a polar orbit. Each country also realized that neither had the ability to launch something that was projected to be 15 tons! This was a technology that was years away from the most powerful countries on the planet. If it didn't belong to the U.S. or the Russians, then whose was it? The reality of the situation must have been very disturbing to the officials. As far as we know today, the Black Knight Satellite is still out there. Is it recording events on Earth? Does it keep a record of our galactic history? Who sent it? Inquiring minds want to know!

Chapter Ten
Extraordinary Experiences
in Space

You need nerves of steel if climbing aboard a rocket is
your career path.
—Kathleen Rubins

We have seen in this book that extraterrestrial and UFO phenomena
are found all over Earth. In the skies, on the land, in the seas and
quite possibly inside the Earth. Since it really does appear that
they are everywhere, one wonders what the only people that have
travelled to space may have encountered. Did extraterrestrials try
to contact Earth's very own space people during their missions? In
our short voyages to space, did they try to interact with or make the
astronauts aware of them? While that question cannot be answered
definitively, I can say that there are some things that have been seen
and heard out there that defy explanation. Earth's space travelers
from space agencies around the world have reported mysterious
sightings and strange incidents while working in space (and at
times while in Earth's skies). It is interesting to look at some of the
reports from those who have traveled to the heavensand hear their
experiences. The following are some of the extraordinary events
that happened during humanity's journeys to space.

NASA Programs
NASA astronauts have observed interesting, unusual, and
often baffling phenomena as they went about their missions. Ever
since the first astronaut went up, these pioneers have met the
inexplicable. The following are a few examples of what they have
experienced in space.

Project Mercury—*Mercury-Atlas 6*
Project Mercury was the first human spaceflight program of
NASA. It ran from 1958 until 1963. *Mercury-Atlas 6* was the first
manned American orbital spaceflight mission. It commenced on

February 20, 1962 and was piloted by John Glenn. While aboard *Mercury-Atlas 6*, Glenn found himself in a unique situation. One that he could not have predicted. While in space, he suddenly found the craft surrounded by thousands of small, lighted objects. Dazzled, perplexed and amazed at what he was seeing, he described them as "little stars." He said that they came by in "showers." He stated that they were luminescent, small (less than a 16th of an inch), and were traveling at a slow rate of around five miles an hour. These enigmatic objects seemed to be attracted to the craft. One wonders if they were a biological being interested in investigating the ship. They stayed with the craft for a time. It did not appear to be something random that Glenn ran into. For all we know it could have been a type of extraterrestrial,1 or even probes.

(*Author's Note*: The same type of phenomenon was also described by contactee George Adamski in the early 1950s. In his book *Flying Saucers Have Landed*, Adamski writes of going on board an extraterrestrial mothership that was as large as a traveling city. At 50,000 miles from Earth, Adamski looked out into space through one of the windows. He described space as being totally dark. Yet in the mist of the blackness, he saw what looked to be billions upon billions of small lights moving about. He observed that they were in a variety of colors and flicking and moving about in many directions. Adamski likened the phenomenon to watching a cosmic show of fireworks. Could both men have encountered the same phenomenon?)

Project Gemini—*Gemini 7*

Project Gemini was NASA's second manned spaceflight program. It operated between the Mercury and Apollo projects. The program was a continuation of preparing for future trips to the Moon. Project Gemini began functioning in 1961, reaching completion in 1966. The Project Gemini spacecraft team consisted of two astronauts. The *Gemini 7* mission was the fourth mission under the Project Gemini program. The *Gemini 7* mission objective was to prove that human beings could survive in a weightless environment for that length of time. *Gemini 7* was in space for 14 days and made 206 orbits. Launching on December 4, 1965, onboard were astronauts Frank Borman and James Lovell Jr. It was during the second orbit that Borman and Lovell encountered the unexpected—a large UFO, and strange smaller particles near the spacecraft. Lovell contacted Mission Control in Cape Kennedy to inform them that they were seeing mysterious objects outside of the capsule. When asked if they were seeing the booster rocket, Lovell responded that they saw not only the booster rocket, but several other objects as well.

In his book *Our Mysterious Spaceship Moon*, ufologist Don Wilson expressed concern over the mysterious sighting the astronauts had during their time aboard *Gemini 7*. States Wilson, "there are three visual sightings made by the astronauts while in orbit which, in the judgment of the writer, have not been adequately explained." One of those sightings was reported by Frank Borman. Wilson writes, "Gemini 7, astronaut Borman saw what he referred to as a 'bogey' flying in formation with the spacecraft." The UFO incident involving *Gemini 7* was described by a NASA spokesperson as "one of the biggest puzzlers" and "certainly…unusual and unexpected." It is clear that whoever was operating the UFO had an interest in our craft.

Gordon Cooper, Mercury-Atlas 9 and Gemini 5

Former astronaut Gordon Cooper first worked as an Air Force test pilot and later for NASA as an astronaut where he flew on the *Mercury-Atlas 9* and *Gemini 5* missions. During his career, Cooper had several UFO sightings. These experiences had a profound effect on him. He felt the necessity to share them with others. Cooper believed the world has a right to know about UFOs. In 1957, he was one of the top test pilots working at Edwards Air Force Base in California. He oversaw several high tech projects. One such project was the installation of a precision landing system. It was during this assignment that Cooper witnessed something extraordinary. He saw an extraterrestrial spacecraft that landed. Cooper had a camera crew videotaping the installation, when they saw the saucer shaped craft. Cooper described it as shimmering, silver, and smooth. It was approximately 30 feet long. The crew first videotaped the craft as it hovered above. The men watched as the ship displayed landing gear and sat down on a dry lakebed. The camera crew slowly made their way toward the craft, until they evidently came too close, because at that point the ship left in a hurry. The encounter lasted just a few moments. Cooper let the authorities in Washington know what had happened. He turned the film over to the officials. Afterward, according to Cooper, he never saw it or heard about it again. About this incident, Cooper was quoted as saying, "A saucer flew right over us, put down three landing gears, and landed out on the dry lake. The cameramen went out there with their cameras toward the UFO… There was no doubt in my mind that it was made someplace other than on this earth."

According to Cooper, when he was still a pilot for the Air Force he was shocked to witness an armada of UFOs. A quote from Cooper states, "I did have an occasion in 1951 to have two days of observation of many flights of them; they were of different sizes, flying in fighter formation, generally from east to west over Europe." He also stated, "Several days in a row we sighted groups of metallic, saucer-shaped vehicles at great altitudes over the base in Germany, 1951, and we tried to get close to them, but they were able to change direction faster than our fighters." About that period, Cooper also stated, "While flying with several other USAF pilots over Germany in 1957, we sighted numerous radiant flying discs above us. We couldn't tell how high they were. We couldn't get anywhere near their altitude." Some years later, Cooper had another UFO experience. This occurred in 1963, while he was inside the *Mercury-Atlas 9* capsule. He witnessed a glowing, green object, shaped like a sphere that seemed to be moving intentionally toward his capsule. His sighting was confirmed when he contacted the tracking station, which was able to locate it on radar.

Cooper famously wrote a letter to the United Nations regarding his concerns about UFOs:

> November 9, 1978
>
> Ambassador Griffith
> Mission of Grenada to the United Nations
> 866 Second Avenue
> Suite 502
> New York, New York 10017
>
> Dear Ambassador Griffith:
>
> I wanted to convey to you my views on our extra-terrestrial visitors popularly referred to as "UFO's", and suggest what might be done to properly deal with them.
> I believe that these extra-terrestrial vehicles and their crews are visiting this planet from other planets,

which obviously are a little more technically advanced than we are here on earth. I feel that we need to have a top level, coordinated program to scientifically collect and analyze data from all over earth concerning any type of encounter, and to determine how best to interface with these visitors in a friendly fashion. We may first have to show them that we have learned to resolve our problems by peaceful means, rather than warfare, before we are accepted as fully qualified universal team members. This acceptance would have tremendous possibilities of advancing our world in all areas. Certainly then it would seem that the UN has a vested interest in handling this subject properly and expeditiously.

I should point out that I am not an experienced UFO professional researcher. I have not yet had the privilege of flying a UFO, nor of meeting the crew of one. I do feel that I am somewhat qualified to discuss them since I have been into the fringes of the vast areas in which they travel. Also, I did have occasion in 1951 to have two days of observation of many flights of them, of different sizes, flying in fighter formation, generally from east to west over Europe. They were at a higher altitude than we could reach with our jet fighters of that time.

I would also like to point out that most astronauts are very reluctant to even discuss UFO's due to the great numbers of people who have indiscriminately sold fake stories and forged documents abusing their names and reputations without hesitation. Those few astronauts who have continued to have a participation in the UFO field have had to do so very cautiously. There are several of us who do believe in UFO's and who have had occasion to see a UFO on the ground, or from an airplane. There was only one occasion from space which may have been a UFO.

If the UN agrees to pursue this project, and to lend their credibility to it, perhaps many more well qualified people will agree to step forth and provide help and information.

I am looking forward to seeing you soon.

Sincerely,

L. Gordon Cooper

Col. USAF (ret)

Astronaut

The Apollo Program

The Apollo Program was NASA's third spaceflight program. It succeeded in its goal of landing people on the Moon.

Apollo 7

Apollo 7 was the first manned flight in the Apollo program. The Apollo program had been put on hold due to a cabin fire that had sadly taken the lives of the three *Apollo 1* astronauts, Virgil I. Grissom, Edward H. White II, and Roger B. Chaffee. *Apollo 7* launched on October 11, 1968. The crew consisted of Commander Walter Schirra Jr.; Lunar Module Pilot R. Walter Cunningham; and Command Module Pilot Donn F. Eisele. Reportedly, the *Apollo 7* crew took photographs that showed a large unidentified flying object that has been variously described as "angelic," "beautiful," "large" and metallic." It is speculated that whatever the mysterious object was, it was made by highly intelligent beings that are far more advanced than mankind. UFO proponents believe that the Earth's space programs are being watched, and that extraterrestrials are especially interested in humanity's progress into space. When looking at the photograph, the craft appears to be hovering in space as if *Apollo 7* was being observed. It is interesting that it was there just as the first Apollo mission went up. A coincidence?

Apollo 8

Apollo 8 commenced on December 21, 1968. Its goal was lunar orbit. The team consisted of Commander Frank Borman, Lunar Module Pilot William Anders and Command Module Pilot James Lovell. During the mission, surprising and mysterious incidents occurred. While in space the men were perplexed to see a fast-moving, circular shaped UFO near their craft. The UFO emitted a light that was so spectacular, and so brilliant, that they could scarcely see inside their own craft. As the UFO passed by, their capsule pitched and yawed, causing the astronauts to nearly lose control of it. One fascinating, thought-provoking aspect of what happened is that at one point, the astronauts heard peculiar, garbled noises coming from the radio. They had no idea what the sounds were, nor where they were coming from. They had no idea what they meant or why they were even happening. Additionally, there was a strange high frequency radio noise that the astronauts described as being "intolerable." Were these mysterious noises the result of the UFO passing by? Were there extraterrestrials inside the UFO that were attempting to signal the astronauts?

Apollo 9

Apollo 9 launched on March 3, 1969. It was the Apollo program's third manned mission. It was tasked with executing fundamental techniques for landing people on the Moon. The team consisted of Commander James McDivitt; Command Module Pilot David Scott; and Lunar Module Pilot Rusty Schweickart. During the mission, the astronauts had an extraordinary UFO sighting. They witnessed several large, cylindrical-shaped UFOs crossing the Moon. Cylindrical-shaped UFOs have been seen throughout history and are often seen in Earth's skies today.

Apollo 10

Apollo 10 launched on May 18, 1969. This was to be the "trial run" for *Apollo 11*, which was to land people on the Moon. It was the Apollo program's fourth crewed mission, and the second time Apollo astronauts would orbit the Moon. The crew included Commander Thomas Stafford; Lunar Module Pilot Eugene Cernan and Command Module Pilot John Young. As they traveled to the Moon, *Apollo 10* experienced a problem when the Lunar Module separated from the Command Module (it was the Lunar Module that would carry Neil Armstrong and Buzz Aldrin to the Moon's surface). As the Lunar Module neared the lunar surface, the crew's equipment stalled. As a result, the astronauts in the Lunar Module became stuck in space. The astronauts attempted manual override and failed. They contacted mission control for guidance with no success. During the excitement, Cernan saw a UFO moving near the craft. The UFO quickly disappeared. Moments later, the equipment began operating normally again and the crew was able to successfully complete the mission.

When the astronauts returned home, a video that Cernan had taken of the mysterious UFO was reviewed. According to the account, there were mixed ideas among officials as to what exactly the astronauts had encountered out there. Some believed that what had occurred in space was a coincidence. After all, previous astronauts had spotted UFOs out there. Others speculated that the UFO appearing at the time it did was no accident. Some believed the UFO to be a ship belonging to extraterrestrials that were attempting to warn the astronauts of some danger. Others theorized that extraterrestrials were attempting to assist the astronauts by mysteriously repairing the stalled machinery. Another possibility is that the UFO was emanating signals that were interfering with their systems. When all of this is said and done, when it comes to the *Apollo 10* mission, some things stand out. We have yet again an experience where extraterrestrials may have been encountered. If they were there to help in some way, if indeed this was their goal and one which they successfully achieved, I might add, then the mission was being watched. These extraterrestrials appear to have known in advance that *Apollo 10* was coming, and they were there to assist if something went wrong. Or, it could have been just the opposite. The ship may have become stuck in space as a warning to stay away.

Apollo 11

Apollo 11 was the historical mission that placed men on the Moon. *Apollo 11* launched on July 16, 1969. The astronauts were charged with exploring the Moon and gathering samples for scientific study. Their destination was the Sea of Tranquility. The crew consisted of Commander Neil Armstrong; Command Module Pilot Michael Collins; and Lunar Module Pilot Buzz Aldrin. On their journey to the Moon, the crew encountered a UFO that was trailing them. In his first autobiography, titled *Return to Earth,* Aldrin wrote about being in the *Columbia* looking out into space when he noticed a strange light outside the craft. In his book he described it as being "brighter than any star," and said that it looked like an "illuminated L."

In a tale that has become legend, after the astronauts landed on the Moon, they purportedly observed spaceships parked on the rim of a crater. In his book *Our Cosmic Ancestors* former NASA Communications Engineer Maurice Chatelain writes, "Moments before Armstrong stepped down the ladder to set foot on the Moon two UFOs hovered overhead." In his book *Visitors from Other Worlds,* author and researcher Brad Steiger writes about Dr. Sergei Bozhich who witnessed the Russians observing the *Apollo 11* Moon landing. Steiger writes, "In his [Bozhich's] opinion, the two UFOs appeared ready to assist the US astronauts in case anything should go wrong with the landing. Once the module appeared to be securely settled on the lunar surface, the alien spacecraft flew away."

While it is impossible to know what the alleged extraterrestrials were doing there, we can guess that they were observing the mission, or as some have theorized, they were there to help. Or perhaps they were considering how to prevent the astronauts from entering their domain.

Apollo 12

Apollo 12 was launched on November 14, 1969. Its destination was the Ocean of Storms, the largest dark spot on the Moon. The team included Commander Charles Conrad Jr.; Command Module Pilot Dick Gordon; and Lunar Module Pilot Alan Bean. From the start, *Apollo 12* was inundated with inexplicable events that seemed to come down to activity coming from extraterrestrials. In his book *Our Mysterious Spaceship Moon,* ufologist Don Wilson writes, "There is widespread agreement by researchers (unquestionably backed up by authenticated evidence from NASA files) that mysterious, unexplainable things did happen on the expedition of *Apollo 12.*"

Just after *Apollo 12* was launched reports came in from observatories from around Europe asserting that there were two UFOs with flashing lights pacing the spacecraft. The next day, the crew confirmed to NASA that they had observed UFOs following them. One of the UFOs was described as spinning as it traveled. The astronauts later stated that they believed that whoever was controlling the UFOs was benevolent. Ufologists believe that, as with the other Apollo missions, extraterrestrials were watching the launch and were there to observe the mission.

Once the *Apollo 12* Lunar Module landed on the Moon's surface, the astronauts went about fulfilling their assignments. However, strange occurrences continued to follow the men. In an image that was taken while the astronauts were on the surface, there is a large UFO hovering above one of the men. On the return trip, while in proximity to Earth, *Apollo 12* ended its journey as it started, with a UFO sighting. Reportedly, again, there was a UFO spotted near the craft. It too had flashing lights.

Apollo 14

Apollo 14 was the replacement for the ill-fated *Apollo 13*.

Apollo 14 commenced on January 31, 1971. Its destination was the Fra Mauro crater. It included crewmembers Commander Alan Shepard; Command Module Pilot Stuart A. Roosa; and Lunar Module Pilot Edgar Mitchell. While on the lunar surface, the astronauts took pictures that showed several mysterious blue lights glowingabove and on the Moon's surface while the astronauts went about their work. Some ufologists have speculated that they may have been alien probes.

Apollo 15

Apollo 15 was the fourth Apollo program mission to land on the Moon. It was more scientifically oriented than the previous missions. *Apollo 15* launched on July 26, 1971. The crew included Commander David R. Scott; Command Module Pilot Alfred Worden; and Lunar Module Pilot James Irwin. The Lunar Module crew landed in the Hadley-Apennine region, a dangerously rugged area filled with crater pocked terrain, rocks and boulders. As astronauts David Scott and James Irwin performed their duties on the surface of the Moon, they were nearly struck by a strange object that flew over them. It was unclear what the object was or where it came from. What we do know is that there should be nothing flying across the Moon.

Apollo 16

Apollo 16 was the fifth Apollo program mission to land on the Moon. It was launched on April 16, 1972. Its crew members included Commander John Young; Command Module Pilot Thomas Kenneth Mattingly; and Lunar Module Pilot Charles M. Duke Jr. Their goal was the Descartes Highlands on the Moon's near side, an area of treacherous terrain encompassing mountains, craters, and boulders. During the *Apollo 16* mission the astronauts gathered soil samples, took photographs and conducted experiments. While in orbit, Mattingly reportedly witnessed mysterious flashes of light. He was unable to locate the source. On another occasion, as Mattingly went about his duties on the Command Module, a weird light suddenly appeared and streaked quickly across the horizon. It disappeared behind the Moon's far side. It was later decided that there was no rational reason for what Mattingly had seen. Were extraterrestrials attempting to signal the astronaut? The prominent

Egyptian-American space scientist, Farouk El Baz, who worked with NASA on the Apollo moon missions, commented on the strange flashes of lights seen during the *Apollo 16* mission, stating, "There is no question about it. Not natural."

Apollo 17

Apollo 17 was the Apollo Program's last mission to the Moon. *Apollo 17* was launched on the night of December 7, 1972. The astronaut's goal was to land in the Moon's Taurus-Littrow valley. The team included Commander Eugene Cernan; Command Module Pilot Ronald Evans; and Lunar Module Pilot Harrison Schmitt. Their assignment was to survey the Moon, photograph areas of interest, and perform special tests on equipment. The astronauts of *Apollo 17* took photographs that showed anomalous lights and unusual objects. One image shows a peculiar, illuminated item located near the lunar surface. Some UFO researchers have likened it to a stargate. In an article titled "Did Apollo 17 find a Stargate on the Moon?" researcher and author Michael Salla writes, "The object appears to be a space portal of some kind with an eerie blue glowing ring around a central darker portion."

More Extraordinary Encounters in Space

Charles J. Camarda, Space Shuttle STS-114

NASA astronaut Charles J. Camarda flew his first mission into space when he served aboard the space shuttle *STS-114*. Although there are no details as to the context of his statement, he was once quoted as saying, "In my official status, I cannot comment on ET contact. However, personally, I can assure you, we are not alone!" Due to this statement, some wonder if Camarda saw an extraterrestrial ship while in space.

Story Musgrave, Space Shuttle Experience

American physician and retired NASA astronaut Story Musgrave has the distinct honor of being the only astronaut to have flown on each of the five Space shuttle missions. At one point while in space, Musgrave saw what has been described as tube shaped eels traveling across space. He saw these objects twice. He reported that there was a white tube which had a propulsion method. At this point no one knows what it is that Musgrave saw out there. However, it can surely be classified as a UFO. One wonders if this was a coincidence in space. Could it have been a probe? A biological life-form? It is one of those occurrences that can be added to the evidence that there is someone out there? Someone created this tube-like object with a propulsion system. On extraterrestrial life, Musgrave was quoted in the December 1, 1993, issue of *The Houston Post*, stating, "I try to communicate with the life that's out there. I'm serious. It is not that far out. When I'm circling around out there, I try in whatever ways I can to get them to come down here and get me." He has also stated, "If we ever start communicating with living creatures from other planets, the number one priority is, how are you going to communicate information? Even between different cultures here on Earth, you get into communication problems."

Brent Jett, STS-115

Brent Jett is a retired NASA astronaut who served aboard several of the space shuttle missions. He was a pilot of *STS-72* (*Endeavour* in 1996) and *STS-81* (*Atlantis* in 1997). He was also the commander of *STS-97* (*Endeavour* in 2000) and *STS-115* (*Atlantis* in 2006). While serving as commander on the *STS-115* flight on Sep 20, 2006, Jett observed three UFOs. The image of the objects, along with Jett's discussion with ground control, was captured on video.

Clark McClelland and the Extraterrestrial Meeting

In a shocking account given by former NASA aerospace engineer Clark McClelland, there was a meeting that he observed that took place between an extraterrestrial and two astronauts. McClelland described the being as approximately nine feet tall and humanoid. He stated that the gathering took place in one of the cargo bay areas of a space shuttle. He noted that the extraterrestrial was wearing a similar spacesuit as those worn by NASA astronauts. In his opinion, the extraterrestrial was the authoritative figure in the group. It was his understanding that the extraterrestrial was communicating directions to the astronauts.

Leroy Chiao, International Space Station (ISS),

In 2005, as he flew aboard the International Space Station (ISS), commander Leroy Chiao reported seeing five mysterious beams of light. Chiao was awestruck by what he had witnessed, as these lights were not located near the Sun, and they appeared to have no point of origin. It was a fascinating anomaly. Chiao reported that they were extremely fast and flew in a methodical arrangement.

Sergey Prokopyev and Dmitri Petelin, International Space Station

On August 9, 2023, cosmonauts Sergey Prokopyev and Dmitri Petelin performed a spacewalk outside of the ISS. The spacewalk was live streamed to the audience. During the process, two silvery, metallic UFOs appeared in the background. In the video the UFOs could clearly be seen and seemed to be observing the cosmonauts at work.

Joseph Walker, X-15

American test pilot Joseph A. Walker purportedly encountered 5 or 6 UFOs during his record-breaking fifty-mile-high flight in April, 1962. According to sources, that was his second time having witnessed and filmed UFOs during a mission. He once said that it was one of his responsibilities to detect UFOs during his *X-15* flights. None of his recordings were released to the public.

China's Shenzhou Program

Liu Yang, Shenzhou 9

As Taikonaut Liu Yang (the first Chinese woman to work in space) flew aboard the *Shenzhou 9* spacecraft in 2012, two UFOs were recorded pacing her craft. In an article titled "China X-files: UFOs spotted at space rocket launch," the opening line states, "UFO watchers believe that extra-terrestrial beings were tracking China's first female astronaut as she rocketed in space." The incident occurred shortly after *Shenzhou 9* launched and left the atmosphere. *Shenzhou 9* was traveling to the *Tiangong 1* space station which was orbiting above Earth.

Yang Liwei, Shenzhou 5

In 2003, Yang Liwei was the first Chinese astronaut to travel to outer space. While alone onboard *Shenzhou 5*, Liwei heard a mysterious banging sound on his spacecraft. He described it as "someone knocking the body of the spaceship just as knocking an iron bucket with a wooden hammer." Mysteriously, Liwei later explained that the noise neither came from outside nor inside the spacecraft.

Vladimir Afanasyevich Lyakhov, A Soyuz Mission

Vladimir Afanasyevich Lyakhov was a Ukrainian Soviet cosmonaut. He served as commander on *Soyuz 32, Soyuz T-9,* and *Soyuz TM-6.* Lyakhov once witnessed a strange phenomenon while observing Earth from his craft. He witnessed two enormous waves rising from the Indian Ocean, and then collapsing into each other. He described the scene, stating that the volume of water following the crash appeared like a huge mountain, which disappeared moments later. The incident was mentioned in the popular Russian magazine *Tekhnika-Molodezhi,* Issue 3, in 1980.

(*Author's Note*: In addition to the strange sighting, what is interesting here is that it is one of many such reported perplexing sightings in Earth's waters. These are usually accompanied by UFOs. Although a UFO is not mentioned here, the story is so strange that one wonders if there had been an extraterrestrial presence nearby that had somehow manipulated the waters, one which Lyakhov had not seen.)

Valery Ryumin and Leonid Popov, Salyut 6

As they served aboard the *Salyut 6* space station in 1980, cosmonauts Valery Ryumin and Leonid Popov reportedly witnessed what has been referred to as "white, glowing dots" near Moscow. They watched as these puzzling objects flew toward them and into space, ending up just above *Salyut 6.* The cosmonauts were unnerved enough that they promptly reported the occurrence to ground control.

Viktor Afanasyev

Former Soviet cosmonaut Viktor Afanasyev, served as a colonel in the Russian Air Force, and was a test cosmonaut at the Yuri Gagarin Cosmonaut Training Center. He was also a crew commander on four Soviet missions. Afanasyev made his position on his beliefs in aliens very clear. He once stated: "I think that we are not alone in the universe. I believe that someone, or something of extraterrestrial origin, has visited Earth." It was on one of his space missions that Afanasyev witnessed a UFO following his spacecraft. Afanasyev gave details about the experience in several interviews. The encounter occurred in April 1979, when he and his team launched from Star City to dock with the Soviet *Salyut*

6 space station. During the trip, Afanasyev witnessed a UFO following his craft. Afanasyev did not mince words about what he had seen that day.

In describing the incident, Afanasyev stated, "It followed us during half of our orbit. We observed it on the light side, and when we entered the shadow side, it disappeared completely. It was an engineered structure, made from some type of metal, approximately 40 meters long with inner hulls. The object was narrow here and wider here, and inside there were openings. Some places had projections like small wings. The object stayed very close to us. We photographed it, and our photos showed it to be 23 to 28 meters away."

According to Afanasyev, the UFO continued to follow the cosmonauts in very close proximity. During this period Afanasyev was in constant contact with ground control, giving them details of the size of the UFO, its shape, and its location. After the mission, he was debriefed and instructed not to talk about what had happened in space. The film from the ship was also confiscated. The images that were taken, as well as his communications with ground control were never made public. It was after the collapse of the Soviet Union that Afanasyev began to talk about his experience.

Cosmonauts, *Salyut 7*

Six Russian cosmonauts claimed to have seen "angels" while on missions in space. Reportedly, there were two separate sightings with two separate crews. The story is said to have been smuggled out of Russia in 1985 by a scientist who was defecting. According to the report, the cosmonauts of the *Salyut 7* space station, which included Vladimir Solevev, Oleg Atkov, and Leonid Kizim, were surprised when a blinding, bright orange light suddenly appeared, beaming into the space station. When they looked out of the portholes to locate the light's source, they saw seven angels.

The angels were described as "seven giant figures," in human form, with a glow around them and wings that were the size of jetliners. The angels were indistinguishable from each other. The angels are said to have followed the space capsule for ten minutes and then mysteriously disappeared. Twelve days later the angels appeared again. This time three different cosmonauts saw them. Again, the brilliant light appeared and the three new cosmonauts, by the names of Svetlana Savitskaya, Igor Volk and Vladimir Dzhanibekov, saw the gigantic angels. Svetlana Savistskaya was quoted as saying, "We were truly overwhelmed. There was a great orange light and through it we could see the figures of seven angels. They were smiling as though they shared a glorious secret." Many people have interpreted the seven angels as benevolent extraterrestrial beings that were observing the spacecraft.

Georgy Beregovoy and Valentin Lebedev, Salyut 7

On July 12, 1982, cosmonauts Georgy Beregovoy and Valentin Lebedev witnessed a drop-shaped UFO while on assignment aboard *Salyut 7*. They observed it flying between the *Salyut 7* and the *Progressor-14* craft. The UFO was estimated to have been traveling from a distance of 200 meters.

Vladimir Kovalyonok, *Salyut 6*

On May 5, 1981, then astronaut Vladimir Kovalyonok had an unforgettable experience during a mission on the *Salyut 6*. At around 6 p., as they flew over South Africa going toward the Indian Ocean, he noticed an elliptical shaped object outside of the craft as he looked through the porthole. From his point of view at that moment it appeared to have been the size of a finger. As he watched it, the strange item suddenly exploded and split into two golden objects. He watched them until they disappeared when they entered the Earth's shadow. Later describing it, he stated, "The object resembled a barbell. I saw it becoming transparent and like with a 'body' inside. At the other end I saw something like gas discharging, like a reactive object. Then something happened that is very difficult for me to describe from the point of view of physics."

At a press conference Kovalyonok described the event stating: "When I was working at the Salyut orbital station, I saw something strange in a porthole one day. The object was the size of a finger. I was surprised to see it was an orbiting object." He also stated that he had asked his colleague on the mission, Viktor Savinykh, to take a look at the object. About the UFO, Kovalyonok also stated:

> I have to recognize that it did not have an artificial origin. It was not artificial because an artificial object couldn't attain this form. I don't know of anything that can make this movement... tightening, then expanding, pulsating. Then as I was observing something happened, two explosions. One explosion, and then 0.5 seconds later,

the second part exploded. I called my colleague Viktor [Savinykh], but he didn't arrive in time to see anything.

He also commented, "It was hard to determine the size and the speed of an object in space. That is why I cannot say exactly which size it actually was. Savinykh prepared to take a picture of it, but the UFO suddenly exploded. Only clouds of smoke were left. The object split into two interconnected pieces. It was reminiscent of a dumb-bell. I reported about it to Mission Control immediately." On the barbell shaped object, he explained: "The object moved in a suborbital path, otherwise I wouldn't have been able to see it. There were two clouds, like smoke, that formed a barbell. It came near me and I watched it."

(*Author's Note*: One wonders what the reason for the display from the UFO may have been. Was this an alien life-form trying to communicate with those aboard *Salyut 6*? Perhaps one of the most fascinating comments from the astronauts that this author has discovered to date, and which comes from Kovalyonok, is where he states, "I do not believe it when astronauts say they have never seen anything extraordinary in space." This is fascinating because it comes from someone who has been there and saw something extraordinary out there. It is telling that not all has been revealed to the public about strange objects seen by Earth's space men and women. Perhaps one day these secrets will come out.)

Georgy Beregovoy and Valentin Lebedev, Salyut 7
On July 12, 1982, during a mission onboard *Salyut 7*, cosmonauts Georgy Beregovoy and Valentin Lebedev saw something strange on the monitor. The UFO was at a distance of 200 meters and was projected at the time to have been the size of a spaceship.

Gennadi Strekalov, Soyuz TM-10
Cosmonaut Gennadi Strekalov served aboard four space missions. From August 1 to December 10, 1990, he was the flight engineer on *Soyuz TM-10's* flight to Mir along with Gennady Manakov and Japanese reporter-cosmonaut Toyohiro Akiyama. It was on this mission that Strekalov saw a UFO. He is quoted as stating, "during the flight of 1990, I called Gennadi Manakov, our Commander to come to the porthole—but we did not manage to put

film in the camera quickly enough. We looked on Newfoundland and the atmosphere was absolutely clear—suddenly a kind of sphere appeared." He went on to describe it as, "beautiful, shiny, and glittering—I saw it for 10 seconds—it disappeared. What was it? What size it had? I don't know, there was nothing I could compare with—it was a perfect sphere."

(*Author's Note*: It appears from this account that whoever is operating the UFOs are quietly observing all of Earth's space agencies.)

In the next few years space agencies around the world are positioned to travel to space, the Moon, Mars and more. This will be a new and exciting time in Earth's galactic history as we head for the cosmos. We only hope that we can prevail out there as we will surely run into more UFOs, anomalous objects and most certainly extraterrestrials... for better or for worse.

Chapter Eleven
The Battle for Earth

"Wars not make one great."
—Yoda

The KGB secret book titled *Book of Alien Races* states, "From 700 AD to the 19th century AD over 50 battles between alien races were fought in Earth's skies and witnessed by thousands of people. Many artists painted and carved these events, but the Catholic Church searched, found and destroyed most of them. In the 20th century only less than 10 were available." This statement is just one example of some of what has been going on with our world since the beginning. There has always been a battle for Earth. Earth, it appears, is a very special place. Sitting on the outskirts of space, it lights up like a magnificent blue marble in the sky. It is not lost to other races out there that it has spectacular life-forms and resources. Earth would be a prime target for nefarious beings to want to own it or pick it apart for many of the elements, minerals, water, gems, energy, and more located here. There are already strange tales of humanity being enslaved at one time, animal mutilations, human abductions and other terrible things that have gone on here. For the most part, Earth is a beautiful place to be. People have come and gone for generations, most being oblivious to any malevolent activities coming from the cosmos. That, of course, is because there has probably been some intervention that we know nothing of. In other words, our world could have been a lot worse if it were not for unseen benevolent forces working on our behalf.

Today, somewhere in the far reaches of space, there is a possibility a war is going on… Scientists are claiming that there appears to be what looks like a star wars happening, as they cannot explain the anomalous, unnatural explosions they are seeing in deep space. An article titled "Nuclear Wars in Antiquity" from the Space2001 website states, "Five or six years ago an article in the *Herald Tribune* said there had been at least 80 unexplained explosions in deep space during the last decade alone! This had baffled many of the leading scientists and astronomers who were at a complete loss to explain the phenomenon!" The most sizable of these blasts happened, "180,000 light years away outside of the *Milky Way* galaxy." The article quoted Nuclear Physicist and Ufologist, Stanton T. Friedmann (1934-2019) as saying "Tremendous activity of this sort could well be life out there involved in a war!" This just tells us that there are wars going on in space. We live in a universe of the good and bad. Just as on Earth we have both, the same applies to the universe. Fortunately, according to the research, our galaxy is mostly filled with benevolent beings, so much so, that they are rumored to have already approached some of Earth's governments about our use of nuclear weapons. They are aware. They came here with a warning. They prefer to keep the galaxy safe.

Are there unseen forces vying for control of Earth? My son told me recently that he doesn't want to live in a universe where there are "star wars." Neither do I. However, the reality is that it appears that this jewel of a planet on which we live may be the focus of unwanted attention, as I said before, due to its resources. There is also the matter of some races in the universe feeling that they have rights to our planet.

If we look back into our ancient history, there is some evidence that Earth at one time was engaged in advanced warfare that involved nuclear weaponry. There is a theory that humanity once had reached an advanced state of technology and lost it due to a global disaster and perhaps had to begin again. It is also thought that this may have happened several times in our history. A passage from *The Moon's Galactic History* states:

> Could a nuclear war in space have happened in our Solar System eons ago… Could there have been a war of the worlds somewhere in our remote past? If humans had the ability of spaceflight, could there have been a conflict at one time that led to the destroyed ruins that we see on Earth, the Moon and possibly Mars? Were there advanced ancient civilizations on Earth that were destroyed in a cosmic war as well? How about Mars? Perhaps this was a war over the territories of the Earth, Moon and Mars? Might this have anything to do with the asteroid belt? Is this all connected to the evidence on Earth of a mysterious ancient atomic war? And finally, in the past, did we go too

far on Earth with nuclear bombs and destroy ourselves, causing Earth civilizations to have to begin again?! This may be the reasons that UFOs are so frequently seen around military installations on Earth. They may be watching our progress.

After creating the atomic bomb, Robert Oppenheimer (1904-1967) cryptically stated, "Now I am become death, the destroyer of worlds." This dreadful passage is from the Hindu writings of the *Bhagavad-Gita*. Oppenheimer certainly presents the correct image of doom that an atomic bomb most certainly is. One wonders why we would find such a line in the *Bhagavad-Gita*. It is because there are tales in Hindu texts that speak of battles where weapons with extremely intense, high heat were used, such as the *Brahmashirsha astra*, a devastating weapon with the ability to obliterate life on Earth and possibly beyond. Researchers believe from these writings and other evidence, that somewhere in mankind's past, some countries had nuclear arsenals.

Evidence of this can be found in South America where ruins of once magnificent cities can be found. These cities were discovered in the isolated and nearly impenetrable Amazonia, otherwise known as the Amazon Jungle. They were found during Spanish expeditions during their search for the "Seven Cities of Cibola." In their journals, the explorers from those travels recounted their discoveries and adventures. Some told of great metropolises that had been reduced to rubble from some past disaster. They noted that the structures seemed to have been melted by what appeared to have been incredibly high heat. There are researchers who believe that this is evidence points to an ancient atomic weapon, where melted stone buildings and vitrified glass are the result. One account spoke of what was once a glorious city where no plant life grew. This was unusual since the city had been surrounded by a lush, overgrown jungle for centuries. Today we know that this can be the result of atomic radiation! Alternately, there were radiated corpses discovered in the Gobi Desert. This appears to be the result of atomic weaponry that was used on the citizens there. Where did humans obtain that kind of weaponry thousands of years ago? According to legend, there were advanced civilizations that had built vast, majestic cities and had nuclear bombs. We have clear evidence that ancient humans had nuclear capabilities. Are these vitrified ruins on both worlds, symbols of a conflict between the two? Also, was Mars involved?

Somehow, some way, Earth was involved in what appears to be a galactic war. It could have been a war for Earth (or Earth as well as other territories such as the Moon and Mars). Whatever happened back then, it was so disastrous that there are groups of extraterrestrials monitoring and protecting Earth today (to a point).

Author's Note. This does not mean that there are groups out there that are not trying, through a multitude of ways, to gain control of Earth. If you talk to many in the area of ufology, they will tell you that from the state of the world today, we may be losing that battle. Many believe that there are nefarious groups here using other means of warfare including ways that are unseen to humans. However, I digress.

Star Wars

If we look back on our history, there are a few instances when we can see the involvement of extraterrestrials who appear to have stepped in on our behalf. There have been times in history when people were going about their daily lives and witnessed spaceships engaged in battle in the skies over Earth. I am speaking here of physical ships in the skies complete with clashing noises and what seems to have been shooting of some sort (beams? rays? lasers?) going on. There have also been times when Earth's countries were at war when military troops were forced to stop fighting in the middle of battles due to UFOs suddenly appearing in the skies to thwart their efforts. There have been occasions in the modern era when nuclear missiles have mysteriously been disarmed. It appears that there are extraterrestrials out there that are assisting us to not be destroyed and preventing us from destroying ourselves and life on Earth. With the information that is coming out about extraterrestrials, we hope that one day soon they will reveal themselves and explain all. The following are a *few* of the amazing accounts that have occurred over the centuries with extraterrestrials having stepped in and intervened in wars, saving many. Remember too, that during these periods in history there were no airplanes, and the people had no idea what they were witnessing.

Italy

During the Punic Wars (a series of three wars fought between Rome and Carthage from 264 BC to 146 BC) there were several UFO sightings. Were the UFOs there to assist in the wars? Were they chronicling Earth's events? Just what was the purpose of extraterrestrials being in the presence of war at that period? Recorded in the *Annales Maximi* published by the Pontifex Maximus of Rome, phantom ships (UFOs) had been seen glowing in the sky. The next year, "round shields were observed in the sky" over the city of Arpi. One chronicle recounts an incident that occurred as the Roman army organized to fight against the military forces of King Mithridates VI in modern-day Turkey. The famed Greek historian and writer Plutarch documented a sighting that was witnessed by thousands of astonished observers. In 74 BC, as Rome's military advanced, suddenly a loud clashing noise was heard, and a mysterious object appeared in the sky. People watched astounded as, according to the account, "the sky burst asunder," and a large "flame-like" object landed between the two armies, preventing their advancements. *What was it? Who was it?* Plutarch provided a thorough, detailed description of this strange object. He described its shape as that of a "wine-jar," and wrote that the color was that of "molten silver." The armies on both sides were petrified and retreated away from it. Was this an intentional intervention? Needless to say, the battle was halted. This is quite an amazing tale! We already know that Plutarch, one of history's most admired writers and historians, can be trusted with this account. What is amazing here is the intervention in or the stopping of the conflict. Were the extraterrestrials attempting to intervene in this war? Also, what was it that they sent down? This would not be the last time that extraterrestrials attempted to interrupt these battles during the Punic Wars. It must be difficult for them not to just step in and help directly with all of Earth's problems.

Judea, 65 AD

In a remarkable account out of Judea, we learn of extraterrestrials battling in the skies. One wonders if they were fighting over Earth, or territory on Earth, or if there were extraterrestrials attempting to take some resource from Earth. Or maybe it was an early attempt at conquering Earth; we just cannot know, but it is so strange an account. I am struck by the last words in the account which sound to this author as if one of the battling sides was attempting to stop the other that may have been posing as gods at some point (perhaps they were attempting to return?). The extraterrestrials attempted to drive them away, and succeeded apparently, stating, "The gods are leaving!" People literally heard a booming voice out of the sky making that comment.

In 65 AD, Flavius Josephus, a Roman–Jewish historian wrote about a remarkable event that took place in the skies of Judea. He referred to it as a "miraculous phenomenon." Josephus wrote that he and many other witnesses had seen what he referred to as "chariots" in the skies; they could be seen throughout the country. He wrote that people had observed "armed battalions hurtling through the clouds" over area townships. He also stated that as clerics were setting up for the feast of Pentecost within their temple, they could hear and feel the ramifications of what was happening in the skies above. He wrote that they "felt a quaking and heard a great noise." It seems here that there were spacecraft battling overhead. The Roman historian Tacitus also documented this event. He wrote, "In the sky appeared a vision of armies in conflict, of glittering armor!" He also documented that "a lightning flash from the clouds lit up the Temple." The shaking was so fierce above that the ground shook causing the doors of temple to open. Also, according to Tacitus a "superhuman voice" was heard announcing, "The gods are leaving!" *Who in the world was that? What was going on?*

Nuremberg, Germany, April 4, 1561

On April 14, 1561, during the early morning hours, the people of Nuremberg, Germany expected to wake to a regular sunny day. Instead, they awakened to a Sun that, instead of being bright yellow, was blood red (according to their description) and the sky was full of strange objects they had never seen before. It terrified them. Unbeknownst to the town's residents, what they were witnessing was an aerial, galactic battle in the sky. The local news of the time referred to it as "a dreadful apparition." What they saw were UFOs of varying shapes and sizes waging war, which must have looked remarkably like a scene from *Star Wars*. The shapes of the UFOs were varied, some were disk-shaped, others were in the shape of an X, while still others were cylindrical shaped. Throughout the conflict smaller spacecraft could be seen leaving the larger ships and joining in the battle. It was an aggressive fight that shocked the people who had never witnessed such a thing and had no inkling about us not being alone in the universe, or anything about UFOs, spaceships, and extraterrestrials. They were totally ignorant as to what they were seeing, which may be the point of the fight in the first place. It has been said that humanity is being educated about the fact that there is more to the universe than we know, than we have been told, than we believe, than we have been taught, through science fiction.

This sounds like something straight out of a modern-day movie. Just imagine a movie in which there are people in a village in another time, watching spaceships wage war over their heads. That is what happened. We live on a wonderous, valuable planet, that at that time was filled with naïve people that had no idea of who they were, or why they were here. They would have been easy pickings for some nefarious race of beings, when all that they had at the time to protect themselves were shields and swords. At the time, of course, the goings on were interpreted as signs from God. The people had no concept of spaceships or UFOs or extraterrestrials.

We do not know what the battle was about that day. This was also not the only time when unknown ships were seen in the skies in those days. We do not know who or what was operating those ships. We can speculate however, that this particuar fight may have been about Earth. We live in a quiet part of the galaxy in a world full of lifeand resources, and there is much potential here. Who knows what lies in space waiting to prey on us? I would, however, guess that there was someone or something up to no good, and someone else stepped in. *This would not be the last time either... Could this have been a part of a battle for Earth? Is this battle still raging today?*

The town newspaper reported on the event. It read as follows:

In the morning of April 14, 1561, at daybreak, between 4 and 5 a.m., a dreadful apparition occurred on the sun, and then this was seen in Nuremberg in the city, before the gates and in the country—by many men and women. At first there appeared in the middle of the sun two blood-red semi-circular arcs, just like the moon in its last quarter. And in the sun, above and below and on both sides, the color was blood, there stood a round ball of partly dull,

271

partly black ferrous color. Likewise, there stood on both sides and as a torus about the sun such blood-red ones and other balls in large number, about three in a line and four in a square, also some alone. In between these globes there were visible a few blood-red crosses, between which there were blood-red strips, becoming thicker to the rear and in the front malleable like the rods of reed-grass, which were intermingled, among them two big rods, one on the right, the other to the left, and within the small and big rods there were three, also four and more globes. These all started to fight among themselves, so that the globes, which were first in the sun, flew out to the ones standing on both sides, thereafter, the globes standing outside the sun, in the small and large rods, flew into the sun.

Besides the globes flew back and forth among themselves and fought vehemently with each other for over an hour. And when the conflict in and again out of the sun was most intense, they became fatigued to such an extent that they all, as said above, fell from the sun down upon the earth 'as if they all burned' and they then wasted away on the earth with immense smoke. After all this there was something like a black spear, very long and thick, sighted; the shaft pointed to the east, the point pointed west. Whatever such signs mean, God alone knows. Although we have seen, shortly one after another, many kinds of signs on the heaven, which are sent to us by the almighty God, to bring us to repentance, we still are, unfortunately, so ungrateful that we despise such high signs and miracles of God. Or we speak of them with ridicule and discard them to the wind, in order that God may send us a frightening punishment on account of our ungratefulness. After all, the God-fearing will by no means discard these signs, but will take it to heart as a warning of their merciful Father in heaven, will mend their lives and faithfully beg God, that He may avert His wrath, including the well-deserved punishment, on us, so that we may temporarily here and perpetually there, live as his children. For it, may God grant us his help, Amen. By Hanns Glaser, letter-painter of Nurnberg.

August 7, 1566, Basil Switzerland

A similar incident occurred in Basil, Switzerland, where several UFOs described as "black spheres" were seen in the skies doing battle with each other. This battle was witnessed by hundreds to thousands of residents in the area. In relaying the event, a newspaper report from the time that was written by a reporter named Samuel Coccius stated, "Many became fiery and red, ending by being consumed and vanishing." This sounds as though some of the spheres (UFOs) exploded when hit with some type of weapon during this battle. Just unbelievable!

The Battle to Save Us from Ourselves

Now, here is a spin on the idea of a battle for Earth. In this scenario I am not referring to a threat coming from space. I am not talking about a race of beings attempting to take over Earth. I am speaking of beings that are attempting to save Earth from us. Since the creation of the atomic bomb in 1945, Earth has been inundated with UFOs. There are also those who claim to have been visited by extraterrestrials and given information to attempt to dissuade humans from using nuclear weapons in an effort to save humanity and all living creatures here. They have been desperate to save us from ourselves. It is even rumored that government leaders were approached by extraterrestrials about this nuclear threat. They have also insinuated that using the nuclear bomb will have a domino effect in the galaxy. It appears that our extraterrestrial history is catching up with us in the form of a battle for Earth. Therefore, some of the UFO activity seen around Earth today may be coming from extraterrestrials that are watching and attempting to prevent us from blowing up ourselves and all life on Earth. We also know that otherworldly intelligences have powered down nuclear armaments right in front of military personnel, rendering them inoperable. It has been stated too that humanity has to grow up or be removed, as the extraterrestrials have stated that they will not allow us to kill off life on Earth. We have free will. They do not want to interfere. However, this, it appears, is where they draw the line.

We can imagine that within the other inhabited worlds and civilizations in the universe, there are some that are friendly, and some that are not. Earth seems for now to be caught between these polarities. Much of this is due to the lack of technology to participate in galactic affairs. I wonder, which way will Earth go? How will Earth fare? What will be our outcome? Thus far, it appears that Earth has been protected by extraterrestrials or we would have been wiped out by now. We do not know who they are, or why they are protecting us, although there are theories. All we know is that they are on our side. They have even protected us from ourselves.

It is difficult to think about there being a possible war in another area of the galaxy. Most people are not aware enough of what is going on in the area of "galactic happenings" to even fathom such a thing. However, they *are* there. They *are* happening, and you will not find it on the mainstream news. Extraterrestrials exist. We can imagine life on other worlds. Presumably, they have homes, they have families, they have ships, they have weaponry, some are political, some are at war, others are at peace. They have methods of traveling the universe that we do not yet understand. Most are many years ahead of us in technology. We are a young species. We are still in the beginning stages. It is another sobering lesson for us to learn this, as most people on Earth consider our planet to be advanced. To listen to news reports, Earth's inhabitants have limited thoughts about the cosmos. People are having a difficult time imagining a universe full of extraterrestrial people, living lives and with capabilities far surpassing ours.

As a result, we are a world that is separate, struggling against each other and vying for power and ownership of territories, often resulting in wars. President Reagan famously stated, "Perhaps we need some outside universal threat to make us recognize this common bond. I occasionally think how quickly our differences worldwide would vanish if we were facing an alien threat from outside this world."

Even Mikhail Gorbachev, the former secretary general of the Soviet Union once stated in an article published in the periodical *Soviet Life Supplement* in May 1987, that he agreed with former U.S. President Ronald Reagan that in the event of an invasion from outer space, the United States and Soviet Union would join forces to repel it. Many people believe that Reagan was aware of something that has not been shared. They say that the government has not disclosed certain information due to public panic. *Perhaps*. But I say that there will be more panic if people are left unaware of our true reality.

I started out this book hoping to keep an upbeat note. I wanted to introduce extraterrestrials as peaceful and show that we live in a galaxy that is for the most part a harmonious one. I still believe this to be true. According to some contactees and experiencers, and channelings from otherworldly beings, our galaxy has more peaceful civilizations in it than not. While that is true, this may not encompass all. And, we have an entire universe and more out there. So, who knows what Earth may one day be truly up against. For now, it appears that there is and has been a kind of battle for Earth for many years. It is said that there are those out there who would like to dominate Earth and have been attempting to for a very long time. It's time that we take a serious look at what we may be up against and invite those on our side to introduce themselves. This may sound like fantasy and wishful thinking; maybe I am a dreamer...

Chapter Twelve
Galactic Hierarchies

"A Central Galactic Information Repository, which keeps
tabs on all habitale worlds and watches for the uprise of
intelligent beings, might someday welcome earth into the
Space Community."
—Carl Sagan

Are there higher authorities that oversee the galaxy? If so, who
are they? Do they send out people to do surveillance on Earth and
other planetary bodies that may hold life? Could Earth fall under
someone else's jurisdiction and we don't even know it? There
could be decisions being made for Earth and we are not even
aware of it. Researchers believe that there are galactic hierarchies
in the galaxy watching over matters and keeping order.

Galactic Hierachies

We must ask ourselves, since the galaxy consists of many
worlds and we are assuming that some are populated, then how
does it operate and keep order? One would think that some sort
of order has been established. Many of these extraterrestrial
civilizations are advanced. Who is regulating them? Who is
regulating the cosmic freeway, if one exists? It appears that there
really are hierarchies in the galaxy with rules and regulations to
keep things in order. If not, there may be some worlds that would
be vulnerable to attacks and takeovers from malevolent groups. On
Earth there are political agendas, wars, and takeovers. As nice as it
is to believe that the galaxy is full of benevolent beings only, this
may not be the case. The famous researcher and hypnotherapist
Dolores Cannon once stated that *Star Trek* is real. If this is the
case, then yes there are good and bad out there, as this was clearly
portrayed in that series. Therefore, it makes sense that a leadership
would have been formed (just as in *Star Trek* with the Federation).
According to the research, there are extraterrestrial groups that are
brought together to have diplomatic conversations about events

involving various worlds and activities going on within the galaxy. This is done by galactic councils and federations. It has been, and continues to be, going on behind the scenes, as we live out our lives on Earth. The following are some of the most well-known of these groups.

The Galactic Federation

The Galactic Federation, also referred to as The Galactic Federation of Light, the Confederation of Planets, the Interstellar Alliance, the Sphere Being Alliance and the Galactic Federation of Worlds, is an organization of space traveling societies from within the Milky Way galaxy. It is made up of hundreds of thousands of adherents intent on keeping the galaxy safe. It comprises many kinds of wonderful beings from all over the galaxy. Some of these beings resemble humans while others are different. It was established millions of years ago, after a succession of wars that occurred in the Lyra constellation. The devastation from that time led the extraterrestrial worlds involved to form the Federation to resolve conflicts within the galaxy by peaceful, nonviolent means. The Galactic Federation is responsible for intervening in conflicts that arise between worlds. They have at their disposal a vast fleet of sophisticated, high-tech spaceships for their work among the cosmos. Some of the ships are enormous and are, for the most part, city ships. These are self-sustainable worlds complete with farming, forests, lakes, recreation areas, work areas, residential quarters and more. Their ships have cloaking abilities, and they traverse the galaxy by using hyperspace and stargates. This makes it conveniently easy to reach their home worlds and other areas of the galaxy. Interestingly, it is said that they have visited Earth for millions of years, sometimes leaving behind things such as structures and other objects. Could they be responsible for some of the anomalous constructions, formations and out-of-place artifacts found around the world?

According to sources, this federation has also established the "Universal Law of Non-Interference," where contact with humanity is said to be kept to a bare minimum. The members of the Galactic Federation mostly use channeling to communicate with humans. Also, it has been stated that some of Earth's governments are aware of the Federation. It is rumored that one of the United States presidents met with representatives from this group. According to SaLuSa, a member of the Galactic Federation who is channeled by

Mike Quinsey, "Normally we would refrain from direct contact, as it is essential to allow developing civilizations to find their own path to understanding and experience as they choose. It would be quite incorrect if in desiring to assist you we altered your course of evolution."

Israeli author Haim Eshed, in an interview where he talked about his book *The Universe Beyond the Horizon*, mentioned the Galactic Federation. For this author hearing the words Galactic Federation coming from the television was a shock. Mr. Eshed had publicly outed a group that most people have never heard of. It appears that Mr. Eshed, a former Israeli space security chief with an impressive and legitimate resume as long as my arm, was disclosing information not commonly known to most people. It is not information that anyone would have believed if they were not current on UFO and extraterrestrial research. Even though what he mentioned takes place on Mars, we are connected.

In an unusual story recounting Mr. Eshed being interviewed by Israel's *Yediot Aharonot* newspaper, Eshed is quoted as stating, "The Unidentified Flying Objects have asked not to publish that they are here, humanity is not ready yet." He went on to comment that the extraterrestrials are curious about humanity and are attempting to comprehend "the fabric of the universe." According to an NBC news article titled "Former Israeli space security chief says extraterrestrials exist, and Trump knows about it" (December 8, 2020), Eshed stated that there is a cooperation agreement that was signed between species, presumably humans from Earth and members of the Federation. This apparently included working in an "underground base in the depths of Mars," where there are American astronauts and extraterrestrial envoys.

Another statement that Eshed made according to the article was, "There is an agreement between the U.S. government and the aliens. They signed a contract with us to do experiments here." According to Eshed, referring to the extraterrestrials of the Galactic Federation, "They have been waiting until today for humanity to develop and reach a stage where we will understand, in general, what space and spaceships are." Eshed also mentioned why he came out with this information in 2020. He was quoted as stating, "I have nothing to lose. I've received my degrees and awards, I am respected in universities abroad."

The Galactic Federation is well known. This name has been around for many years. It is said that they have ships in our Solar

System and that they are not visible to us. They have also been said to channel information.

Author's Note: Perhaps the idea of extraterrestrials and astronauts from Earth working in the depths of Mars is not so far-fetched. After all, the former head of Lockheed Skunk Groups, Ben Rich, once stated, "We have things flying that are 50 years beyond what you could possibly even dream of. If you've seen it on *Star Wars* or *Star Trek*, we've been there, done that." Therefore, there are things going on that we are not privy to. It looks like Eshed was trying to convey the message that we are not alone in the universe.

The Council of Nine (The Nine)

One such group of entities is known as the Council of Nine. They are "Tribunal Teachers" governing our immediate galactic region. They are known as "The Nine." They are intelligent, wise beings of light. They are said to "exist beyond our understanding and at a velocity even that is beyond light." They are perhaps the most well-known and the most important of all of the groups given here. They have quite an amazing history and may just be in charge of or above the rest of the groups in the hierarchy. First introduced to the modern world through several recognizable names including Uri Geller, Dr. H.R. Hurtak, Dr. Andrija Puharich, Gene Roddenberry, Phyllis Schlemmer and Dr. D.G. Vinod, they are said to be one of Earth's great influencers. They are perhaps the highest level of entities involved with Earth. According to the Nine, via channeled information, their Earth liaisons reach back to the time of ancient Egypt where they were recognized as the Ennead (also Great Ennead), which were a group of nine Egyptian gods. Their names during that time in history were Atum, Geb, Isis, Nephthys, Nut, Osiris, Tefnut, Set, and Shu, all Egyptian gods. This connection to ancient Egypt is particularly significant when it comes to the Nine and their history with Earth. Modern era communications from the Nine are usually conveyed through the means of channeling. The Nine maintain that they are extremely advanced, highly evolved intelligences that are basically "god." According to sources, they have power over the Earth and humanity. Because they are non-physical, they require other species of beings to intermingle with the physical universe.

In yet another revelation from the Nine, one of the means in which the Nine were able to function in ancient Egypt was through

Egypt's pyramids. According to the Nine, the Great Pyramid of Giza was constructed by them as a stargate. They also noted that the Pyramid's design is intentional. The design enables them to connect with and utilize universal energies, which act as a power source for them. This power source links them to the Akashic Records.

Gene Roddenberry (the creator of *Star Trek*) is said to have sat in on channeling sessions with the Nine when they were relaying information through Phyllis Schlemmer in 1974 and 1975. The concept of the Nine is believed to have found its way into the early *Star Trek* shows, the movies, as well as the *Star Trek: The Next Generation* and *Deep Space Nine* series.

Ashtar Command

According to certain information, the Ashtar Command is made up of thousands of starships. It has a workforce of races from different worlds and civilizations. The Command is under the direction of Ashtar after whom it is named. Ashtar is also a member of several Intergalactic Councils. The second in command is Sananda. They are stationed within our Solar System with ships positioned in the skies over Earth. They are charged with protecting Earth from nefarious races and other forces. They are also here to assist Earth and humankind through the ascension process. They are in position and ready to lift people off the planet at the first sign of a global disaster. The Ashtar Command also has several million of their people on Earth going about their missions of helping to bring light and peace to the planet as well as educate the public that they are not alone in the universe. These are their "ground troops." They are referred to by the Command as "The Terran Eagles." They are said to be well trained for their missions on Earth.

Alliance for Peace

The Alliance for Peace is a part of the Intergalactic Council which is in service to the Light and to Earth. The Alliance for Peace is disallowed from interfering in the affairs of the people of any planet so as not to disrupt their evolution (much like in the original *Star Trek* television and movie series). In order to interfere in any way, the Alliance must have permission from the governments of that planet. The Alliance has many spaceships invisible to the human eye. They are said to have been encircling our planet for many years. They have "mother ships" in the Earth's atmospheres that are 100 miles across. These ships are believed to contain entire cities that can accommodate millions of people. The authority of the Alliance for Peace comes from the Spiritual Hierarchy of the Solar System. There is said to be a serious penalty if a member of the alliance interferes with developing species. There is an exception to this rule, however, and it involves the Laws of the Universe. When the Laws of the Universe are violated by a planetary race such as humankind, the Alliance can interpose themselves with the aid of other members of the Alliance. An example of this would be an atomic war. It was the atomic bomb that first drew the attention of the Alliance for Peace bringing them into Earth's atmosphere. It is a violation of universal law when a species puts at risk the entire spectrum of life-forms of a planet. The chaotic results of this would be felt throughout the immediate galaxy as a domino effect. The elimination of life is a direct violation of the law and is not tolerated by the Alliance of Peace. Another name for The Alliance of Peace is simply The Alliance.

Author's Note: There may be extraterrestrials here that are living among us in human form. Some are here to move forward the agenda of saving Earth and to help humankind move into a galactic, spacefaring future and join the galactic community. There are those that are here to assist for those reasons. Some have had their lives extended but are unable to tell the world who they really are and their purpose for being here; they are living in what is sort of like a witness protection program. They have chosen to remain here after the death of the physical body, or perhaps reached an agreement before death to have their lives here secretly extended for a special mission or purpose. These people cannot reveal themselves due to the violence this knowledge would create, and the possibility that there may be something akin to witch hunts and trials. So, they remain quiet as they go about their business performing their work here in secret. These are not necessarily beings that have an agreement with the governments of this world but are working for federations and hierarchies in the cosmos.

The Author's Last Words

Could the extraterrestrials be discreetly attempting to bring us disclosure? Some believe that they are as more and more UFOs are showing themselves all over the world. I am under the impression that this is not a coincidence that we are learning so much about our galactic history today and so rapidly. There may just be an unseen guiding force behind all of this. This may be the time in Earth's history for us to learn the astonishing story of our origins, the ancient past and our extraterrestrial connection. Could it be that we are as children being fed information slowly as we grow to reach a state of advancement?

There are many researchers today that are making discoveries that we simply do not see on the mainstream news. These people are the forerunners and perhaps even the catalysts into the world waking up to understanding that things are not what we have been taught, and that there is more going on in our world than most are aware of. These are very exciting and important times. However, it is not without growing pains. We can see the resistance of this new information and findings. There are still rumors of cover-ups about UFOs, UAPs, USOs, extraterrestrial encounters, messages from space, and even archeological discoveries that do not fit into the mainstream of things. Let's hope that sometime in the near future, there will be a larger sharing of information so that we can grow and change for the better on planet Earth.

Author Biography

Constance Victoria Briggs is an author, researcher and public speaker specializing in cosmic mysteries including, galactic and Moon mysteries, ancient astronauts, extraterrestrials, angels, and the unseen world. She is the author of, *Earth's Galactic History and Its Extraterrestrial Connection; The Moon's Galactic History: A Look at the Moon's Extraterrestrial Past and Its Connection to Earth; The Encyclopedia of Moon Mysteries: Secrets, Conspiracy Theories, Anomalies, Extraterrestrials and More.*; *Encyclopedia of the Unseen World*: *The Ultimate Guide to Apparitions, Death Bed Visions, Mediums, Shadow People, Wandering Spirits, and Much, Much More; Encyclopedia of God: An A-Z Guide to Thoughts, Ideas, and Beliefs about God; The Encyclopedia of Angels: An A-to-Z Guide with Nearly 4,000 Entries.* Briggs is a regular invited guest speaker on numerous radio shows, podcasts, and YouTube shows. Some of the prominent shows Briggs has been featured on include *Coast to Coast am with George Noory, The Leak Project, Earth Ancients, Broadcast Team Alpha, Forbidden Knowledge, Spaced Out Radio,* and others. Briggs has also been featured in *Shadows of Your Mind Magazine* and *UNX Magazine.* Briggs has been a speaker at conferences such as *Total Disclosure, Inner Truth Summit,* and *Watchers Talk Humanity Unplugged Conference.* Briggs is also in the *Women on the Fringe Anthology.* It is Briggs's goal to investigate the mysteries of the universe and how they connect to humanity.

Bibliography Books

A Signal from Mars, Tesla's Collected Articles on Alien Communication, Kenneth Arnold, Saucerian Publisher, Las Vegas, NV, 2021

Alien Agenda: Investigating the Extraterrestrial Presence Among Us, Jim Marrs, Harper, New York, NY, 1997

Alien Encounters, Chuck Missler, Mark Eastman, Koinonia House, Minneapolis, Minnesota, 2003

The Ancient Alien Question, Philip Coppens, New Age, 2021

Atlantis and the Silver City, Peter Daughtrey, Pegasus Books, New York, NY 2013

The Book of Alien Races, Gil Carlson, Blue Planet Press, Hampton VA, 2017

Children of the Matrix: How an interdimensional race has controlled the world for thousands of years–and still does, David Icke, Bridge of Love Publications, Wildwood, MO, 2001

The Complete Idiot's Guide to Extraterrestrial Intelligence, Michael Kurland, Alpha Books, New York, NY, 1999

The Encyclopedia of Extraterrestrial Encounters: A Definitive, Illustrated A-Z Guide to All Things Alien, Edited by Ronald D. Story, New American Library, New York, NY, 2001

The Encyclopedia of Moon Mysteries: Secrets, Conspiracy Theories, Anomalies, Extraterrestrials and More, Constance Victoria Briggs, Adventures Unlimited Press, Kempton, IL, 2019

ETs and Aliens: Who Are They? And Why Are They Here? Noel Huntley, Ph.D., Xlibris Corporation, US, 2002

The Extraterrestrial Encyclopedia: An Alphabetical Reference to All Life in the Universe, David Darling, Ph.D., Three Rivers Press, New York, NY, 2000

Exopolitics: Politics, Government, and Law in the Universe, Alfred Lambremont Webre, Universebooks, Vancouver, BC, Canada, 2005.

Extraordinary Encounters: An Encyclopedia of Extraterrestrials and Otherworldly Beings, Jerome Clark, ABC-CLIO, Santa Barbara, CA, 2000

Everything You Know is Still Wrong, Lloyd Pye, Edited by Amy Vickers, Las Vegas, NV, 2023

The Gaia Project, 2012, The Earth's Coming Great Changes, Hwee-Yong Jang, Translated by Mira Tyson, Llewellyn

Publications, Woodbury, Minnesota, 2007

God Made the Aliens: Making Sense of Extraterrestrial Contact, Brian M. Rossiter, Independently Published, San Bernardino, CA, 2020

Impossible Truths: Amazing Evidence of Extraterrestrial Contact, Erich von Daniken, Watkins London, England, 2018

Is Jehovah an ET?, Dorothy Leon, Ozark Mountain Publishing, Huntsville, AL, 2002

Invader Moon, Rob Shelsky, Permuted Press, Brentwood, TN, 2016

Lying Wonders of the Red Planet, Exposing the Lie of Ancient Aliens, LS. Douglas Woodward, Faith Happens, Oklahoma City, OK, 2014

The Mammoth Encyclopedia of Extraterrestrial Encounters, Edited by Ronald D. Story, Robinson, London, England, 2002

The Martians: Evidence of Life on the Red Planet, Nick Redfern, Red/Wheel/Weiser, LLC, Newburyport, MA, 2020

The Missing Lands: Uncovering Earth's Pre-Flood Civilization, Freddy Silva, Invisible Temple, 2019

The Moon's Galactic History: A Look at the Moon's Extraterrestrial Past and Its Connection to Earth, Constance Victoria Briggs, Adventures Unlimited Press, Kempton, IL, 2022

New Evidence That the Holy Bible is an Extraterrestrial Transmission, C.L. Turnage, Timeless Voyager Press, Santa Barbara, CA, 2017

The Only Planet of Choice: Essential Briefings from Deep Space, Compiled by Phyllis V. Schlemmer & Palden Jenkins, Gateway Books, Bath, England, 1993

Real Alien Worlds: A Brief Encyclopaedia, David McCready, McCready Publishing, London, United Kingdom, 2016

Secrets of the Lost Races: New Discoveries of Advanced Technology in Ancient Civilizations, Rene Noorbergen, Researched by Joey R. Jochmans, Teach Services, Inc. Publishing, 2001

Signs of the Earth: Deciphering the Message of Virgin Mary Apparitions, UFO Encounters, and Crop Circles, Richard Leviton, Hampton Roads Publishing Company, Inc., Charlottesville, VA, 2005

The Source: Journey Through the Unexplained, Art Bell and
    Brad Steiger, New American Library, New York, NY, 2002
Star Trek Encyclopedia: A Reference Guide to the Future,
    Michael Okuda, Denise Okuda, Pocket Books, a division of
    Simon & Schuster, Inc., New York, NY, 1994
The UFO Magazine: UFO Encyclopedia, Edited by William J.
    Birnes, Pocket Books, New York, NY, 2004
We, The Arcturians (A True Experience), Dr. Norma J.
    Milanovich with Betty Rice and Cynthia Ploski, Athena
    Publishing, Scottsdale, AZ, 1990
*Witnesses, Organizations, Publications, and Government
    Research,* Margaret Sachs, Perigee Books, New York, NY,
    1980

Bibliography Magazines and Periodicals
"EX-NASA Official Speculates on UFOs," Caleb Trainer, *Desert
    Sun,* Number 287, July 13, 1981
"Nikola Tesla at 75," *Time Magazine*, July 20, 1931, New York,
    NY
SAGA's 1973 UFO Special, USA, 1973
"Science: Message from a Star," *Time Magazine*, April 9, 1973
"Spacemen Throughout History, Ancient Astronauts," *UFO
    Magazine Special Edition*, USA, September 1977

Bibliography Videos Alphabetical Order
5 Aliens Life Forms on Moon and Mars Caught by NASA, Mind Boggler,
https://www.youtube.com/watch?v=wWdsGfzdReU
5 Weird Things Astronauts Encountered in Space, https://www.bing.com/
videos/ Crazy+Things+From+Outer+Space
*10 Mysterious Things Astronauts Have Seen in Space | Space
Discoveries,* Factnomenal, https://www.youtube.com/watch?v=qcxm-
LM6DQ8
Alex Collier on the Andromedans, Starseed Alliance, https://www.
youtube.com/watch?v=KuTyoBHMWaQ
"Alien Antenna" Found on Sea Floor in Antarctica?, Mystery History,
https://www.youtube.com/watch?v=tAQDp4l9uwY&t=267s
Alien Moon Structures–Apollo 17, by Benjamin Redman, https://www.
youtube.com/watch?v=lVyaWOlnuo0.
"Alien Relic" Spotted in Cairo Museum? Mystery History, https://www.
youtube.com/watch?v=n3xxDXLlvi0
Alien Truth: Church Bishop Suddenly Quit Pulpit, https://www.youtube.
com/watch?v=XW0mrt4yOO8&t=8s
Aliens – Stonehenge, Mike Davis, February 22, 2015, https://www.

youtube.com/watch?v=kE0iUEv0abA

Aliens Threaten Global Invasion | Countdown to Armageddon, History, https://www.youtube.com/watch?v=eO1ElsB6FzY&t=473s

Ancient Aliens: Alien Tech in Ancient Greece (Season 10) | *History,* https://www.youtube.com/watch?v=wY7LXJI8Ago&t=112s

Ancient Aliens: Did Aliens Terraform Earth? (Season 10) | History*,* https://www.youtube.com/watch?v=pMy2Lf40Xts

Ancient Aliens: Egyptian Mysteries Hide Proof of UFOs, History, https://www.youtube.com/watch?v=J-RixrDfeDQ

Ancient Aliens: Terrifying Humanoids Emerge from Subterranean Realm (Season 18*)*, History, https://www.youtube.com/watch?v=IROLRx0Bypw

Angel Hair & The Ufo Connection (UFOS&ALIENS#8), Mad Cat Mysteries, https://www.youtube.com/watch?v=FDgkHFPl190&t=402s

Another World that Exists Beneath the Surface of Our Earth, Fascinating Mysteries, https://www.youtube.com/watch?v=pjMxdYCW2rI

Antarctica's Secret Alien Cover-Up | Ancient Aliens, https://www.youtube.com/watch?v=TozSkCROyqU

Black Knight Decoded Message, L. Jung, https://www.youtube.com/watch?v=4qITuy75v1M

The Book of Alien Races - Over 82 Species on Earth (Full Documentary), Visible Thought, https://www.youtube.com/watch?v=r6tB2lKKKmw

The Book of Enoch: The Watchers, Noah, & Nephilim | Astral Legends, AstralLegends, 2023, https://www.youtube.com/watch?v=jbUAB89hxeM&list=PLVVizx_1Cw_QxlJFN7PYdETGhX2c-Jv8W&index=1

Brian O'Leary NASA Astronaut Blows Whistle on UFO, GH, VJ, https://www.youtube.com/watch?v=iGKH-lkPkG0

Charles Hall & the Tall White Aliens | REAL Story, The Alien Hunter, *https*://www.youtube.com/watch?v=kVy1T9gErxM

Close Encounters at the Nuclear Bases, National Geographic, S1E3, https://www.nationalgeographic.com/tv/shows/ufos-investigating-the-unknown/episode-guide/season-01/episode-03-close-encounters-at-the-nuclear-bases/vdka32402854

Columbus' UFO Sightings, History, //www.history.com/videos/columbus-ufo-sightings

Crabwood Alien Crop Circle - Inside Out 2002, https://www.youtube.com/watch?v=8Uv5X4FAZzI

Crop Circle Theorist Thinks the Truth is Out There, Vice, https://www.youtube.com/watch?v=KDqZvGJW4gk,

Did Ancient Aliens Build the Pyramids? - UFOlogy (Episode 2), Extreme Mysteries, https://www.youtube.com/watch?v=uwNXDjsh6MI

Dogon Tribe & the Sirius Mystery, https://www.youtube.com/watch?v=kzQ3lmB8_pU&t=186s

Dr. Delbert Blair, Inner Earth Worlds, July 17, 1998, Detroit, Sirius Times Media, https://www.youtube.com/watch?v=padhQ5ihDow

Dr. Michael Salla—the Science of Traversable Wormholes & Stargates for Secret Space Programs, UAMN TV, https://www.youtube.com/watch?v=Q31KSDx2RfI

The Earth May Be Hollow! | A Journey Inside! | The Conspiracy Show | S2E11, Richard Syrett, Sci-Fi Central, https://www.youtube.com/watch?v=PNlcZg87MH4

Earthfiles, May 30, 2018: Linda Moulton Howe - Mysterious Outpost Interview, https://www.youtube.com/watch?v=d9lclpajgN8

Evidence We Were NEVER Alone, Gaia, https://www.youtube.com/watch?v=IUSzBAM0S9k

Filiberto Cardenas Abduction and Contact Case, Todd Shaw, October 9, 2014, YouTube, https://www.youtube.com/watch?v=le22E3UeP1Y

Gaia, *Evidence We Were NEVER Alone*, February 18, 2022, https://www.youtube.com/watch?v=IUSzBAM0S9k

Hidden in Plain Sight: Some things Public MUST NOT KNOW... Jordan Maxwell's Fond Farewell Lecture, https://www.youtube.com/watch?v=exjD1TcogSk

Is life possible on Venus? Interesting Engineering, https://www.youtube.com/watch?v=DUplel6ioOQ&t=13s

Is THIS A Mysterious Abandoned Alien Base? Extreme Mysteries, *https://www.youtube.com/watch?v=RV4JTIfRb5I*

Linda Moulton Howe: Exploring Encounters with Nordic Tall Whites Extraterrestrial Beings, PortalToAscension, April, 2023, https://www.youtube.com/watch?v=PZa5-RzOAJ8

May 30, 2018: Linda Moulton Howe - Mysterious Outpost Interview, Earthfiles, https://www.youtube.com/watch?v=d9lclpajgN8

C-SPAN: Buzz Aldrin Reveals Existence of Monolith on Mars Moon, https://www.youtube.com/watch?v=bDIXvpjnRws

NASA UFO Original Footage STS115, https://www.youtube.com/watch?v=98QgiJSm-m0.

Nikola Tesla's Extraterrestrial Signals, UncoveringTheWholeTruth, https://www.youtube.com/watch?v=A7JIQ-2QAec

Dive into the Deep Dark Ocean in a High-Tech Submersible! August 24, 2017, Shot & edited by Greg Foot. Additional footage courtesy of Nekton / XL Catlin Deep Ocean Survey. Alex4D. https://www.youtube.com/watch?v=eDb7VRxW9Cw

UFOs: History and Background/Part 1, https://www.citizenhearing.org/watch-the-testimony

Paul Wallis & Billy Carson/Anunnaki Gods, Consciousness & The Holographic Universe – July 2022, The 5th Kind, https://www.youtube.com/watch?v=SOxUTuiZvZ4

Planetary Awakening, (See Salla's Webinar)

Prince Sabu's disc (Schist disc), Ancient Architecture, https://www.

youtube.com/watch?v=lLO1h0sC5h4
The schoolkids Who Said They Saw 'Aliens', BBC News, https://www.bbc.com/news/av/stories-57749238
Special Rebroadcast - May 30, 2018 - Mysterious Outpost Interview, Earthfiles, https://www.youtube.com/watch?v=E140ELOV_kM
Stargates and Portals That Exist on Earth Today! Deano Upended, https://www.youtube.com/watch?v=83mT1sYe-9U
Star Trek, Strange New Worlds, Season 1, Episode 8, "The Elysian Kingdom"
"They Are Coming" - Brian Cox FINALLY Breaks Silence On Aliens!" Future Unity, https://www.youtube.com/watch?v=LU4RGYz7lwE
Top 4 Most SHOCKING Mysteries of South America | The Proof Is Out There, https://www.youtube.com/watch?v=TSK6d8O_ogQ
Top 10 Scariest Space Mysteries That Will Freak You Out, https://youtu.be/vsZbEJyc_EY
Top 10 Scary Signals from Space, https://www.bing.com/
Top 10 Unexplained Mysteries of the Moon, Mind Boggler, https://www.youtube.com/watch?v=etifRufySPE
U.F.O. Confrontation: Mansfield/Bodega Bay Ghost/Prophecy of Hope/Dream Murder/Power to Heal/Encounters in Space (1994), Sightings TV, S3E10, https://www.youtube.com/watch?v=ZBWM9iKlvRg&list=PLg9HJ97sVpY647-TvqeKVg59S36xCV1-H&index=44
The UnXplained: Ancient Alien Civilizations Hidden On Mars (Season 3), History, https://www.youtube.com/watch?v=LnDZTR77ehg&t=24s
US Archeologists Discover Ancient Alien Coins in Egypt, Tales from Out There, https://www.youtube.com/watch?v=NjSeFIrgth0
Were Anunnaki Progenitors of the Human Race? Gaia, https://www.youtube.com/watch?v=I-nfNEwE3cs, https://cs-link.gaia.com/3TqI4Of
What is the Council of Nine? January 24, 2022, Call Me Stormy: Finding righteous currents in turbulent times, https://callmestormy.net/2022/01/24/what-is-the-council-of-nine
What You Need to Know About The REPTILIAN ALIEN RACE, WoodwardTV Published on Jul 12, 2018, https://www.youtube.com/watch?v=-eGs4jdPNmQ
Who or What Is Knocking on His Spacecraft? | NASA's Unexplained Files, Factnomenal, https://www.youtube.com/watch?v=ioJsRQ53IEM
Why Do We Imagine Aliens as 'Little Green Men'?, https://www.youtube.com/watch?v=SeAQVXGXTyI
You Have To See This! Our History Is NOT What We Are Told! Ancient Civilizations—Graham Hancock, The 5th Kind, https://www.youtube.com/watch?v=P0CnZlX0gXU

Get these fascinating books from your nearest bookstore or directly from: Adventures Unlimited Press
www.adventuresunlimitedpress.com

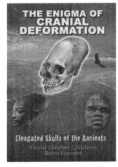

COVERT WARS AND BREAKAWAY CIVILIZATIONS
By Joseph P. Farrell
Farrell delves into the creation of breakaway civilizations by the Nazis in South America and other parts of the world. He discusses the advanced technology that they took with them at the end of the war and the psychological war that they waged for decades on America and NATO. He investigates the secret space programs currently sponsored by the breakaway civilizations and the current militaries in control of planet Earth. Plenty of astounding accounts, documents and speculation on the incredible alternative history of hidden conflicts and secret space programs that began when World War II officially "ended."
292 Pages. 6x9 Paperback. Illustrated. $19.95. Code: BCCW

THE ENIGMA OF CRANIAL DEFORMATION
Elongated Skulls of the Ancients
By David Hatcher Childress and Brien Foerster
In a book filled with over a hundred astonishing photos and a color photo section, Childress and Foerster take us to Peru, Bolivia, Egypt, Malta, China, Mexico and other places in search of strange elongated skulls and other cranial deformation. The puzzle of why diverse ancient people—even on remote Pacific Islands—would use head-binding to create elongated heads is mystifying. Where did they even get this idea? Did some people naturally look this way—with long narrow heads? Were they some alien race? Were they an elite race that roamed the entire planet? Why do anthropologists rarely talk about cranial deformation and know so little about it? Color Section.
250 Pages. 6x9 Paperback. Illustrated. $19.95. Code: ECD

THE GIZA DEATH STAR REVISITED
An Updated Revision of the Weapon Hypothesis of the Great Pyramid
By Joseph P. Farrell
A summary, revision, and update of his original *Giza Death Star* trilogy in this one-volume compendium of the argument, the physics, and the all-important ancient texts, from the Edfu Temple texts to the Lugal-e and the Enuma Elish that he believes may have made the Great Pyramid a tremendously powerful weapon of mass destruction. Those texts, Farrell argues, provide the clues to the powerful physics of longitudinal waves in the medium that only began to be unlocked centuries later by Sir Isaac Newton and his well-known studies of the Great Pyramid, and even later by Nikola Tesla's "electro-acoustic" experiments. Chapters and sections include: A Remarkable, and Remarkably Strange, Structure; The Hypothesized Functions of the Great Pyramid's Topological-Analogical Code of Ancient Texts; Greaves, Gravity, and Newton; Meta-Materials, Crystals, and Torsion; The Top Secret Cold War Soviet Pyramid Research, and much, much more!
360 Pages. 6x9 Paperback. Illustrated.. $19.95. Code: GDSR

HESS AND THE PENGUINS
The Holocaust, Antarctica and the Strange Case of Rudolf Hess
By Joseph P. Farrell

Farrell looks at Hess' mission to make peace with Britain and get rid of Hitler—even a plot to fly Hitler to Britain for capture! How much did Göring and Hitler know of Rudolf Hess' subversive plot, and what happened to Hess? Why was a doppleganger put in Spandau Prison and then "suicided"? Did the British use an early form of mind control on Hess' double? John Foster Dulles of the OSS and CIA suspected as much. Farrell also uncovers the strange death of Admiral Richard Byrd's son in 1988, about the same time of the death of Hess.

288 Pages. 6x9 Paperback. Illustrated. $19.95. Code: HAPG

HIDDEN FINANCE, ROGUE NETWORKS & SECRET SORCERY
The Fascist International, 9/11, & Penetrated Operations
By Joseph P. Farrell

Farrell investigates the theory that there were not *two* levels to the 9/11 event, but *three*. He says that the twin towers were downed by the force of an exotic energy weapon, one similar to the Tesla energy weapon suggested by Dr. Judy Wood, and ties together the tangled web of missing money, secret technology and involvement of portions of the Saudi royal family. Farrell unravels the many layers behind the 9-11 attack, layers that include the Deutschebank, the Bush family, the German industrialist Carl Duisberg, Saudi Arabian princes and the energy weapons developed by Tesla before WWII.

296 Pages. 6x9 Paperback. Illustrated. $19.95. Code: HFRN

THRICE GREAT HERMETICA & THE JANUS AGE
By Joseph P. Farrell

What do the Fourth Crusade, the exploration of the New World, secret excavations of the Holy Land, and the pontificate of Innocent the Third all have in common? Answer: Venice and the Templars. What do they have in common with Jesus, Gottfried Leibniz, Sir Isaac Newton, Rene Descartes, and the Earl of Oxford? Answer: Egypt and a body of doctrine known as Hermeticism. The hidden role of Venice and Hermeticism reached far and wide, into the plays of Shakespeare (a.k.a. Edward DeVere, Earl of Oxford), into the quest of the three great mathematicians of the Early Enlightenment for a lost form of analysis, and back into the end of the classical era, to little known Egyptian influences at work during the time of Jesus.

354 Pages. 6x9 Paperback. Illustrated. $19.95. Code: TGHJ

REICH OF THE BLACK SUN
Nazi Secret Weapons & the Cold War Allied Legend
by Joseph P. Farrell

Why were the Allies worried about an atom bomb attack by the Germans in 1944? Why did the Soviets threaten to use poison gas against the Germans? Why did Hitler in 1945 insist that holding Prague could win the war for the Third Reich? Why did US General George Patton's Third Army race for the Skoda works at Pilsen in Czechoslovakia instead of Berlin? Why did the US Army not test the uranium atom bomb it dropped on Hiroshima? Why did the Luftwaffe fly a non-stop round trip mission to within twenty miles of New York City in 1944? Farrel takes the reader on a scientific-historical journey in order to answer these questions. Arguing that Nazi Germany won the race for the atom bomb in late 1944,

352 PAGES. 6x9 PAPERBACK. ILLUSTRATED. $16.95. CODE: ROBS

ANDROMEDA: THE SECRET FILES
The Flying Submarines of the SS
By David Hatcher Childress

Childress brings us the amazing story of the German Andromeda craft, designed and built during WWII. Along with flying discs, the Germans were making long, cylindrical airships that are commonly called motherships—large craft that house several smaller disc craft. It was not until 1989 that a German researcher named Ralf Ettl, living in London, received an anonymous packet of photographs and documents concerning the planning and development of at least three types of unusual craft—including the Andromeda. Chapters include: Gravity's Rainbow; The Motherships; The MJ-12, UFOs and the Korean War; The Strange Case of Reinhold Schmidt; Secret Cities of the Winged Serpent; The Green Fireballs; Submarines That Can Fly; The Breakaway Civilization; more. Includes a 16-page color section.

382 Pages. 6x9 Paperback. Illustrated. $22.00 Code: ASF

GODS AND SPACEMEN THROUGHOUT HISTORY
Did Ancient Aliens Visit Earth in the Past?
By W. Raymond Drake

From prehistory, flying saucers have been seen in our skies. As mankind sends probes beyond the fringes of our galaxy, we must ask ourselves: "Has all this happened before? Could extraterrestrials have landed on Earth centuries ago?" Drake spent many years digging through huge archives of material, looking for supposed anomalies that could support his scenarios of space aliens impacting human history. Chapters include: Spacemen; The Golden Age; Sons of the Gods; Lemuria; Atlantis; Ancient America; Aztecs and Incas; India; Tibet; China; Japan; Egypt; The Great Pyramid; Babylon; Israel; Greece; Italy; Ancient Rome; Scandinavia; Britain; Saxon Times; Norman Times; The Middle Ages; The Age of Reason; Today; Tomorrow; more.

280 Pages. 6x9 Paperback. Illustrated. $18.95. Code: GSTH

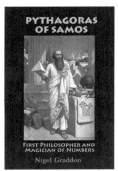

PYTHAGORAS OF SAMOS
First Philosopher and Magician of Numbers
By Nigel Graddon

This comprehensive account comprises both the historical and metaphysical aspects of Pythagoras' philosophy and teachings. In Part 1, the work draws on all known biographical sources as well as key extracts from the esoteric record to paint a fascinating picture of the Master's amazing life and work. Topics covered include the unique circumstances of Pythagoras' birth, his forty-year period of initiations into all the world's ancient mysteries, his remarkable meeting with a physician from the mysterious Etruscan community, Part 2 comprises, for the first time in a publicly available work, a metaphysical interpretation of Pythagoras' Science of Numbers.

294 Pages. 6x9 Paperback. Illustrated. $18.95. Code: PYOS

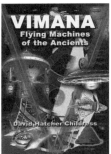

VIMANA:
Flying Machines of the Ancients
by David Hatcher Childress

According to early Sanskrit texts the ancients had several types of airships called vimanas. Like aircraft of today, vimanas were used to fly through the air from city to city; to conduct aerial surveys of uncharted lands; and as delivery vehicles for awesome weapons. David Hatcher Childress, popular *Lost Cities* author, takes us on an astounding investigation into tales of ancient flying machines. In his new book, packed with photos and diagrams, he consults ancient texts and modern stories and presents astonishing evidence that aircraft, similar to the ones we use today, were used thousands of years ago in India, Sumeria, China and other countries. Includes a 24-page color section.

408 Pages. 6x9 Paperback. Illustrated. $22.95. Code: VMA

LOST PAITITI & THE NON-HUMAN REMAINS OF NAZCA
By Thierry Jamin

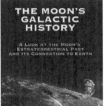

French explorer Jamin relates findings from his years in Peru in search of the lost Inca city of Paitit,i plus his most recent escapades with non-human skeletons at Nazca on the coast. Chapters include: On the Tracks of the Lost City of the Incas; Machu Picchu and the Mystery of the Secret Room; The Strange Square Mountain; Where It All Begins; In the Footsteps of "Mario"; Summit Meeting; Strange Relics; The New B.E.; A Mysterious Man in Black; Three Eggs!; The Incredible Hybrid; The Lima Conference; The Real False Site; The "Familia"; Transfer of the Mummies; The Ica Conference; The Flight Over the Gran Paititi; The Case of Nazca Continues; more. Color photo section.

384 Pages. 6x9 Paperback. Illustrated. $22.00. Code: LPNZ

THE MOON'S GALACTIC HISTORY
By Constance Victoria Briggs

The book examines such questions as, "Are there Moon inhabitants?" "Are the UFOs seen today connected to the Moon?" "Is there a city on the Moon?" and more. Additionally, Briggs discusses thing observed on the Moon, including anomalous strange lights, unidentified flying objects, odd constructions, artifacts, symbols and more. This book examines new thoughts and ideas from researchers and what their ideas are today about the extraterrestrial Moon-Earth connection, and what it means for us. Did you know that: Apollo 10 astronauts heard strange "space music" when traveling on the far side of the Moon?; mysterious anomalous activity has been seen on the Moon for centuries?; there are said to be ruins of structures on the Moon?; and more.

324 Pages. 6x9 Paperback. Illustrated. $22.00. Code: MGH

THE ENCYCLOPEDIA OF MOON MYSTERIES
Secrets, Anomalies, Extraterrestrials and More
By Constance Victoria Briggs

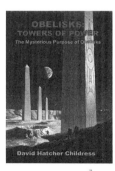

Our moon is an enigma. The ancients viewed it as a light to guide them in the darkness, and a god to be worshipped. Did you know that: Aristotle and Plato wrote about a time when there was no Moon? Several of the NASA astronauts reported seeing UFOs while traveling to the Moon?; the Moon might be hollow?; Apollo 10 astronauts heard strange "space music" when traveling on the far side of the Moon?; strange and unexplained lights have been seen on the Moon for centuries?; there are said to be ruins of structures on the Moon?; there is an ancient tale that suggests that the first human was created on the Moon?; Tons more. Tons of illustrations with A to Z sections for easy reference and reading.

152 Pages. 7x10 Paperback. Illustrated. $19.95. Code: EOMM

OBELISKS: TOWERS OF POWER
The Mysterious Purpose of Obelisks
By David Hatcher Childress

Some obelisks weigh over 500 tons and are massive blocks of polished granite that would be extremely difficult to quarry and erect even with modern equipment. Why did ancient civilizations in Egypt, Ethiopia and elsewhere undertake the massive enterprise it would have been to erect a single obelisk, much less dozens of them? Were they energy towers that could receive or transmit energy? With discussions on Tesla's wireless power, and the use of obelisks as gigantic acupuncture needles for earth, Chapters include: Megaliths Around the World and their Purpose; The Crystal Towers of Egypt; The Obelisks of Ethiopia; Obelisks in Europe and Asia; Mysterious Obelisks in the Americas; The Terrible Crystal Towers of Atlantis; Tesla's Wireless Power Distribution System; Obelisks on the Moon; more. 8-page color section.

336 Pages. 6x9 Paperback. Illustrated. $22.00 Code: OBK

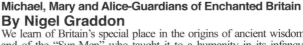

THE GODS IN THE FIELDS
Michael, Mary and Alice-Guardians of Enchanted Britain
By Nigel Graddon

We learn of Britain's special place in the origins of ancient wisdom and of the "Sun-Men" who taught it to a humanity in its infancy. Aspects of these teachings are found all along the St. Michael ley: at Glastonbury, the location of Merlin and Arthur's Avalon; in the design and layout of the extraordinary Somerset Zodiac of which Glastonbury is a major part; in the amazing stone circles and serpentine avenues at Avebury and nearby Silbury Hill: portals to unimaginable worlds of mystery and enchantment; Chapters include: Michael, Mary and Merlin; England's West Country; The Glastonbury Zodiac; Wiltshire; The Gods in the Fields; Michael, Mary and Alice; East of the Line; Table of Michael and Mary Locations; more.
280 Pages. 6x9 Paperback. Illustrated. $19.95. Code: GIF

AXIS OF THE WORLD
The Search for the Oldest American Civilization
by Igor Witkowski

Polish author Witkowski's research reveals remnants of a high civilization that was able to exert its influence on almost the entire planet, and did so with full consciousness. Sites around South America show that this was not just one of the places influenced by this culture, but a place where they built their crowning achievements. Easter Island, in the southeastern Pacific, constitutes one of them. The Rongo-Rongo language that developed there points westward to the Indus Valley. Taken together, the facts presented by Witkowski provide a fresh, new proof that an antediluvian, great civilization flourished several millennia ago.
220 pages. 6x9 Paperback. Illustrated. $18.95. Code: AXOW

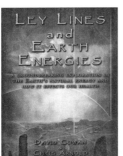

LEY LINE & EARTH ENERGIES
An Extraordinary Journey into the Earth's Natural Energy System
by David Cowan & Chris Arnold

The mysterious standing stones, burial grounds and stone circles that lace Europe, the British Isles and other areas have intrigued scientists, writers, artists and travellers through the centuries. How do ley lines work? How did our ancestors use Earth energy to map their sacred sites and burial grounds? How do ghosts and poltergeists interact with Earth energy? How can Earth spirals and black spots affect our health? This exploration shows how natural forces affect our behavior, how they can be used to enhance our health and well being.
368 pages. 6x9 Paperback. Illustrated. $18.95. Code: LLEE

THE BRINGER OF LIFE
A Cosmic History of the Divine Feminine
By Hayley A. Ramsey

Who and what is the divine feminine? What does She represent, and where can She be found? Hayley Ramsey starts at the beginning of time itself and explains the origins of goddess veneration and follows What caused the shift from matriarchal society to a patriarchal society? What was the relationship between religions such as Christianity and the suppression of the goddess? Ramsey examines the connections between Mary Magdalene, Jesus, and the Holy Grail while considering the importance of astrological precession. Many believe that She disappeared, but perhaps Her veneration went underground. Ramsey proposes the goddess and Her followers never disappeared, but instead She became shrouded in allegory and symbolism by different secret societies that still exist today. Is there a connection between the medieval Knights Templar, the divine feminine, and modern Freemasonry?
338 Pages. 6x9 Paperback. Illustrated. $18.95. Code: BOLF

ORDER FORM

**10% Discount
When You Order
3 or More Items!**

One Adventure Place
P.O. Box 74
Kempton, Illinois 60946
United States of America
Tel.: 815-253-6390 • Fax: 815-253-6300
Email: auphq@frontiernet.net
http://www.adventuresunlimitedpress.com

ORDERING INSTRUCTIONS

✓ Remit by USD$ Check, Money Order or Credit Card

✓ Visa, Master Card, Discover & AmEx Accepted

✓ Paypal Payments Can Be Made To:
info@wexclub.com

✓ Prices May Change Without Notice

✓ 10% Discount for 3 or More Items

SHIPPING CHARGES

United States

✓ POSTAL BOOK RATE

✓ Postal Book Rate { $5.00 First Item
50¢ Each Additional Item

✓ Priority Mail { $8.50 First Item
$2.00 Each Additional Item

✓ UPS { $9.00 First Item (Minimum 5 Books)
$1.50 Each Additional Item

NOTE: UPS Delivery Available to Mainland USA Only

Canada

✓ Postal Air Mail { $19.00 First Item
$3.00 Each Additional Item

✓ Personal Checks or Bank Drafts MUST BE

US$ and Drawn on a US Bank

✓ Canadian Postal Money Orders OK

✓ Payment MUST BE US$

All Other Countries

✓ Sorry, No Surface Delivery!

✓ Postal Air Mail { $29.00 First Item
$7.00 Each Additional Item

✓ Checks and Money Orders MUST BE US$
and Drawn on a US Bank or branch.

✓ Paypal Payments Can Be Made in US$ To:
info@wexclub.com

SPECIAL NOTES

✓ RETAILERS: Standard Discounts Available

✓ BACKORDERS: We Backorder all Out-of-
Stock Items Unless Otherwise Requested

✓ PRO FORMA INVOICES: Available on Request

✓ DVD Return Policy: Replace defective DVDs only

ORDER ONLINE AT: www.adventuresunlimitedpress.com

**10% Discount When You Order
3 or More Items!**

Please check: ✓

☐ This is my first order   ☐ I have ordered before

Name

Address

City

State/Province | Postal Code

Country

Phone: Day | Evening

Fax | Email

Item Code	Item Description	Qty	Total

Please check: ✓

☐ Postal-Surface

☐ Postal-Air Mail
(Priority in USA)

☐ UPS
(Mainland USA only)

☐ Visa/MasterCard/Discover/American Express

Subtotal ▶	
Less Discount-10% for 3 or more items ▶	
Balance ▶	
Illinois Residents 6.25% Sales Tax ▶	
Previous Credit ▶	
Shipping ▶	
Total (check/MO in USD$ only) ▶	

Card Number:

Expiration Date: | Security Code:

✓ SEND A CATALOG TO A FRIEND: